UNDERSTANDING
FOUR VIEWS
ON THE LORD'S SUPPER

Books in the Counterpoints Series

Church Life

Evaluating the Church Growth Movement

Exploring the Worship Spectrum

Remarriage after Divorce in Today's Church

Understanding Four Views on Baptism

Understanding Four Views on the Lord's Supper

Who Runs the Church?

Exploring Theology

Are Miraculous Gifts for Today?

Five Views on Apologetics

Five Views on Law and Gospel

Five Views on Sanctification

Four Views on Eternal Security

Four Views on Hell

Four Views on Salvation in a Pluralistic World

Four Views on the Book of Revelation

How Jewish Is Christianity?

Show Them No Mercy

Three Views on Creation and Evolution

Three Views on Eastern Orthodoxy and Evangelicalism

Three Views on the Millennium and Beyond

Three Views on the Rapture

Two Views on Women in Ministry

UNDERSTANDING FOUR VIEWS ON
THE
LORD'S SUPPER

- **Russell D. Moore**
- **I. John Hesselink**
- **David P. Scaer**
- **Thomas A. Baima**

- **Paul E. Engle,** *series editor*
- **John H. Armstrong,** *general editor*

ZONDERVAN.com/
AUTHORTRACKER
follow your favorite authors

Understanding Four Views on the Lord's Supper
Copyright © 2007 by John H. Armstrong

Requests for information should be addressed to:
Zondervan, *Grand Rapids, Michigan 49530*

Library of Congress Cataloging-in-Publication Data

Moore, Russell, 1971–.
    Understanding four views on the Lord's Supper / Russell D. Moore.
       p. cm. — (Counterpoints : church life)
    Includes bibliographical references and index.
    ISBN-10: 0-310-26268-2
    ISBN-13: 978-0-310-26268-8
    1. Lord's Supper. I. Title.
  BV825.3.M66 2007
  234'.163 — dc22

                                     2007014707

Printed in the United States of America

12 · 23 22 21 20 19 18 17 16 15 14 13 12 11 10 9 8 7 6

CONTENTS

Abbreviations   7

Introduction: Do This in Remembrance of Me   11
   JOHN H. ARMSTRONG

1. **BAPTIST VIEW:**
   Christ's Presence as Memorial   29
   RUSSELL D. MOORE

   A Reformed Response: 45
     I. JOHN HESSELINK

   A Lutheran Response: 48
     DAVID P. SCAER

   A Roman Catholic Response: 53
     THOMAS A. BAIMA

2. **REFORMED VIEW:**
   The Real Presence of Christ   59
   I. JOHN HESSELINK

   A Baptist Response: 72
     RUSSELL D. MOORE

   A Lutheran Response: 75
     DAVID P. SCAER

   A Roman Catholic Response: 79
     THOMAS A. BAIMA

3. **LUTHERAN VIEW:**
   Finding the Right Word   87
   DAVID P. SCAER

   A Baptist Response: 102
     RUSSELL D. MOORE

   A Reformed Response: 106
     I. JOHN HESSELINK

   A Roman Catholic Response: 109
     THOMAS A. BAIMA

4. ROMAN CATHOLIC VIEW:
Christ's True, Real, and Substantial Presence   119

THOMAS A. BAIMA

A Baptist Response: 137
RUSSELL D. MOORE

A Reformed Response: 141
I. JOHN HESSELINK

A Lutheran Response: 144
DAVID P. SCAER

Conclusion: The Two Most Important Questions   153

JOHN H. ARMSTRONG

Appendix 1: Statements on the Lord's Supper in Creeds,   160
    Confessions, and Catechisms

Appendix 2: Quotations on the Lord's Supper   182

Resources for Further Study   205

About the Contributors   209

Discussion and Reflection Questions   212

Scripture Index   215

Subject Index   00

ABBREVIATIONS

Bible Texts, Versions, Etc.

ESV	English Standard Version
KJV	King James Version
NASB	New American Standard Bible
NIV	New International Version
NRSV	New Revised Standard Version
NT	New Testament
OT	Old Testament

Old Testament, New Testament

Gen.	Genesis
Exod.	Exodus
Lev.	Leviticus
Num.	Numbers
Deut.	Deuteronomy
Josh.	Joshua
Judg.	Judges
Ruth	Ruth
1–2 Sam.	1–2 Samuel
1–2 Kgs.	1–2 Kings
1–2 Chr.	1–2 Chronicles
Ezra	Ezra
Neh.	Nehemiah
Esth.	Esther
Job	Job
Ps./Pss.	Psalm/Psalms
Prov.	Proverbs
Eccl.	Ecclesiastes

Song	Song of Songs
Isa.	Isaiah
Jer.	Jeremiah
Lam.	Lamentations
Ezek.	Ezekiel
Dan.	Daniel
Hos.	Hosea
Joel	Joel
Amos	Amos
Obad.	Obadiah
Jonah	Jonah
Mic.	Micah
Nah.	Nahum
Hab.	Habakkuk
Zeph.	Zephaniah
Hag.	Haggai
Zech.	Zechariah
Mal.	Malachi
Matt.	Matthew
Mark	Mark
Luke	Luke
John	John
Acts	Acts
Rom.	Romans
1–2 Cor.	1–2 Corinthians
Gal.	Galatians
Eph.	Ephesians
Phil.	Philippians
Col.	Colossians
1–2 Thess.	1–2 Thessalonians
1–2 Tim.	1–2 Timothy
Titus	Titus
Phlm.	Philemon
Heb.	Hebrews
Jas.	James
1–2 Pet.	1–2 Peter
1–2–3 John	1–2–3 John
Jude	Jude
Rev.	Revelation

General

AD	*anno Domini* (in the year of [our] Lord)
BC	before Christ
ca.	*circa* (around, about, approximately)
cf.	*confer,* compare
chap.	chapter
ed(s).	editor(s), edited by
e.g.	*exempli gratia,* for example
esp.	especially
Gk.	Greek
ibid.	*ibidem,* in the same place
i.e.	*id est,* that is
n.	note
N.B.	*nota bene,* note carefully
p(p).	page(s)
sec.	section
trans.	translator(s), translated by
v(v).	verse(s)

INTRODUCTION:
DO THIS IN REMEMBRANCE OF ME

John H. Armstrong

From my earliest remembrance, as I was growing up in an evangelical Christian church, I thought often about the Lord's Supper. In front of me every week, in a plain and mostly unadorned sanctuary, were the words of the Lord Jesus, carved into the table below the pulpit: "Do This in Remembrance of Me." This meal was not celebrated very often in my home church, but when it was included in our worship, it had a strong attraction for me. I remembering asking my parents, "When can I take it?" and, "What does this mean?" Or even, "Why do we do this?" (I even recall asking, "Why do we do this so infrequently?") The answers I got were not entirely satisfactory. But the attraction I felt to this celebration grew even stronger over time. To many of my friends the ceremony seemed somber, but to me it was thrilling, a time filled with hope and joy. I understood that it was vitally important for my life as a Christian, but I had no idea why. I also knew that I wanted to partake of it as a Christian who truly loves the Lord.

How odd it is that we Christians need to be reminded by a simple and recurring meal. We have been redeemed through the precious blood of our Messiah, Jesus, yet we are prone to forget his great act of sacrifice. But our Lord understands perfectly well our weakness and thus made provision for us to come again and again to this table so that we do not forget.

11

More than five decades later, I am still thinking about this awesome and simple meal. Why is this ceremony so important for Christians? What is the appeal in the taking of bread and wine to remember Christ's death in our gathered church meetings? And why is it that this particular meal is still practiced by almost every Christian alive today when Christians have consistently disagreed about its precise meaning for nearly twenty centuries?

Donald Bridge and David Phypers, in a helpful overview of the Lord's Supper, describe an imaginary viewer watching a religious channel on television. He sees many sights, sounds, and forms coming from various Christian groups all over the world. In the midst of this wide-ranging diversity, he takes note of the following:

> [There] is one thing the oddly different groups do have in common. They all make rather special use of bread and wine. The use they make of it is bewilderingly different, but they all use it. If [this viewer] sticks with the program for a few weeks, he will soon discover that Christians have not only done different things with the bread and wine, but have done terrible things to each other because of it. Men and women have been imprisoned, whipped, pilloried, tortured, and burned alive because of differing opinions about what really happens when Christians eat bread and drink wine and remember their Lord.[1]

All Christians the world over trace their practice of the Lord's Supper back to that evening prior to Jesus' horrific death when he shared a final meal with his disciples in a "large upper room" (Luke 22:12). During that meal Jesus said to his followers, first of the bread that he gave to them, "This is my body" (Matt. 26:26), then later of the cup, which he also gave to them, "This is my blood of the covenant" (Matt. 26:28). In so doing, Jesus commanded his followers that they should "do this in remembrance of me" (Luke 22:19). It appears he intended that they would celebrate this meal again and again. This is how the apostle Paul understood the event, since we read that both the bread and the cup should be taken "in remembrance of me [Jesus]," just as Jesus commanded (1 Cor. 11:24–25).

This meal has been called by several appropriate names. The simplest expression occurs in 1 Corinthians 11:20, where it is called "the Lord's Supper." In 1 Corinthians 10:21 it is called "the Lord's table." In 1 Corinthians 10:16 it is a *koinonia* (a "communion"), literally referring to "a sharing together" or a "participation" (NIV). Most scholars agree that an allusion to this same meal also occurs in Acts 2:42, where it is referred to as "the breaking of bread." Later the church called this meal the "Eucharist," because this particular word expressed the most characteristic element of the Lord's Supper, namely, the giving of thanks (Matt. 26:27; 1 Cor. 11:24; cf. the Greek *eucharisteō*, "to give thanks"). (The term "Mass," which comes from the Latin ending of the Roman rite, came later and was taken from the words, "Go, you are dismissed.") A number of allusions to this Supper also occur in the New Testament.

The chief thing to be noticed in all of these texts is the rich variety of expressions for the Lord's Supper, all pointing to Jesus and his sacrifice. Almost every Christian, regardless of how they understand this Supper, agrees with this much—Christ instituted it, and the New Testament commands his followers to celebrate it. The very word that was on the table in my childhood church said we were to "do" this, not "debate" this. Both repetition and command are located in this one word, "do." Furthermore, the belief that we all must come to this table is plainly rooted in the instructions the apostle Paul gave to one of the earliest Christian congregations when he wrote, "For whenever you eat this bread and drink this cup, you proclaim the Lord's death until he comes" (1 Cor. 11:26).

Reading these words makes it seem all so simple, so obvious. For sure, Christ's commands are not burdensome or complicated. Yet earnest and faithful Christians have disagreed. They disagree over the *meaning* of the Supper as well as the *importance* of it. They disagree over *who* should take it and *when*. And they strongly disagree over *what happens* to the elements themselves when they are prayed over and taken by the people of God. Careful consideration of the biblical texts and the practice of the earliest Christians reveal that almost every action and phrase in the biblical text is "alive with meaning and vibrant with implication."[2]

A COMMANDED REMEMBRANCE

"Do this in remembrance of me." Our Lord's command seems very simple, as I've said. Any faithful Christian can comply if they so desire. But the understanding of what these words meant, and how we are to obey them, has not been so simple throughout the course of two thousand years of church history. At times it would seem the better part of real wisdom to simply lay aside all the controversies and obey the command.

The earliest references we have of Christians remembering Christ in this sacred meal occur in the book of Acts. Here we read that they regularly "devoted themselves to the apostles' teaching and to the fellowship, to the breaking of bread and to prayer" (Acts 2:42). Biblical scholars have no doubt that this reference to "the breaking of bread" is a reference to the Lord's Supper.

In Acts 20, we read that the Christians in Troas gathered "on the first day of the week ... to break bread" (Acts 20:7). Here the expressed purpose for the church's gathering seems to have been "to break bread," indicating that this meal was central to the church's public assembly. Luke, the human author of these words, is the same writer who recorded in the third gospel the Lord's clear command to celebrate this meal (Luke 22:19). This makes it quite obvious that the church's gathering "to break bread" is understood by him as the *fulfillment of Jesus' command* to "do this in remembrance of me."

Some biblical scholars have surmised that the early church celebrated the Lord's Supper daily (Acts 2:46–47). This would indicate that the Supper was immediately separated from the Passover, which was only celebrated annually. It is clear that, several decades into the Christian era, believers appear to have been receiving the bread and the cup every week, on the first day, which had become the Lord's Day (cf. Acts 20:7, 11; 1 Cor. 16:2). And in both 1 Corinthians 10 and 11, where Paul devotes the most descriptive textual material in all of the New Testament to the Supper, there is little doubt that this celebration of Christ's body and blood was a regular occurrence. Yet virtually all biblical scholars agree there is no clear command regarding the frequency of the Lord's Supper within the New Testament. Paul simply says, "For I received from the Lord ... " (1 Cor. 11:23), which implies that he had a trust received directly from the Lord Jesus himself. In fact, one way to read this statement would be, "I, even I Paul, have *received* from the Lord [Jesus Christ] that which I now *deliver* to you." (It is commonly agreed that *received* and *delivered* were technical terms used to describe the passing on of an oral tradition. Where Paul received this we do not know, but it could well have been from either the church in Damascus or the church in Antioch.) So I believe we are required to make much of this meal precisely because Jesus, and his faithful apostles who labored to build the church's one foundation on him, made much of it.

What Is the Lord's Supper?

What exactly is the Lord's Supper? Put very simply, it is an uncomplicated ceremony in which bread and wine are taken by gathered worshipers in a sacred act of communion, remembrance, and thanksgiving. This sacred act is rooted in the words and actions of Jesus. Justin Martyr, writing in his classic work *Apology*, put it this way: "We do not receive these things as common bread or common drink, but as Jesus Christ our Savior who became incarnate by God's Word and took flesh and blood for our salvation."[3]

There is no real doubt about this simple historical fact—through the centuries this meal has been *the central and characteristic action of the church at worship*. If the church is a community that remembers Jesus as Lord, then the chief way this has been done in public worship has been through this Supper. And this remembrance is not designed for sentimental reflection but as a divinely invoked "recalling" of the historic event of Christ's life and work, particularly his passion, resurrection, and ascension.

The Origins of the Supper

Most scholars agree that the Lord's Supper has its roots in the Jewish Passover celebration. The Passover meal consisted of lamb, bitter herbs, and unleavened bread. It was instituted to celebrate and commemorate God's liberation of the Israelites from slavery in Egypt. The story is told in Exodus 28. The meal was celebrated as a thanksgiving for the gifts of food, fellowship, and freedom. When Israelite children would later ask their parents, "What does this ceremony mean to you?" (Exod. 12:26), the parents were to refer them to these great events.

When Jesus instituted the meal that we call the Lord's Supper, it was not a Passover meal he celebrated but rather an entirely new ceremony within the context of the Passover. It was not celebrated yearly, as the Passover, and it involved only two simple elements—bread and wine. And though Jesus is "the Lamb of God," who sacrifices himself for our sins (John 1:29), a literal Passover lamb was not involved in the Lord's Supper, as in the Passover. The differences between the two meals are important to note, but the parallels are also worth careful consideration:

> During the Passover meal, someone, usually the youngest son, was designated to ask the question, "Why is this night different from other nights?" At this point the host would retell the story of Israel's deliverance out of Egypt and the meaning of the various elements of the meal. As the host of the Last Supper, Jesus would have retold the story. Later, the parallels between the Passover and the Last Supper which Jesus was establishing would be quite apparent.[4]

A VISIBLE REMEMBRANCE

Though we sometimes forget this, this meal is not a private ceremony. It is a church-based celebration wherein believers remember their Lord together in a visible manner. In this corporate family meal we celebrate Christ's sacrifice for our sins.

Over many centuries, the celebration of this church meal became more and more elaborate. The reasons will be explored, to some extent, in the chapters that follow. Part of the reason Christians differ about the meaning of the meal is connected to the way they choose to celebrate it. But this much must never be lost in our disagreements—the Lord's Supper emphasizes participation by the entire congregation in the meal. The pattern is clearly established in Mark 14:23, where we read, "Then he took the cup, gave thanks and offered it to them, and they all drank from it." This is a communion that expresses the unity of God's family and thereby anticipates the end of this age, the final and complete unity of all Christians in their Lord.

But what does this remembrance really mean to us as Christians? I suggest that at least three things are clearly in view.

1. Commemoration

Since Jesus instructed us to always celebrate this meal "in remembrance of me" (1 Cor. 11:24), the Lord's Supper should always remind us of the final meal Jesus celebrated with his disciples before he died on the cross. When these texts are read and understood in their redemptive context, the words and actions of our Lord have powerful significance. They are plainly meant to bring to the minds of the disciples, and ours as well, all the events of his incredible life, his suffering and ignominious death, and his glorious and victorious resurrection. Thus, by this meal, we now recognize, observe, and remember his life and death for us.

2. Renewal

As surely as we commemorate and remember Christ's sacrifice for our salvation, we also renew our faith and offer ourselves up to him again when we come to this table (cf. Rom. 12:1–2). The Lord's Supper enriches our Christian lives through our meeting with Christ at this appointed place. Here we receive his grace again, and here he reveals to us that we belong to him through mystical union. This inspires us to be committed followers of the Savior. Each of us has an obligation to love and serve the Savior and to minister to one another. Gathered around this table, we receive the ability to love God and our neighbors. Having received these tokens of his love, in the bread and the wine we are given gifts that empower us to serve. Our faith is renewed.

3. Thanksgiving

Mark 14:23 reads, "Then he [Jesus] took the cup, gave thanks and offered it to them [the disciples]." Note carefully that he gave the cup to them after he had given thanks. Thus we see an obvious reason why the church has always seen, as a central element in the Lord's Supper, the idea of thanksgiving. Thus the word *Eucharist*, which comes from the Greek *eucharisteō*, meaning "to give thanks," has always been closely associated with the Lord's Supper for a very good reason. It is here that we give thanks and praise to God through our prayer. It is here that we thank God for creating us, for making us in God's image, for being a good and faithful God, for forgiving our sins for Christ's sake, and for giving us a future and a hope to be fully revealed in the kingdom of Christ, both now and in the age to come.

A STRENGTHENING REMEMBRANCE

Whereas our baptism is given only once and marks the beginning of our Christian journey, the Lord's Supper is given regularly and assures us of the Holy Spirit's ongoing presence in our lives. By this meal we are regularly given the grace and strength of Christ in communion with him. It is a meal that feeds us so that we can grow in the love and knowledge of Christ. The bread signifies the physical body of Christ as well as the mystical body of his church. The cup stands for his blood and thus the forgiveness of our sins and the life-giving power of his sacrifice for us.

Spiritual nourishment and growth come to us at this Supper in at least four ways:

1. It Enables

The Lord's Supper enables our faith in a way designed by God to strengthen us. Through reverent and faithful participation in this meal, we are enabled to proclaim our Lord's death until he comes. We are empowered to be more faithful in our witness to the gospel and called to serve others as Christ has served and given himself up for us. In a powerful way, if we come in humble faith, we reflect on our confession at the Lord's Table and ask God to enable us to live more faithfully for him. As we experience afresh God's love at the Eucharist, we find fresh peace with God. By this we are enabled to live our lives in the power of his love.

Regardless of how we understand the Supper, we who gather around this table receive the power of Christ—a power that enables us to give ourselves more completely to God and to our neighbors. By this divinely appointed means we are able to carry God's love into the world so that others may receive the benefit of Christ's gifts through us. By this means, the Lord's Supper also enables our mission to be carried out as we go out into the world.

2. It Unites

The bread we eat is one loaf, and the cup we drink is one cup. These elements symbolize our oneness with Christ and each other. The bread is not just for me individually but for the whole church, thus expressing our unity. The cup symbolizes the shedding of Christ's blood for the sins of all, not just for mine. This is the life of the whole church.

The *Didache*, a second-century document that served as a kind of manual of church order, makes extensive reference to the Eucharist. In connection with the piece of bread, broken from the one loaf and given to the worshiper, this liturgy reads as follows:

> We thank you, our Father, for the life and knowledge which you have revealed through Jesus, your child. To you be the glory forever.
>
> As this piece [of bread] was scattered over the hills and then was brought together and made one, so let your church be brought together from the ends of the earth into your Kingdom. For yours is the glory and the power through Jesus Christ forever.

The Lord's Supper is a fellowship (cf. 1 Cor. 10:15–17). It seems to have served from the very beginning as the sacred act of Christian fellowship, the bond of love between the members of a society. At this meal we share in the fellowship of Christ and of each other. What a tragedy that this meal constitutes a cause for division in the church of our day! A pastor of an earlier era stated the matter well when he wrote, "Herein is placed an inescapable obligation on every Christian that this act of Holy Communion become again, as it was in the Apostolic Church, a bond of union and a seal of Christian consecration to a common Lord."[5]

3. It Nourishes

It has been observed by many who have reflected on this meal that we are nourished by Christ at the feast of the Lord's Supper. Here we grow in our ability to nourish others and to be nourished by other Christians, who also share the grace of God with us. But the greater nourishment comes from God himself.

Here, in Christian worship, the whole of our relationship with God is summed up in one simple action—that of eating bread and drinking wine together as followers of Christ.

The famous German poet and novelist Goethe once said, "The highest cannot be spoken; it can only be acted." This is actually true of all human love, especially that of Jesus, who, "while we were still sinners,... died for us" (Rom. 5:8). Words and thoughts ultimately fail us when it comes to the mystery of such love; thus it seems that God gave to us a spiritual drama wherein we can be nourished again and again by his love.[6]

It's a demonstration a Picture
an acting out.

4. It Prepares

Wedd-
ing
feast!

The Scripture teaches that we prepare for the coming of the Lord and his earthly kingdom by taking the bread and the wine of this meal. Paul writes, "For whenever you eat this bread and drink this cup, you proclaim the Lord's death *until he comes*" (1 Cor. 11:26, italics added). We make a declaration at this table and prepare our body and soul for the coming day of the Lord. Jesus plainly gave to the Last Supper an eschatological orientation (cf. Mark 14:25). Here, I believe, is the right way to look at this matter of preparation:

> The wine, we are to understand, is to partake of the newness of the new heavens and the new earth which will be revealed in the Day of the Lord. Here Jesus is not viewing this great day on the side that is now turned toward us—this side which threatens judgment and prompts us to repentance—but on the bright side, which will not be visible to us till after the regeneration. His decisive orientation toward the future may explain why Jesus did not speak of the sacrament as a retrospective memorial of him, although it was sure to acquire this significance eventually. Paul emphasizes the memorial character of the sacrament when he says, "Ye do show the Lord's death till he comes" (1 Cor. 11:26). But the second coming is prospective, and even the proclamation of the Lord's death is not wholly retrospective, being an instance of the proclamation of the gospel, which always has in view a future salvation. This is the sense in which the bread and the wine—Jesus' body and blood—are given and spoken and eaten in remembrance of him.[7]

[handwritten margin notes: "If someone from the crowd was imprisoned and took it, it would be singular the plural ing not be proclaim to unbelievers"]

A PERSONAL REMEMBRANCE

This meal is given for you. It is intensely personal, though it should never be private or individualistic in its orientation or setting. When Paul states, "For whenever you eat this bread and drink this cup, you proclaim the Lord's death until he comes" (1 Cor. 11:26), he uses the plural "you," which in the context meant the Christians in Corinth. But we must not overlook the personal significance of the Lord's Supper. The Supper is surely for *you* as an individual Christian, but having said that, you must remember it is *not for you alone*. It is for you to share with your brothers and sisters in Christ.

How Do We Prepare for this Supper?

Each of us must personally prepare for this celebration if we are to take the bread and the wine as we ought. There are several ways to prepare. First, we should meditate on the meaning of Jesus' life, death, and resurrection. By this type of reflection and prayerful thought we can draw fresh inspiration and encouragement from his sacrifice for us. Second, we can consider again the message of Christ and how this good news informs the living of our lives today. Third, we can explore the various areas of our lives that need change and improvement through repentance. Finally, we can pray for the Spirit-given faith to receive the elements of the Supper with a deeper love for Christ and one another.[8]

There are thousands of written prayers and devotional helps that can be employed to assist one's personal remembrance of Christ in coming to this table. I particularly like the ancient prayer of Saint John Chrysostom, a great preacher and theologian in the Christian East, which expresses and summarizes almost every thought I've offered to this point. He wrote these words for all of us to pray as we come to this table:

> We praise and adore the ever blessed Trinity for the redemption of the world by our Lord Jesus Christ, and we come, O blessed Savior, now to take and eat thy body, which was broken for us. We come joyfully to drink of that cup which is the new testament in thy blood, which blood thou hast shed for the remission of the sins of

"Manna in the arc"

many. O merciful Jesus, create in us a mighty hunger after this bread of life, this bread which came down from heaven. Let this immortal food instill in our weak and languishing souls new supplies of grace, new life, new love, new vigor, and new resolutions. Amen.[9]

When Do We Celebrate the Supper?

The Bible does not answer a number of questions that we have about the Supper. One of the questions most often asked over the course of the centuries has to do with the frequency of the celebration: How often should we come to the table, and should it be only on the first day of the week?

Paul writes in 1 Corinthians 11:26, "For whenever you eat this bread and drink this cup ...." The word *whenever* appears to be open-ended. It means simply that you may take the meal as often as conscience and common practice determine. Churches differ in their customs, but one thing we do know — the earliest Christians took the Supper very often. It is possible that in some settings they took it almost every day. It seems fairly obvious when we read the historical records that initially they took it every Lord's Day. Paul's counsel does not determine the precise number of times the church should take the meal, but it places no limits on frequent celebration either.

A common argument I've encountered among some evangelical Protestants is that frequent celebration will make the Supper ordinary or less important. I have always found this argument weak, if not outright appalling. How can you remember the Lord's death too frequently? How can I express my devotion and love for Christ too much? The problem in making it too ordinary may lie in our hearts, not in how often we actually come to the table.

The other important truth underscored in Paul's counsel is that we are to "proclaim the Lord's death until he comes." This meal has both a past and a future perspective in it. We must regularly remember the Lord's death. But we should also look forward to his coming again, when we will no longer need this oft-repeated meal to remind us of the Lamb's victory. This idea introduces us to the great "wedding [supper] of the Lamb" (Rev. 19:7) which will come when all the redeemed celebrate the Lord's death and resurrection with him in heaven.

A SPIRITUAL REMEMBRANCE

The apostle Paul provides important instruction about taking this meal as a proper spiritual remembrance:

> A man ought to examine himself before he eats of the bread and drinks of the cup. For anyone who eats and drinks without recognizing the body of the Lord eats and drinks judgment on himself. That is why many among you are weak and sick, and a number of you have fallen asleep. But if we judged ourselves, we would not come under judgment. When we are judged by the Lord, we are being disciplined so that we will not be condemned with the world.
>
> *1 Corinthians 11:28–32*

The context of this counsel, often misunderstood by modern Christians who fear that they have committed a particular sin that must keep them from coming to the Lord's Table, is about the unity of the church (see 1 Cor. 10:17; 11:21). The great sin in Corinth was the way the church humiliated the poor in their midst. Well-off Corinthians appear to have prevented the less fortunate from celebrating the various feasts. This problem carried over into the Lord's Supper context. Their behavior was utterly selfish and a scandalous contradiction of the meaning of this meal. This action equates to what Paul calls "despising" the church of God in 1 Corinthians 11:22. What this underscores is not personal sin but actions and attitudes that would keep a person from fellowship with all the members of the congregation. This meal is a fellowship—with Christ and one another. It is a meal of peace; thus, to refuse to be at peace with our brothers and sisters is to eat and drink "judgment" on ourselves. Given the fact that schism and pride plague every congregation on earth, the Lord's Supper is an appointed time for reconciliation and renewed fellowship. Here God's grace is given to heal and to unite us again to our Lord and to each other.

A REAL FELLOWSHIP

One of the differences of opinion you'll encounter in the four views on the Lord's Supper presented in this book surrounds the meaning of our fellowship with Christ at this table.

There is room for discussion about this matter, but there seems to be little room for disagreement about one particular fact: in some way we fellowship with Christ himself at this meal.

Here is how the Bible puts it:

> Is not the cup of thanksgiving for which we give thanks a participation in the blood of Christ? And is not the bread that we break a participation in the body of Christ? Because there is one loaf, we, who are many, are one body, for we all partake of the one loaf.
>
> *1 Corinthians 10:16–17*

The word "participation" here is the translation of *koinonia*, a word familiar to many readers. *Christ is present at this Supper*. We may debate *how* he is present, but the teaching of 1 Corinthians is clear at this point. And what we read from the earliest records of Christian thought outside of sacred Scripture demonstrates that Christians believed the living Christ communed or fellowshipped with his people when they ate this bread and drank this cup. Somehow more is going on here than what can be processed in our brains. There is mystery here, beyond doubt. The attempt to explain away this mystery is neither correct nor spiritually fruitful. All who wrestle with the four views discussed in this book will want to keep this in mind as they read and reflect. This Supper renews our life in Christ and assures us of the Holy Spirit's presence in us as we continue to draw near to God every day.

At this Supper, Christians commemorate Christ's life, death, and resurrection. We are to come in faith, seeking fellowship with Christ in thanksgiving. There is much here that may still divide one Christian understanding from another, but also much to encourage us to actively and faithfully participate with reverence. This is one reason why Communion seasons have often been times of revival in the history of Christianity. Here God has come to his people, and love for Christ has been renewed in a season of divine refreshing sent by the Lord. May it happen again in our day, as we humbly draw near to God, who gave us this holy meal to keep us close to Christ our Lord.

Notes: Introduction: Do This in Remembrance of Me

1. Donald Bridge and David Phypers, *Communion: The Meal That Unites?* (Wheaton, Ill.: Shaw, 1983), 9–10.

2. Ibid., 10.

3. Cited in "Reflections: Quotations to Stir Heart and Mind," *Christianity Today* (June 2005), 54.

4. Robert H. Stein, "Last Supper," in *Dictionary of Jesus and the Gospels*, ed Joel B. Green, Scot McKnight, and I. Howard Marshall (Downers Grove, Ill.: InterVarsity, 1992), 447.

5. Hugh Thompson Kerr, *The Christian Sacraments* (Philadelphia: Westminster, 1944), 94.

6. See Charles L. Wallis, ed., *The Table of the Lord* (New York: Harper & Brothers, 1958), 116.

7. Walter Lowrie, cited in *Table of the Lord*, 140.

8. These suggestions come from the booklet "What Every Presbyterian Should Know about the Sacrament of the Lord's Supper" (South Deerfield, Mass.: Channing L. Bete, 1984).

9. Saint John Chrysostom, cited in *Table of the Lord*, 44.

Chapter One

BAPTIST VIEW

Christ's Presence as Memorial

BAPTIST VIEW

Christ's Presence as Memorial

Russell D. Moore

[handwritten annotation: symbol]

Novelist Flannery O'Connor was at a dinner party when "the conversation turned on the Eucharist." In response to a comment from the ex-Catholic intellectual Mary McCarthy in which she said she thought of the bread of Communion as a pretty good symbol, O'Connor said, "Well, if it's a symbol, to hell with it."[1] Many Christians can sympathize with O'Connor's reflexively Catholic dismissal of a "symbolic" view of the Lord's Supper. And, in one sense, she is exactly right. If the bread and the wine are simply "symbols" — along the lines of a contemporary corporate logo — whose point is to remind us of a significant historical event, then the Lord's Table really isn't all that defining for Christian identity. But this, of course, is not at all what Baptists and others in the broad Zwinglian tradition have meant when we have affirmed that the Lord's Supper is a "memorial meal," or an ordinance of Christ. In order to understand the Baptist view, we must take into account the biblical pattern of signs, and how it relates to the role of proclamation for the creation and sustenance of faith. But in order to recapture the meaning of the so-called "memorial" view, more than just understanding is in order. Churches must consciously reclaim the Lord's Supper as a central aspect of the church's identity in Christ.

THE LORD'S SUPPER AS SIGN

Biblical Foundations

The very term *memorial* can be misleading. Many contemporary Christians have thus chafed at the idea of the Supper as a bare means to remembrance—prompting even some Baptists to embrace a more sacramental understanding of the Supper.[2] But the historic Baptist concept of the Lord's Supper serves less as a "memorial" than as a sign—a sign pointing both backward and forward. In the Old Testament, this function of the sign serves as a "reminder" and a proclamation to both covenant parties—Yahweh and his people—of the promises of God. The rainbow sign of the Noahic covenant, for instance, served to remind the entire surviving creation that they had been spared from the wrath of God in the deluge, and to remind them that God promised never to destroy his creation by water again. But the most significant aspect of the bow was the "reminder" to God himself: "Whenever the rainbow appears in the clouds, I will see it and remember the everlasting covenant between God and all living creatures of every kind on the earth" (Gen. 9:16). As theologian Michael Williams points out, the bow in the sky is "a sign of God's grace in the midst of judgment," a treaty of peace between the Creator and his human image bearers along with the creation they are called to govern under his lordship.[3]

The sign nature of the Supper is in continuity then with the rest of God's redemptive purposes in the canon, purposes that often are linked with the concept of eating and feeding. In the primeval garden of Eden, the man and the woman were sustained by the fruit of the trees, especially by that of the Tree of Life. One of the earliest and most specific acts of God's lordship over humanity entailed what they were to eat and what they were to avoid eating.[4] After their rebellion, they were cut off from the garden sanctuary, but most specifically from the life-giving tree.

In the redemption of Israel from among the nations, God gave various signs that he was for them, centering on the act of eating and feeding. The Passover meal indicated God's presence on behalf of the Israelites. Manna in the wilderness, along with the provision of water and of quail, demonstrated that God cared for his covenant people. Moreover, God promised a future restoration that included eating and drinking of bread and of wine. In his prophecy of God's overturning of the reign of death, Isaiah mentions that God will lay out a banquet for all peoples on the holy mountain, a feast that includes "the finest of wines" (Isa. 25:6). The messianic feast points even beyond the bounty of Canaan, "a land of grain and new wine, where the heavens drop dew" (Deut. 33:28). Speaking of the glorious future that awaits God's people, Zechariah writes, "The seed will grow well, the vine will yield its fruit, the ground will produce its crops, and the heavens will drop their dew. I will give all these things as an inheritance to the remnant of this people" (Zech. 8:12). With Israel restored, "Grain will make the young men thrive, and new wine the young women" (9:17). When the Davidic kingdom is exalted in the last days, Amos announces, "New wine will drip from the mountains and flow from all the hills" (Amos 9:13), and the restored nation of Israel "will plant vineyards and drink their wine" (v. 14).

With the curse on the ground (Gen. 3:17–18) now lifted, the people will feast, because their covenant God feeds them— and does so without stinginess. Whereas in the old age, people labored against the ground for bread and for wine ("through painful toil you will eat of it all the days of your life" [Gen. 3:17]), at the messianic banquet the earth itself will joyfully give forth the provision of the covenant God.

The coming of Jesus promises the onset of this new reality. Jesus changes water to wine at a wedding feast, pointing to a greater feast to come (John 2:1–11). He feeds thousands by multiplying food with a word (John 6:1–13). He identifies himself and his people with the vine of God (John 15:1–8), an image previously given to the nation of Israel (Isa. 5:1–7; Jer. 2:21), identifying himself as the fulfillment of the promise that the vine would one day yield fruit (Isa. 27:6; Gal. 5:22–23). In Christ, this new age is a reality, although a veiled reality seen only to those who have the eyes of faith. The meal Jesus feeds us then is a sign of an eschatological banquet, with the church acknowledging the "already" and pining for the "not yet."

All of this is set in the context of a cosmic warfare schema of Scripture. The story line is a battle between the Serpent and the dragon-slayer son of Eve (Gen. 3:15; Rev. 12), a war that rages from the very earliest pages of the biblical story. Even in the tracks just outside of Eden, the murderous Serpent leads a fallen humanity to the shedding of blood, a killing that, ironically, finds its root in two views on ritual sacrifice. Cain brings to Yahweh the vegetation and grain of the earth, as though he does not recognize that he now lives in a cursed era. Abel the righteous, however, recognizing that something is awry, brings before his God a bloody sacrifice (Gen. 4:3–5). In the Lord's Supper, both the restoration of Eden and the recognition of human sin coincide in a ritual meal that is indeed the produce of the earth, perhaps pointing backward to our pre-carnivorous past and to our post-carnivorous future (Isa. 11:7), and yet symbolizing spilled blood and a mangled body, pointing to the fact that we are forever approaching our God through a Mediator (Rev. 5:9–10).

The banquet of the Lord's Supper signals that, for the church, the warfare is over, and yet it still rages on. While not all things in the outside world have yet been placed under the feet of our King, we have come into his rest. And as we gather around his table, he announces to us his victory, pointing us to the day when we will eat at a table spread for us in the presence of our enemies (Ps. 23:5). In this sense, the Lord's Supper is the antithesis of an ongoing sacrifice of Christ. It is instead the sign that the sacrifice has been accepted once for all and that we now share in the spoils of a crucifixion that crushed the Serpent's head. This warfare motif is why Jesus assigns the Supper with such kingdom significance, even in the midst of an ongoing tumult against the principalities and powers. After he celebrates the Supper, Jesus announces to his disciples, "You are those who have stood by me in my trials. And I confer on you a kingdom, just as my Father conferred one on me, so that you may eat and drink at my table in my kingdom and sit on thrones, judging the twelve tribes of Israel" (Luke 22:28–30). Immediately after this declaration, Jesus promises Peter that he will stand against a Satan who desires to destroy him (v. 31), assuring him and us that through Jesus the kingdom will prevail. Through the eating of a messianic banquet meal, the church announces—not just to itself but to the principalities and powers (Eph. 3:10)—that the kingdom has invaded, the new order is dawning, and the rulers of this age are being cast out. That is more than a symbol; it is a sign.

Contemporary Implications

The sign aspect of the Lord's Supper is often obscured in contemporary churches—and not only in those who hold to the Zwinglian/Baptist view of the Supper as a memorial meal. Often this has as much to do with the ethos of the Supper as with any teaching regarding it. Often Lord's Supper services are characterized by a funereal atmosphere, complete with somber, droning organ music as the ministers or deacons distribute the elements to the congregation. The congregation is sometimes led to believe (if for no other reason than the omission of pastoral teaching) that the point of the meal is to screw up one's face and try to feel sorry for Jesus. This is often accompanied by a psychological attempt to meditate on the physical pain of Jesus' sufferings—an emphasis that is markedly understated in the biblical text itself.

In order to recover a biblical model of the Lord's Supper, churches need not tacitly accept a sacramental understanding of the "real presence of Christ" in the elements of bread and wine. Instead, they must recapture the vision of the eschatological messianic banquet—and seek to recover the joyfulness and triumph of this event within their own churches. This would mean that the Lord's Supper would be characterized by even more celebrative singing, and even laughter, than the rest of the service. The congregation would be taught to understand that the Supper is a victory lap—announcing the triumph of Christ over the powers of sin, death, and Satan. At the same time, the Supper would maintain the gravity of the moment, as the congregation recognizes that it is performing a sign of God's freeing us from slavery through Christ—a sign of a new covenant that addresses not only other believers but God himself, the unseen demonic rulers, and even unbelievers who might marvel from outside at the meaning we find in this ancient rite.

THE LORD'S SUPPER AS PROCLAMATION

Biblical Foundations

The function of the Supper as proclamation is particularly acute in the old covenant precursor to the Lord's Supper—the

Passover meal. Yahweh delivers the people of Israel from the curse on the firstborn through a substitutionary sacrifice, the death of a lamb. He then commands them to continue the meal as a statute—a memorial to the deliverance from the curse on Egypt (Exod. 12:43–50). The point of the meal was explicitly commemorative. The Israelites are told how to respond when future generations ask what the meal means: "Then tell them, 'It is the Passover sacrifice to the LORD, who passed over the houses of the Israelites in Egypt and spared our homes when he struck down the Egyptians'" (12:27). But the meal did not simply point backward. Yahweh reminds the people that they will continue to celebrate the Passover when *their children* are in *the land of promise*. In so doing, Israel's God signifies that he will keep his covenant to multiply the nation and to deliver them into a land flowing with milk and honey. Moreover, the meal was to prompt the Israelite community to worship in light of Yahweh's redemptive act (v. 27, "the people bowed down and worshiped"). As one commentator observes, "The annual Passover celebrations, then, were a constant summons to Israel to *look back* and were never meant to be anything other than a 'Getting out of Egypt' feast, a commemoration of their deliverance and redemption."[5] The feast was to continue even after the conquest of the Promised Land, to remind the people of Israel in perpetuity that they were a redeemed people.

It is no accident that the first Lord's Supper was a Passover meal. Luke specifically tells us that it was "the day of Unleavened Bread on which the Passover lamb had to be sacrificed" (Luke 22:7). It is not incidental that the institution of the meal coincided with Passover since Jesus explicitly called it the Passover meal, an identification Matthew repeated in retrospect (Matt. 26:18–19). Again, just as with the Passover meal, Jesus ties the significance of the meal with its function as proclamation. If Jesus intends to suggest that the elements of bread and wine are literally his body and his blood, he certainly avoids the obvious question as to how then the disciples see his body still before them, at that point neither broken nor poured out. But he does suggest that the bread and the wine function as covenant markers (Luke 22:20), that the disciples should "do this in remembrance of me" (Luke 22:19). Moreover, Jesus points forward to the messianic banquet to come by noting that he will not eat or drink with his disciples "until it finds fulfillment in the kingdom of God" (Luke 22:16).

It seems, then, that for Jesus the institution of the Lord's Supper functioned for the new covenant Israelite community precisely as it had for the old covenant Israelite community. Yes, the meal strengthened faith, but it did so through a visible sign of an invisible covenant promise—the promise of the kingdom of Christ. The question, then, is not whether the Lord's Supper is a means of grace but *how* it functions as a means of grace. The Supper does indeed ground, buttress, and establish Christian faith—but it does so through the proclamation of the finished redemption of Christ and the promise of the kingdom to come. In this sense, the eating and drinking of the Lord's Supper create faith within the body, and this is analogous to the verbal proclamation of the word of truth. The church's faith is established through the preaching of the gospel—a proclamation that includes the eating of the bread and the drinking of the wine.

This gets at the very definition of faith itself. In a passage identified by various Christian groups as eucharistic, Jesus contends that his disciples must "eat the flesh of the Son of Man and drink his blood" (John 6:53–55). To equate this feeding on Christ with the physical act of consuming the elements of the Lord's Supper confuses the context of the event and obscures the force of Jesus' teaching. Immediately after feeding the crowd of five thousand, Jesus identifies himself as the true bread from heaven, as distinct from the manna in the wilderness. He then points the crowd to the issue of belief, a belief that includes looking to and trusting in Jesus as Messiah and Lord (John 6:40). In the act of feeding, Jesus illuminates the very meaning of faith itself and therefore of gospel proclamation.

From Eden onward, a fatal flaw of humanity remained the appetites, specifically the refusal to trust God for the provision of food and drink. Noah, the founder of a new humanity after the deluge, becomes drunk with wine (Gen. 9:21). Esau throws aside his birthright for the sake of a hunger for stew (Gen. 25:33–34), a pattern that the New Testament warns believers not to emulate (Heb. 12:16–17). Indeed, the apostle Paul indicts unbelievers, specifically false teachers within the church, because they are governed by the appetites, persons whose "god is their stomach" (Phil. 3:19). The Israelites grumbled in the wilderness that

God was not for them, specifically because they did not believe he would feed them (Num. 11:4–5). In the temptation (Matt. 4:2–4), Jesus demonstrates trust in his Father, where Israel demonstrated distrust, by refusing to eat the food of demons, trusting instead that by living by every word that comes from the mouth of the Father he would gain "a good land—… a land with wheat and barley, vines and fig trees, pomegranates, olive oil and honey; a land where bread will not be scarce and you will lack nothing" (Deut. 8:7–9).[6] When the church feeds on the bread and the wine given by Christ, we are confessing to one another, calling forth faith within the church, that the God who brought us out of slavery now says to us: "Open wide your mouth and I will fill it" (Ps. 81:10).

Contemporary Implications

The first way the church can incorporate a more biblical understanding of the Lord's Supper as an event of proclamation is to restore the Supper to the biblical rhythm of congregational life. The ordinary pattern of the Supper recorded in the book of Acts is a weekly observance (Acts 2:42), accompanied by the preaching of the gospel, prayer, and the fellowship of the body. Often churches neglect the Supper—observing it monthly, quarterly, or even less often—out of fear that it will be seen as sacramental, or, conversely, that it will callous the congregation to the meaning of the ritual. If the Supper is gospel proclamation meant to call forth and strengthen the faith of believers, how could such an event become rote? The key to this question is not so much in an evangelical fear of sacerdotal tendencies as in an evangelical ignorance of the role of gospel preaching *for the believer*. Evangelicals understand that the gospel is "the power of God for … salvation" (Rom. 1:16) at the moment of conversion. What we often do not comprehend is that this same gospel is what continues believers in the faith, moving them to conformity with the image of Christ. So often our Lord's Supper practices are so ambiguous simply because we are unsure of how to preach the gospel to believers. We believe that the message of John 3:16 is too elementary, so we move on to "practical life tips" from the Scriptures. And yet the Bible never envisions a church of believers not constantly nourished by the gospel of

Christ crucified—both through verbal preaching and through the ordinances.

Such a reorientation will necessitate pastors and church leaders who explain the meaning of the Supper, both to lifelong members and for the benefit of those who may come from more sacramental backgrounds. The Lord's Supper should never be an afterthought, tagged on to the end of a service, perhaps after the final musical number of a visiting youth choir. Instead, the Supper should require the same pattern as the Passover and Jesus' institution of the Supper: explanation of God's redemptive act followed by the enactment of the redemption in the meal. Sinners should be called to see in the bread and in the wine their own crucifixion through the crucifixion of the Christ in whom they are hidden (Col. 3:3). It should be an opportunity to present to sinners the tangible evidence that their transgressions are forgiven. Imagine, for instance, a pastor at the beginning of the Supper assuring women in the congregation who have had abortions in their past to trust in the Christ whose body was given and whose blood was shed for the remission of all of their sins, including this one that dare not be named.

In this sense, the Supper of blood and flesh drives us in faith to confess our sins and to rest in Christ. It serves to convict us of the truth that we approach God through a veil of blood and death; we do not stand before him with our own covenantal righteousness. In this sense, we are similar to our old covenant ancestors, who were reminded by the slit throats of goats and calves that they were sinners reconciled to God. Our eating of bread and drinking of wine are not sacrifices—precisely because we cannot repeat the infinite sacrifice of Jesus—but they point us backward to the truth that we come to God now only because of a judgment that fell on our King at Golgotha. In 2004, filmmaker Mel Gibson released his film *The Passion of the Christ*, a project derided by critics as sadistic and gory. And yet, the film, with its intense depictions of the bloody sacrifice of Christ, resonated with Christian audiences—especially evangelical Protestants—across America. Could it be that, for many Christians, this film reminded them that theirs is a bloody religion, a truth too long obscured in our churches except in occasional evangelistic presentations to unbelievers? Could it be that this longing in evangelical audiences is the result of a loss of the

Lord's Supper as a robust and meaningful proclamation of the bloody death of our Christ?

As the Supper functions as proclamation, the presence of Christ in the indwelling Spirit not only assures of forgiveness through the Word; he also convicts of unbiblical patterns of life and thought. The Supper must be verbally interpreted by pastors and church leaders to mean that the church renews its commitment to seek first the kingdom of God, knowing that only from him can we find our daily bread. This is especially relevant in an American society so fattened by our consumerism, materialism, and wealth that we are plagued with problems with food—problems ranging from childhood obesity to teenage anorexia to middle-aged bulimia. Jesus spoke of children who ask their fathers for bread and are not given stones (Matt. 7:9). Too often in our culture of self-sufficiency, children never need to ask fathers for bread at all—they simply grab another Twinkie from the cabinet. The Lord's Supper can serve as a much-needed gospel corrective to all of us, reminding us, through faith, that we are but hungry children who reject the Evil One's delicacies as we wait for our Father to feed us until we want no more.[7]

THE LORD'S SUPPER AS COMMUNION

Biblical Foundations

The apostle Paul grounds the Supper's meaning in the new covenant identity of the body of Christ. The problem with not "recognizing the body" in the Corinthian church is that the community did not recognize how the Supper distinguished them from the condemned world (1 Cor. 11:29–32). For Paul, the point is not a metaphysical question about the secret makeup of the elements. Rather, he, like Jesus, points to remembrance and to promise. The bread and the cup are signs of remembrance of the atonement (1 Cor. 11:24–25) and point to the coming of the kingdom (1 Cor. 11:26). There is no question that in the Supper we commune with one another and with Christ. The question is *how*. The apostle Paul does not intend to teach that the elements physically become Jesus' body and blood; nor does he intend to teach that believers are spiritually transported to the heavenly places to commune with Christ. Instead, it seems that the New

Testament assumes that Christ is *always present* with his people (Matt. 28:20), organically and mystically united to his church as a head is united to a body (Eph. 5:23).

In the Supper, we experience the presence of Christ through the proclamation that Christ is united with his people, the church. We, through faith, confess the identity of the people of God and our union with the crucified Messiah. Once again, there is continuity with an aspect of old covenant Israel's Passover feast. Bible scholar Peter Craigie puts it this way: "After the exodus and forming of the covenant at Sinai, Israel became a single nation, the family of God; thus the Passover became the act, symbolically speaking, of the one large family of God, celebrated in one place where the sanctuary or house of God was located."[8] The Lord's Supper identifies the temple presence of God in his new sanctuary, the church.

Through the Lord's Supper then, the church feasts, specifically because we recognize the presence of Christ. In the temptation in the wilderness, Jesus refuses to eat because God will give him eschatological bread (Matt. 4:2–4). In the Supper, we confess that God has fed us through the broken body and spilled blood of his Messiah. Jesus tells us that the wedding party fasts when the bridegroom is away but feasts in his presence (Matt. 9:14–15). The kingdom community feasts because our Christ is always with us, although this presence is not yet evident to the watching world.

This is the reason why some in the Corinthian church were "guilty of sinning against the body and blood" of Christ, by not "recognizing the body" and thus eating and drinking judgment on themselves (1 Cor. 11:27, 29). The issue was not that they did not recognize some metaphysical reality within the elements; nor was it that they were not transported to another spiritual realm. The problem was instead that there were divisions within the body (v. 18). These people were using the Supper to feed their individual appetites rather than to care for one another (vv. 20–21). This kind of fighting to get ahead of one another, to feed one's own belly, means that the Supper is "not the Lord's Supper you eat" but something entirely different. The divisions within the body are repudiated, Paul notes, because of the way the Supper forms the identity of the people of God. Immediately after noting that the broken bread is "a participation in the body of Christ" (1 Cor. 10:16), Paul goes on to elaborate—identifying this body with the church itself: "Because there is one loaf, we, who are many, are one body, for we all partake of the one loaf" (v. 17).

The bread, the apostle notes, is "a participation in the body of Christ" and the cup "a participation in the blood of Christ" (1 Cor. 10:16). But how is this so? In the same way that eating food sacrificed to idols means becoming "participants with demons" (v. 20). It is not that the meat itself is the real presence of the demonic beings; nor is it that the eaters are transported to the demonic realm to commune with them. Rather, the eaters of this pagan meat participate in consuming a sacrifice intended to exalt and identify with the demons who masquerade as gods (cf. Deut. 32:32–33). It is in this way that the believer has "fellowship" with Christ—through the presence of his body, the church. Thus, the eating of the Supper points back to the Old Testament imagery of the worshiper "fellowshipping" with God through the meal of a sacrifice, a meal the meat of which the worshiper actually consumes. The idea of a shared meal as fellowship, as Bible scholar Mark Rooker notes, "sheds light on Paul's warning in 1 Corinthians 10:18–22 that partaking of a sacrifice offered to an idol or a demon is in effect having fellowship with it."[9]

This is also why the apostle Paul ties the Lord's Supper to the discipline of the congregation. The immoral man is to be cut off from the community—specifically in terms of barring him from eating with the congregation (1 Cor. 5:11). Why? The apostle points to the Passover imagery once again (vv. 6–7), both in terms of the unleavened bread and in terms of the sacrificed Passover lamb. Since the meal defines the people of God, the one who refuses to repent is delivered to Satan, to the world outside—the world that is waiting to be judged (vv. 5, 12–13). In this way, the congregation is "recognizing the body" of Christ by defining the boundaries of communion at the table in terms of those who are in union with Christ. In so doing, the church by faith acknowledges what Jesus once accused his religious interlocutors of ignoring: "I say to you that many will come from the east and the west, and will take their places at the feast with Abraham, Isaac and Jacob in the kingdom of heaven" (Matt.

8:11). This is one reason why the breaking of bread between Jews and Gentiles was such a crucial aspect of the unity of the early church.

Contemporary Implications

Often the rejection of the "memorial view" of the Lord's Supper has less to do with the view itself than with the sick Western individualism that attaches itself to it. It seems that if the Lord's Supper is a "reminder" or even a sign of the future, it must necessarily be an individual act, devoted simply to causing the individual to exercise his cognition in a more holy fashion. This is not, of course, necessarily the case. Indeed, the alternative viewpoints have found themselves just as vulnerable to American individualism—as is evidenced by Roman Catholic churches in which the communicants line up for the Eucharist and its sacramental blessings without ever knowing one another.[10]

The need for a community focus around the table cannot, however, be eradicated. Baptist churches that celebrate a curt "Communion" every three months still find themselves with this need for a truly communitarian Lord's Supper. Often these churches seek to fill this need for table fellowship with a "Dinner on the Grounds" Sunday meal or coffee and doughnuts before the Sunday school hour or lunch after services at the local steakhouse. These moments of fellowship are crucial, but they cannot take the place of the Supper Jesus has given us. Part of the problem is the individualized way we present the elements themselves. Most contemporary Baptist churches—and many other evangelical Protestant churches—distribute chewing gum-sized pellets of bread and thimble-sized shot glasses of juice. Increasingly this practice is even more individualized by companies that sell to churches "disposable" Communion "sets," a plastic container filled with juice with a wafer wrapped in cellophane on top (ideal, we are told, for the college group's summer retreat in the mountains).

This practice nullifies the thrust of the New Testament emphasis on a common cup and a common loaf, both of which signify the unity of the congregation in Christ. It also mitigates the meaning of the Supper as a *supper*, as a meal. The meaning of the Supper would go a long way toward recovery in our churches if we asked the congregation to tear apart the bread and to drink together from a common cup of wine—practices that would have been commonplace in the early New Testament communities. Some would shrink from such a practice, no doubt, out of fear of illness or discomfort with such close contact with others. But that is precisely the kind of American individualism that is obliterated by the gospel emphasis on the church as the household of God, a family united through the Spirit. As we encourage the congregation to eat together around the table of Christ, we call them to faith, asking them to recognize and welcome the presence of Christ—not in the elements or in the heavens above them, but in the body he has called together, the assembly he rules and protects even now as King. Only then will we understand what the New Testament Scriptures mean when they call us to "fellowship." Perhaps if we recover the community focus of the Lord's Supper, we will have less and less need for professional conflict resolution experts and others to "consult" with our congregations on alleviating divisions among the congregants. After all, for the apostle Paul, the starting point for unity in the church was the common table. It could be once more.

At the same time, the recovery of the Lord's Supper necessitates the recovery of church discipline. The two are inseparable in the New Testament and, if the Supper is to effect real fellowship in the Spirit, they must be inseparable once more. Often in our contemporary ecclesial culture the act of barring a member from the table seems quaint or even meaningless. After all, who really cares if he is deprived of a wafer and a splash of grape juice? If the table, however, is once again seen as the locus of church fellowship, as the place where we experience Christ present in one another around the eating of an inaugurated banquet feast, the fencing of the table takes on a very different—and much more biblical—hue. If the identity of the presence of Christ in "the brothers" is seen by who is admitted to the Lord's Table, then we will understand the importance of the church far more than if we simply see the bread and the wine as some undefined ritual—something we do because Jesus told us to, although we can't quite remember why.

The nexus of church discipline and the Lord's Supper is bound then to militate against the individualistic grain of contemporary evangelicalism. It will mean that churches must discuss, for instance, the meaning of baptism as the boundary marker for the church—with churches that believe in a regenerate church membership and credo-baptism affirming such a stance even when such affirmation is seen as sectarian by those who would ask, "So you wouldn't admit Jonathan Edwards to the Lord's Table?" Ironically, such discussions would not mean more division in the church but *less*. Churches that recognize the importance of the ordinances of baptism and the Lord's Supper for Christian identity have far more prospect for eventual unity than churches that seek to find unity in carefully written manifestos or carefully orchestrated press conferences.

CONCLUSION

The Lord's Supper is about more than how we view a ritual of the Christian church. Instead, our view of the Supper affects and explains how we think about the most basic realities of our common Christian faith. In 1832, Ralph Waldo Emerson resigned as a Unitarian minister because he could not administer the bread and the wine, since his religion was wholly spiritual and not material at all. Historian John Lukacs argues that Emerson's anti-material spirituality, seen in his view of the Supper, represented a trend in liberal Protestantism that eventually led to the widespread acceptance of Darwinism. After all, Christianity was "spiritual" and "commemorative," not earthly or physical.[11] This kind of pseudo-Gnosticism erodes Christianity at its very core.

It is this kind of anti-material "spiritual" Christianity that once drove Flannery O'Connor to rage. But the alternatives are not merely some metaphysical understanding of "real presence" or the idea that the Supper is "just a symbol." The Lord's Supper is no more "just a symbol" than the gospel account is "just a story." The gospel, presented in verbal declaration or in the messianic table meal, points to something that makes sense of all reality—indeed the reality to which everything else points. In order to reclaim the centrality of the Lord's Table, we must think anew about what it means to be a fellowship of believers, united through the Spirit around a crucified and triumphant Messiah. It is true that, in one sense, "the kingdom of God is not a matter of eating and drinking" (Rom. 14:17). But we must remember that, in another sense, the sounds of the kingdom of God are not those of eerie cosmic silences but of the murmur of voices, the clinking of cups, and the tearing of bread.

A REFORMED RESPONSE

I. John Hesselink

It is reassuring to see Russell Moore immediately dismissing an all too popular Protestant understanding of the Lord's Supper as being simply symbolic. The Baptists and others in "the broad Zwinglian tradition" (whatever that means), he tells us, believe that the sacrament does not merely "remind us of a significant historical event" (p. 29). Later in the chapter, however, the position taken regarding the Supper is problematic from a Reformed, not to mention Catholic and Lutheran, standpoint.

Nevertheless, when Moore states that "the historic Baptist concept of the Lord's Supper serves less as a 'memorial' than as a sign—a sign pointing both backward and forward" (p. 30), we resonate with that.[1] The subsequent biblical exposition, which takes up much of the chapter, is interesting and helpful, but it does not clarify how the signs in the Lord's Supper relate to what is signified. The biblical exposition concludes with the statements, "Through the eating of a messianic banquet meal, the church announces ... that the kingdom has invaded, the new order is dawning, and the rulers of this age are being cast out." And then, "That is more than a symbol; it is a sign" (p. 32).

Fine, but a sign of what? Simply of a "vision of the eschatological messianic banquet" (p. 33)? The eschatological emphasis and the stress on the joyful, triumphant nature of the sacrament are salutary. However, the question remains, What happens in the Lord's Supper? Moore states, "In order to recover a biblical model of the Lord's Supper, churches need not tacitly accept a sacramental understanding of the 'real presence of Christ' in the elements of bread and wine" (p. 33). Then follows the sentence, "Instead, they must recapture the vision of the eschatological messianic banquet." This raises another question: Does the Supper only point to a future celebration?

The discussion that follows makes much of the Passover celebrations that were a precursor to Jesus' celebration of the Last Supper with his disciples. The bread and wine then "function as covenant markers" (p. 34), and the meal is accordingly "a visible sign of an invisible covenant promise—the promise of the kingdom of Christ" (p. 35). The main point of this whole section, however, is that the function of the Lord's Supper is proclamation. It is significant, however, that this proclamation refers to a past event—Christ's redemption—and a future event—the promise of the kingdom. So again the question remains, What happens in the present? Note that, for Moore, the Supper as "gospel proclamation" is "meant to call forth and strengthen the faith of believers" (p. 36). It also "drives us in faith to confess our sins and to rest in Christ" (p. 37). At one point, Moore speaks of "the presence of Christ," but not in the partaking of the Lord's Supper but "in the indwelling Spirit" (p. 38)—a vague and curious expression.

What it finally comes down to is a general presence of Christ with the church: "We, through faith, confess the identity of the people of God and our union with the crucified Messiah" (p. 39). And "the kingdom community feasts because our Christ is always with us" (p. 39). All this is true, but there is nothing uniquely sacramental about all of this. Calvin, too, emphasized the role of the covenant, the sacrificial atoning death of Christ, and our faith union with Christ, but he didn't stop there. For Calvin (and Luther and Aquinas), participating in the Lord's Supper brings something extra to the table, something not experienced simply by the proclamation of the Word or the fellowship of the covenant community. It is a mysterious, miraculous communion with the flesh and blood of our Lord Jesus Christ—and that is what I find missing in Moore's presentation.

All these caveats notwithstanding, I still find much that I can affirm, above all the biblical background and eschatological emphasis. In our own liturgy for the Lord's Supper we say together, "Christ has died. Christ is risen. Christ will come again." The section on the meaning of the sacrament begins with the sentence, "Beloved in the Lord Jesus Christ, the holy Supper which we are about to celebrate is a feast of remembrance, of communion, and of hope." Each of these themes is then developed with a full paragraph. The same motifs reappear in the prayer before Communion. Such reminders should foster a more celebrative experience of the Supper.

I also agree that ideally there should be a common loaf and a common cup in the celebration of the Supper. In most of our congregations this is not the practice, but at Western Seminary, where we celebrate the sacrament every Friday, we pass around the one loaf and then dip the portion we have torn off from that loaf in the one cup that is passed around. As each person hands the bread and later the cup to the next person, they say, "The body of Christ broken for you," and "The blood of Christ shed for you." The service concludes with a prayer and hymn of thanksgiving. This is an appropriate ending for any Communion service, since the Eucharist, among other things, is also a *eucharistia* (thanksgiving) for God's gift of salvation in Jesus Christ.

A LUTHERAN RESPONSE

David P. Scaer

Offering these chapters from different perspectives brings to light not only unresolved historical differences but areas in which one tradition can enhance that of the others. My hope is that our discussions will not simply reiterate Reformation-era differences, but Russell Moore opens this door by putting forth Zwingli's view as the Baptist position. This takes matters back to the impasse at the Marburg Colloquy of October 1529 at which Ulrich Zwingli and Martin Luther could not agree on the Lord's Supper. The Lutheran Reformers were asked to tolerate Zwingli's views so that the princes could form a united front against armies of the emperor and pope, who were intent on eradicating their reformations. In spite of the threat, Luther did not capitulate to Zwingli's memorial view of the Lord's Supper.

This was only the tip of the iceberg. Agreement on the first fourteen and the first two parts of the fifteenth article of faith proved to be superficial, especially on Christology. Zwingli was influenced by the Renaissance humanism, with its revival of Neoplatonism, which allowed neither Christ's human nature to embrace his divine nature nor the sacramental bread to be recognized as his body. In Reformed churches, including baptistic and paedobaptist ones, Zwingli's view that Christ is present by way of memory in the Lord's Supper exists side by side with Calvin's belief that Christ is present spiritually. In spite of their differences, Zwingli and Calvin agreed that the elements could not be identified with Christ's body.

Since Marburg, the Reformed have sought Lutheran recognition of both Zwingli's and Calvin's views, but confessional Lutheran churches have not reciprocated. Recognition of Zwingli's position that the Lord's Supper is hardly more than a memorial meal and a sign would be a surrender of the Lutheran belief that the elements of bread and wine become Christ's body and blood in this sacrament.

Lutherans can agree with Russell Moore that the Lord's Supper is a memorial, a sign, and proclamation, within a constellation of other signs in both the Old and New Testaments. Memory or recollection of Christ's death belongs to the celebration of the sacrament. From the beginning, God provided signs to evoke the memory of past events as evidences of his mercy. So Moore rightly understands the Lord's Supper as the culminating act of God's feeding his people, to which belong the manna given to Israel in the wilderness and Christ's miraculous feeding of the thousands.

A full understanding of this rite requires seeing it within the broad scope of salvation history. Old Testament signs point forward to the Lord's Supper. The Supper embodies such past events as the Passover and the sacrifices, and it points to the complete union of God with his people at the end of time. However, such signs are more than memory devices, because Christ is present in all these signs, giving grace, salvation, the Holy Spirit, and himself to create union with the Father. Jesus was already present in the Old Testament signs, but the Lord's Supper is the pinnacle of all signs because the one who was born of the Virgin Mary, crucified under Pontius Pilate, and raised from the dead is actually present with his sacrificial body and blood in the bread and wine. It is the most sacred of signs, because the signs correspond to the divine realities they contain. What the reading of the Gospels causes to be recalled in the church's memory becomes present, tangible, edible reality in the Lord's Supper. All of the events of Christ's life recorded in Scripture pour into the moment of the sacrament so that he who is remembered in the hearing of believers takes on form in bread and wine and is received not only by mouth into the body but also into the soul. In this sacrament the memory of Christ becomes reality so that he is really with us in every aspect of the celebration, including the elements.

Zwingli's view is sometimes called the *anamnēsis*, taken from Christ's words of institution: "do this in remembrance [*anamnēsis*] of me" (Luke 22:19). This cannot only mean that we remember him but, in following the pattern of the Psalms, that we also ask God to remember his promises to us. As we remember Christ in the sacrament, we ask God to remember the promises he made in Christ to forgive us. After all, prayer is reminding God of his love to us—and this is most appropriate as he looks at us through Christ, who is embodied in this sacrament.

Challenges to Lutheran views not only come in formal ways from Reformed churches who desire fellowship with Lutheran churches but also from evangelicals who share with Lutherans a commitment to biblical authority, inspiration, and inerrancy but who remain Zwingli's and Calvin's heirs in their doctrines of Christ and the sacraments, especially the Lord's Supper. Alliances with them require that distinctive Lutheran doctrines of the regenerative power of baptism and of the Lord's Supper as Christ's actual body and blood be submerged to serve a greater unity against destructive methods of biblical criticism. Though Luther is revered in Reformed churches, including Baptist ones, for his doctrine of justification in opposition to Rome, his views on the Lord's Supper are as intolerable as the Roman Catholic view. Identification of the elements with Christ's body and blood falls under the Reformed censure of forbidding idolatry, which comprises their second commandment. Any reference to the "bread god" to describe the Catholic doctrine of the Lord's Supper also targets the Lutheran view.

For Zwingli, both baptism and the Lord's Supper had historical and eschatological significance in pointing back to what God had done and ahead to what God was going to do, but God was not present in the rites and its elements—hence they were not essential for salvation. It is hard to avoid the implication that one sacramental sign can be substituted for the other and that the order of their administration is a matter of indifference. Today's Baptists, like Zwingli, regard both rites as memorials, signs and proclamations, making baptism's function virtually indistinguishable from that of the Lord's Supper. Thus within a Zwinglian context, it is not surprising that the Lord's Supper can be given to one without baptism. These rites may be necessary by way of command and so properly called ordinances rather than sacraments—a word implying that in them God is granting salvation.

The Lord's Supper is the proclamation of Christ's death, but it is a proclamation bringing the historical moment of the cross into the present. If the Lord's Supper is a proclamation and memorial only in the sense that the hearers recall information about a past event or figure in history, then it is hardly distinguishable from or more useful than a sermon. For Lutherans, the sermon, the proclaimed Word (i.e., the gospel), is Christ himself and is in this sense sacramental. He who is present in preaching and enters the ears of his hearers invites them to receive him by their lips and mouths in the sacrament.

Lutherans can agree with Moore that those leading immoral lives are excluded from the Lord's Supper, but with the understanding that a sense of guilt for sin and unacceptability by God rather than a sense of moral rectitude best equips one for receiving the Lord's Supper. This sacrament is not an ordinance in the sense of the Ten Commandments but an institution that forgives sins committed against the law. In following ancient church practice, closed communion for Lutherans means excluding unbelievers and those who have not been baptized or belong to churches with erring beliefs—especially about the Lord's Supper. Baptist practice, on the other hand, allows the unbaptized to receive it.

Since the Lord's Supper in a Zwinglian sense is understood as hardly more than a memorial or sign without real content, instructions about its administration, recipients, and elements are not pressing issues. A layperson is as qualified to administer the rite as an ordained minister. Grape juice is as acceptable as wine, though the preference of the former over the latter seems motivated more by principles of the prohibition movement than biblical reasons. Wine that gladdens human hearts (see Ps. 104:15) is the fit vehicle for Christ's blood, by which we are taken into the mystery of the atonement in which are embedded the glories of heaven. In some Reformed, and embarrassingly Lutheran, churches, beverages other than wine, such as soda or orange juice, are substituted. Where Christ's institution of the Lord's Supper with regard to its elements, beliefs, administrators, and recipients is not followed, it is compromised.

Moore eloquently declares that "in the Lord's Supper, both the restoration of Eden and the recognition of human sin coincide in a ritual meal" (p. 32). Following this line of reasoning, we can say that all prior Old Testament rituals are assumed into this sacrament so they initiate a participation with Christ that will be completed when the one whom we devour with our mouths will be seen by our eyes. As valuable as bringing the full biblical panorama into a discussion on the Lord's Supper is, a word might have been said about Zwingli's position vis-à-vis Luther in interpreting the word "is" in the phrase "this is my body" as "signify." (Calvin agreed with Luther on "is" but took body to be Christ's "spiritual body.")

Now for a personal note. Perhaps the vast majority of Lutheran pastors in receiving members from churches that adhere to Zwinglian or Calvinist teachings on the Lord's Supper often discover that these members did not hold Reformed teachings but already held to the Lutheran belief that the ordinary elements of bread and wine are those extraordinary things of Christ's body and blood. In other words, they actually believe Christ's words, "This is my body." Of course, the reverse is also tragically true of both Lutherans and Catholics who do not believe that the elements are Christ's body and blood, as surveys indicate. This should serve as a reminder that every sermon accompanying the celebration of the Lord's Supper must contain this teaching.

A ROMAN CATHOLIC RESPONSE

Thomas A. Baima

One of my hopes for this book was that the authors could treat questions from the perspective of the various churches and ecclesial communities as they are, rather than as either an idealized version or as they were in the sixteenth century. I must say I have been pleased by each of the chapters by the other authors, who have done exactly that. Hence, this response can focus on my appreciation for the author's insights and questions that still need resolution. In short, each author has made dialogue possible.

I will admit to being surprised by Russell Moore's chapter, especially in its generous use of liturgical and sacramental terms. At the outset, I found myself agreeing with his contention that the Lord's Supper defines Christian identity and expressing appreciation for his presentation on the biblical pattern of signs. Any Catholic scholar would feel comfortable with his description of what is called *anamnēsis* (see pp. 34–35), the sign that points backward and forward, though we would also want to talk further about the sign of something *now*. And I was surprised and pleased by his appreciative use of the writings of both Flannery O'Connor and Pope Benedict XVI.

I also appreciated the chronological reading of the Old Testament and his use of the allegorical method so loved by the Fathers of the church. Certain other points he makes would find a hearing with Catholic scholars, such as his use of semi-realized eschatology and his reflections on sacrifice.

An insight I found distinctive in his chapter was the warfare motif. This approach to the spiritual life during the time of the church—the time between the two comings of Christ—is very similar to themes in Eastern Orthodox spirituality and which, while present in the Western Catholic tradition, have been less emphasized today. Indeed, the warfare motif is also suggestive of other points as well, specifically those around church discipline and the notion that the church is for believers. These three themes could be of great interest to Catholic Christians who are involved in the ministry of Christian initiation of adults.

The chapter also raised some questions for me. Moore is clear to say that the Holy Communion is "more than a symbol"—that "it is a sign" (p. 32). It is not clear to me to what the subject of the sentence (the "messianic banquet meal") is referring to. What is the sign? Is it the elements, or is it the meal? At one point he says that the meal creates faith and establishes faith (p. 35), and in another that Christ is always present with his people and that in the meal we recognize his presence (p. 39). Later, Moore is much clearer when he writes, "[We ask] them to recognize and welcome the presence of Christ—not in the elements or in the heavens above them, but in the body he has called together, the assembly he rules and protects even now as King" (p. 42). But then, is the meal the sign, or is the assembly the sign? And if it is the assembly, how is the presence of Christ different in the meal from the service of preaching?

Also, more conversation is needed on the Last Supper. Moore correctly identifies the Last Supper as a Passover meal. He also draws theological significance from the Passover. Where we need more conversation is in the fact that the Passover was a sacrifice and a meal. *Pesach* is the term used for both the meal ("Passover") and the sacrificial victim ("Passover lamb"). Consequently, I think he moves too quickly over the institution narrative ("This is my body ...") when he concludes "that the elements of bread and wine are [not] literally his body and his blood" (p. 34). The significance of the Passover was more than proclamation; it was a participation in the sacrifice through the sharing in the sacred meal.

This matter of sacrifice keeps emerging in the dialogue about the Lord's Supper. Each time, theologians set it aside for some future time. But the question will not be denied. Already in the World Council of Churches' "Lima Document" (titled *Baptism, Eucharist and Ministry*) we read the following:

It is in the light of the significance of the Eucharist as intercession that the references to the Eucharist in Catholic theology as "propitiatory sacrifice" may be understood. The understanding is that there is only one expiation, that of the unique sacrifice of the cross, made actual in the Eucharist and presented before the Father in the intercession of Christ and of the church for all humanity. In the light of the biblical conception of memorial, all churches might want to review the old controversies about "sacrifice" and deepen their understanding of the reasons why other traditions than their own have either used or rejected this term.[1]

As I will say in my own chapter, this is a matter for another time—a time that should not be far off. We are saved by Christ's sacrificial death on the cross. Just as Moore pointed us to the Passover as a means to understanding the Lord's Supper as a memorial meal, we need to do the same, in dialogue with each other, around our understanding of the sacrifice that the meal of the new covenant makes present and effective.

Notes: Chapter 1: Baptist View (Russell D. Moore)

1. Flannery O'Connor, *The Habit of Being* (New York: Farrar, Straus, Giroux, 1979), 125.

2. See, e.g., Anthony R. Cross and Philip E. Thompson, eds., *Baptist Sacramentalists* (Carlisle: Paternoster, 2003).

3. Michael D. Williams, *Far as the Curse Is Found: The Covenant Story of Redemption* (Phillipsburg, N.J.: P & R Publishing, 2005), 96–97.

4. This is true even in the vegetarian diet of the primeval creation. Of early humanity and animal life, ethics philosopher Leon Kass makes this comment: "But that they needed to be told what to eat is perhaps a sign that, left to their own devices, their appetites might have extended to incorporate one another" (Leon R. Kass, *The Hungry Soul: Eating and the Perfecting of Our Nature* (Chicago: Univ. of Chicago Press, 1999), 207.

5. Alec Motyer, *The Message of Exodus* (Downers Grove, Ill.: InterVarsity, 2005), 147.

6. This is, of course, part of the full context of the Deuteronomy citation Jesus delivered to the Serpent in the wilderness.

7. Based on the final line of the first stanza of the hymn "Guide Me, O Thou Great Jehovah," lyrics by William Williams.

8. Peter C. Craigie, *The Book of Deuteronomy* (New International Commentary on the Old Testament; Grand Rapids: Eerdmans, 1976), 242.

9. Mark F. Rooker, *Leviticus* (New American Commentary; Nashville: Broadman & Holman, 2000), 103.

10. This is not to say this is inherent in the Roman Catholic view of the Eucharist. To the contrary, I'm simply saying that Western individualism is an acid that can distort any view of the Lord's Supper unless careful vigilance is maintained. Pope Benedict XVI has addressed the need for a community focus of the Eucharist in his *God Is Near Us: The Eucharist and the Heart of Life* (San Francisco: Ignatius, 2003).

11. John Lukacs, *A New Republic: A History of the United States in the Twentieth Century* (New Haven, Conn.: Yale Univ. Press, 2004), 345.

Notes: Chapter 1: A Reformed Response (I. John Hesselink)

1. It would have been nice if Moore had explained what the historic Baptist position is concerning the Lord's Supper. Although Baptists do not generally regard themselves as a confessional church, they do have confessions (e.g. the Schleitheim Confession [1527] and the Dordrecht Confession [1612]). Both have articles on the Lord's Supper. These confessions are found in John H. Leith, ed., *Creeds of the Churches* (Richmond, Va.: John Knox, 1973).

Notes: Chapter 1: A Roman Catholic Response (Thomas A. Baima)

1. *Baptism, Eucharist and Ministry* (Faith and Order Paper 111; Geneva: World Council of Churches, 1982), 11.

Chapter Two

REFORMED VIEW

The Real Presence of Christ

REFORMED VIEW

The Real Presence of Christ

I. John Hesselink

At the outset it is necessary to clarify the Reformed view of the Lord's Supper. This will require an explanation of the notion of <u>Christ's real presence in the Lord's Supper</u>, a presence that is spiritual in nature. However, this view is not universally held by all Reformed theologians. For example, Ulrich Zwingli (1484–1531), who initiated the Reformed reformation in Zurich in 1519, held a view of the Lord's Supper that is generally known as a memorialist position—one that takes a purely symbolic interpretation of the Supper. This view was sharply rejected by Martin Luther at the Marburg Colloquy in 1529 and was regarded unfavorably by John Calvin.

Since this view was represented earlier in this book, I will <u>focus on the view of John Calvin</u>. This view of a spiritual partaking of the flesh and blood of the risen Christ in the Supper is also generally taught in most Reformed confessions, including the Heidelberg Catechism (1563) and the later Westminster Confession of Faith (1648). Hence Calvin's view is today usually considered *the* Reformed view, although some Reformed and Presbyterian theologians lean toward the Zwinglian view. Keith Mathison in his book *Given for You: Reclaiming Calvin's Doctrine of the Lord's Supper* documents the falling away from Calvin's view by a number of nineteenth- and early twentieth-century theologians, who found Calvin's view too complicated and mystical.[1] Thus, one cannot describe the view here espoused as being Reformed when that label is broadly conceived. However, among contemporary Reformed-Presbyterian theologians, Calvin's view of the real presence is almost universally the preferred understanding of the sacrament. Moreover, the high view of the Lord's Supper that Calvin espoused was not his alone but was essentially that of his friend and mentor Martin Bucer; his successor in Geneva, Theodore Beza; and another Reformed contemporary, Peter Martyr, whose sacramental theology is often regarded as having made a singular contribution to Reformed theology.[2]

CALVIN'S VIEW OF THE SACRAMENTS

Before proceeding to Calvin's doctrine of the Lord's Supper, it will be helpful to see how he understands "sacrament." Calvin had a high view of the sacraments, as high in most respects as Luther's. (The same cannot be said of many modern Reformed-Presbyterian Christians, in contrast to their Lutheran counterparts, not to mention Episcopalians and Roman Catholics).

In his chapter on the sacraments in the *Institutes*, Calvin begins with a statement found already in the first edition: "We have in the sacraments another aid to our faith related to the preaching of the gospel."[3] He expands on this with a more formal definition. "It seems to me," he says, "that a simple and proper definition would be to say that it is an outward sign by which the Lord seals on our consciences the promises of his good will toward us in order to sustain the weakness of our faith; and we in turn attest our piety in the presence of the Lord and of his angels and before men" (*Inst.* IV.14.1). He then refers to the famous definition of Augustine — "a visible sign of a sacred thing" or "a visible form of an invisible grace" — but feels that it is too brief and hence somewhat obscure (IV.14.1). Later, however, he expresses approval of Augustine's description of sacraments as "a visible word" because a sacrament "represents God's promises as painted in a picture and sets them before our sight, portrayed graphically and in the manner of images" (IV.14.6).

Calvin also uses other images and metaphors to describe the sacraments. He suggests that we might call them "the pillars of our faith":

> For as a building stands and rests upon its own foundation but is more surely established by columns placed

underneath, so faith rests upon the Word of God as a foundation; but when the sacraments are added, it rests more firmly upon them as upon columns. Or [he adds] we might call them mirrors in which we may contemplate the riches of God's grace, which he lavishes upon us. (IV.14.6)

I need to point out three more things before taking up Calvin's doctrine of the Lord's Supper, namely, the role of the Holy Spirit, the importance of faith, and the place of Christ in making the sacraments powerful and efficacious. In the lengthy chapter on the sacraments in the *Institutes*, the motif of the Holy Spirit becomes prominent. Here Calvin repeats that the sacraments were given by God to establish and increase our faith, but, he adds, they only properly fulfill their office "when the Spirit, that inward teacher, comes to them, by whose power alone hearts are penetrated and affections moved and our souls opened for the sacraments to enter in. If the Spirit be lacking, the sacraments can accomplish nothing more in our minds than the splendor of the sun shining upon blind eyes, or a voice sounding in deaf ears" (*Inst.* IV.14.9). In short, "the sacraments profit not a whit without the power of the Holy Spirit" (IV.14.9). Or, as Calvin puts it in his Geneva Catechism, "The power and efficacy of a sacrament does not lie in the external elements, but wholly emanates from the Spirit of God" (Q. 313).[4]

On the human side, however, faith is also indispensable. For it is "certain that the Lord offers us mercy and the pledge of his grace both in his Sacred Word and in his sacraments. But it is understood only by those who take Word and sacraments with sure faith." Then Calvin cites Augustine to the same effect, that "the efficacy of the Word is brought to light in the sacrament, not because it is spoken, but because it is believed" (*Inst.* IV.14.7). The Reformer expresses himself even more forcibly in a polemical treatise: "He who separates faith from the sacraments does just as if he were to take the soul away from the body."[5]

Sacraments are thus not magical means by which recipients are automatically blessed. On God's side, the Word and the Spirit are crucial; on our side, faith is essential if the promises of God in Jesus Christ are to be realized. Yet even the faith by which we believe is a gift of the Holy Spirit, for "faith is the proper and entire work of the Holy Spirit, illumined by whom we recognize

God and the treasures of his kindness and without whose light our mind is so blinded that it can see nothing, so dull that it can sense nothing of spiritual things" (*Inst.* IV.14.8).

The third idea that is fundamental to Calvin's understanding of the sacraments is that they find their meaning in Christ. For "Christ is the matter [*materiam*] or (if you prefer) the substance [*substantiam*] of all the sacraments; for in him they have all their firmness [*soliditatem*], and they do not promise anything apart from him" (*Inst.* IV.14.16). For the benefits of the sacraments "are conferred through the Holy Spirit, who makes us partakers in Christ; conferred, indeed, with the help of outward signs, if they allure us to Christ; but when they are twisted in another direction, their whole worth is shamefully destroyed" (IV.14.16). In other words, if we focus on the elements and not on the Christ to whom they point, we misunderstand and misconstrue the sacraments.

THE LORD'S SUPPER

It cannot be overemphasized that Calvin does not teach that the bread and the wine are mere symbols of Christ's body and blood. In this regard, Calvin is closer to Luther than to Zwingli, for he believed in a real presence of Christ in the Supper. Luther and Calvin differed on the nature of that presence, but they both believed that Christ is really present in some sense in the elements of the bread and wine when they are received by faith. Calvin emphasized the role of the Holy Spirit more than Luther did, but at the same time he warned against conceiving of the sacraments as no more than a purely spiritual communion with the spirit of Christ.

Note how Calvin expresses the matter in his First Catechism: in the symbols of the bread and the wine "the Lord exhibits the true communication of his body and his blood—but a spiritual one" (sec. 29).[6] These words might be interpreted in a "spiritual," that is, nonobjective way, but he later writes, "Accordingly, body and blood are represented under bread and wine, so that we may learn not only that they are ours, but that they are life and food for us" (sec. 29). The same truth is expressed more clearly later in the *Institutes*: "If it is true that a visible sign is given to us to seal the gift of a thing invisible, when we have received the symbol of the body, let us no less surely trust that the body itself is also given to us" (IV.17.10).

At times Calvin seems to be engaging in a direct polemic against Zwingli's more symbolic view, where the recipient's faith is the key factor. Calvin also emphasizes the necessity of faith for the sacrament to be efficacious, but his emphasis is on God's grace and the inherent power in the sacrament. He also criticizes the Roman view and that of his high Lutheran critic Joachim Westphal,[7] but he does not hesitate to use concrete, graphic language and metaphors to show how seriously he believes that when we partake of the elements in the Lord's Supper, we truly feed on the Lord Jesus himself.

A Real Presence

Here are a few examples: Just as bread nourishes our bodies, so the body of Christ nourishes and quickens our souls. Similarly, as wine "strengthens, refreshes, and rejoices a man physically, so [Christ's] blood is our joy, our refreshing, and our spiritual strength" (Geneva Catechism, Q. 341). When the sacrament reminds us that Christ "was made the bread of life which we continually eat, and which gives us a relish and savor of that bread, it causes us to feel the power of that bread.... By true partaking of him, his life passes into us and is made ours—just as bread when taken as food imparts vigor to the body" (*Inst.* IV.17.5).

Calvin can even say that "Christ's flesh enters into us to be our food" (IV.17.24). Taking his cue from Cyril of Alexandria and using the analogy of a spring, Calvin concludes, "In like manner the flesh of Christ is like a rich and inexhaustible fountain that pours into us the life springing forth from the Godhead into itself. Now who does not see that communion of Christ's flesh and blood is necessary for all who aspire to heavenly life?" (IV.17.9).[8]

This kind of realistic language about the "eating of Christ's flesh" through faith (IV.17.5) and having Christ's blood offered "for us to taste" has been offensive to some later Reformed theologians and may shock some contemporary Reformed-Presbyterian faithful.[9] Calvin himself concedes that "it seems unbelievable that Christ's flesh, separated from us by such great distance, penetrates to us so that it becomes our food" (IV.17.10).

One would think that the passages cited above would dispose of criticisms from Calvin's Lutheran critics in particular who maintain that Calvin does not believe in a "real presence" of Christ in the Supper.[10] Granted, the real presence and partaking of Christ's flesh and blood in the Supper should not be interpreted materialistically but spiritually; but "spiritual" in this sense does not mean unreal or that Christ is present only in spirit. At the same time, Calvin resists the notion that the body and blood of Christ are contained in the elements. Rather, the elements "are as instruments by which our Lord Jesus Christ distributes them to us."[11] Nevertheless, Christ is present to us in the Supper even though physically distant from us. The clue to Calvin's theology of the sacrament here, as with so many doctrines, is the Holy Spirit.

The Role of the Holy Spirit

One of Calvin's fundamental presuppositions with regard to the Lord's Supper is that the ascended body of Christ is localized, so to speak, in heaven. Hence the body of Christ cannot be ubiquitous, as it was for Luther. Calvin repeats in various later works what he affirms briefly in his 1538 Catechism: "For although Christ, having ascended into heaven, ceases to reside on earth, . . . still no distance can prevent his powers from feeding his believers on himself and bringing it about that they still enjoy ever present communication with him, though he is absent from that place" (sec. 29).

What is missing here, however, is how the distant, ascended Christ becomes one with us in the Supper. The answer is the Holy Spirit. In Calvin's *Short Treatise on the Lord's Supper*, written only two years later, the role of the Holy Spirit in this connection is still largely absent. Calvin only alludes to the fact that it is the Holy Spirit who "gives efficacy to his ordinance" and that "the virtue [or power] of the Holy Spirit is joined to the sacraments when they are duly received."[12] In his Geneva Catechism, however, written the following year (French edition, 1542) Calvin is much more explicit as to "how we are made partakers of Christ's substance," even though "Christ's body is in heaven and we are still pilgrims on earth." This gap is bridged "by the miraculous and secret virtue of [Christ's] Spirit, for whom it is not difficult to associate things that are otherwise separated by an interval of space" (Qs. 353–55).[13]

In his commentary (written in 1546) on Paul's account of the Lord's Supper in 1 Corinthians 11, Calvin is more precise about the way the Holy Spirit unites things separated in the celebration of the sacrament. Here he succinctly and clearly explains how the flesh of the ascended Lord spiritually nourishes us. In the following passage, note particularly how he first rejects Roman Catholic and Lutheran views of the real presence and then states his own view:

> The sharing in the Lord's body, which, I maintain, is offered to us in the Supper, demands neither a local presence, nor the descent of Christ, nor an infinite extension of his body, nor anything of that sort; for, in view of the fact that the Supper is a heavenly act, there is nothing absurd about saying that Christ remains in heaven and is yet received by us. For the way in which he imparts himself to us is by the secret power of the Holy Spirit, a power which is able not only to bring together, but also to join together, things which are separated by distance, and by a great distance at that.[14]

Elsewhere in his commentary, Calvin is even more explicit in distancing himself from Zwinglians and those who see in the Supper "only a memorial of something that is absent":

> My conclusion is that the body of Christ is really [*realiter*], to use the usual word, i.e., truly [*vere*] given to us in the Supper, so that it may be health-giving food for our souls. I am adopting the usual terms, but I mean that our souls are fed by the substance of his body, so that we are truly [*vere*] made one with him; or, what amounts to the same thing, that a life-giving power from the flesh of Christ [*vim ex Christi carne vivificam*] is poured into us through the medium of the Spirit, even though it is at a great distance from us, and is not mixed with us [*nec misceatur nobiscum*].[15]

Calvin's final edition of the *Institutes* amplifies this thesis. Here Calvin refers to the Holy Spirit as "the bond of this connection," which is "like a channel through which all that Christ himself is and has is conveyed to us." Calvin's key text here is Romans 8:9, which "teaches that the Spirit alone causes us to possess Christ completely and have him dwelling in us" (IV.17.12). More specifically, in reference to the Supper, Calvin reiterates that this spiritual eating is no less real even though Christ remains in heaven and is not "enclosed" in the elements in a carnal fashion. The solution again is the "secret" and "incomprehensible power" of the Spirit (IV.17.33).[16]

Here a slight complication arises. Do we then only lift up our hearts (*sursum corda!*) to the ascended Christ and somehow feed on him there? Or is there a sense in which the risen Christ by his Spirit descends to us and nourishes us spiritually through the partaking of the elements? Both are true, but the accent is on the former. For the most part, Calvin teaches that "in order to enjoy the reality of the signs our minds must be raised to heaven where Christ is" (*Geneva Catechism*, Q. 355). Calvin is so averse to any notion that Christ is physically contained or enclosed in the elements that he ridicules those who would "drag" Christ down from heaven (*Inst.* IV.17.31). "But if we are lifted up to heaven with our eyes and minds, to seek Christ there in the glory of his Kingdom, as the symbols invite us to him in his wholeness, so under the symbol of bread we shall be fed by his body, under the symbol of wine we shall separately drink his blood, to enjoy him at last in his wholeness" (IV.17.18).[17]

Yet Calvin can also speak figuratively of Christ's coming down to us in order to nourish us in the Supper.[18] For "in order to be present with us, [Christ] does not change his place, but from heaven *he sends down* the efficacy of his flesh to be present in us."[19] And again, "We say Christ descends to us both by the outward symbol and by his Spirit, that he may truly quicken our souls by the substance of his flesh and blood" (IV.17.24). But this "descent" must not be misunderstood in such a way that Christ is literally brought down and enclosed within the elements. Those who so believe "do not understand the manner of descent by which he lifts us up to himself" (IV.17.16).

This may leave some readers confused — and understandably so — for this is a very complex matter. It may be of some comfort to see that Calvin himself did not pretend to understand all of this. One cannot "reduce to words so great a mystery," he concedes, and then humbly adds, "which I see I do not even sufficiently comprehend with my mind. I therefore freely admit that no man should measure its sublimity by the little measure of my childishness." Calvin concludes with these words:

> Rather, I urge my readers not to confine their mental interest within these too narrow limits, but to strive to rise much higher than I can lead them. For, whenever this matter is discussed, when I have tried to say all, I feel that I have as yet said little in proportion to its worth. And although my mind can think beyond what my tongue can utter, yet even my mind is conquered and overwhelmed by the greatness of the thing. Therefore, nothing remains but to break forth in wonder at this mystery, which plainly neither the mind is able to conceive nor the tongue to express (*Inst.* IV.17.7).[20]

Since this heavenly mystery is beyond comprehension but is at the same time such a precious gift of God's generosity and kindness, our proper response should not be frustration because of our inability to understand the mysteries of the sacrament, but rather gratitude and a reverent openness to what God would give us through it. We should emulate the spirit of Calvin, who was "not ashamed to confess" that the nature of Christ's presence in the Supper is "a secret too lofty for either my mind to comprehend or my words to declare." In short, he concludes, "I rather experience than understand it" (*Inst.* IV.17.32).[21]

PASTORAL ISSUES

Frequency of Celebration

Calvin's high view of the sacrament of the Lord's Supper is also reflected in his desire to celebrate the sacrament at each Lord's Day worship service. In the church order he introduced shortly after his arrival in Geneva—the "Articles concerning the Organization of the Church and of Worship at Geneva 1537"—he proposed the following:

> It would be good to require that the Communion of the Holy Supper of Jesus Christ be held every Sunday.... When the church assembles together for the great

consolation which the faithful receive and the profit which proceeds from it, in every respect according to the promises which are there presented to our faith, then we are really made participants of the body and blood of Jesus, of his death, of his life, of his Spirit, and of all his benefits.[22]

However, this was rejected by the City Council and Calvin never got his way with regard to this issue. When Calvin returned to Geneva in 1541 after his three-year stay in Strasbourg, he proposed a revised church order, the "Draft Ecclesiastical Ordinances" of 1541. Here he proposes a compromise: "that it always be administered in the city once a month, in such a way that every three months it takes place in each parish."[23] Thus Calvin's compromise became the established order in most Reformed and Presbyterian churches until about the middle of the twentieth century.

As a result of liturgical renewal in the Reformed tradition[24] and a growing appreciation of the significance of the Lord's Supper in local Reformed and Presbyterian churches, a more frequent celebration of the Supper has become common. In several Presbyterian/Reformed churches around the world a monthly celebration is practiced. According to Keith Mathison, "There are a growing number of Reformed churches that observe the Supper on a weekly basis,"[25] but I'm not aware of many. However, in some Reformed and Presbyterian seminaries, including my own (Western Theological Seminary in Holland, Michigan), the sacrament is celebrated once a week in the context of a regular chapel service.

Manner of Celebration

In the Reformed tradition, there is no set manner as to how the sacrament is to be celebrated. On the continent, the tradition has been for the celebrants to come forward, receive the elements (from a minister assisted by elders), partake while standing, and return by a side aisle. In some cases, elements are in trays; in other cases, the recipient will receive a small piece of bread and dip it in the cup of wine or grape juice (the intincture method). This is also the practice in some other parts of the world (e.g., in the Presbyterian Church in Brazil) and is increasingly being done this way in North America. However, in most American Presbyterian and Reformed churches the common practice is to have the elements served by elders to the parishioners as they remain seated in their pews. The elements consist of tiny pieces of precut bread and tiny cups of wine or grape juice—usually the latter.[26] Unfortunately, this undercuts the significance of breaking a single loaf in front of the congregation. Robert Letham feels very strongly about this and believes that this practice "is redolent of post-Enlightenment individualism, where religion is conceived of as a private, inward matter between the individual soul and God."[27]

In any case, there is considerable freedom in this regard, so that where it is feasible, groups may come forward and form a circle around the Communion table and first pass a loaf of bread to the next person saying, "The body of Christ broken/given for you." The celebrant then tears off a piece of bread from the loaf and dips it in the cup of wine or juice as the words "the blood of Christ shed for you" are spoken by the person holding the cup.

In a few churches, both on the continent and in the United States, small groups of believers will come forward and take turns sitting at a large Communion table and partake of the elements there. The practice of "the common cup," where people drink from the same cup, is still practiced in some Reformed-Presbyterian churches both here and in Europe.

Who May Participate?

Here we deal with the issue of "the fencing of the table." At one time, particularly in Scotland and the Netherlands, elders would visit members of the congregation prior to each celebration of the Supper to determine whether they were fit to partake of the Supper on the next Lord's Day. They were given Communion tokens, which they would present at the worship service to indicate that they had been approved for the partaking of the sacrament. Sadly, in some conservative branches of the Reformed and Presbyterian churches only a few older, "saintly" characters felt worthy of partaking, which meant that the majority of the congregation never experienced the blessings of the sacrament until they reached that stage in life.

In some conservative Reformed denominations, such as the Christian Reformed Church in North America, the practice of "close," not closed, communion was practiced. Only those who had been checked out by an elder beforehand were permitted to partake. Today, the practice in most Presbyterian and Reformed churches, including Christian Reformed, is to welcome anyone to the Lord's Table who has been baptized and is a professing member of a Christian church.

In some churches in the Reformed tradition, including my own (the Reformed Church in America), during the worship one week before the celebration of Communion, an "Exhortation to Self-Examination" is read prior to the prayer of confession. One of the opening lines is this: "That we may celebrate the Sacrament to our comfort, it is necessary that we rightly examine ourselves."[28] However, where the sacrament is celebrated more frequently than four times a year this practice tends to fall out. Also, churches that are into contemporary worship often play fast and loose with liturgical matters. For example, they will omit the section on "The Meaning of the Sacrament" and the fairly elaborate Communion prayer.

Then there is the matter of children's participation in the Lord's Supper—a relatively new development in Reformed and Presbyterian churches. The question of whether it was appropriate for children to participate in the Lord's Supper was first raised in the United Presbyterian Church in the 1960s and in the Presbyterian Church U.S. (Southern) in the 1970s. By the time of the reunion of the two churches in 1983, it was a generally accepted practice. In the Reformed Church in America, the issue came to the fore in the early 1970s and was hotly debated for over a decade. Finally, in 1988, the General Synod accepted the most recent report of the Commission on Theology.[29] The Christian Reformed Church, with more specific restrictions, approved the practice in the 1990s. Conservative Presbyterian denominations such as the Orthodox Presbyterian Church are opposed to the practice.[30]

The Requisites for a Proper Celebration of the Sacrament

In an earlier age it was often believed that the Lord's Supper could only be celebrated in the context of a worship service in a church. The officiants were an ordained minister assisted by elders. That limitation has given way in the last half of the twentieth century to celebrations of the Supper at conferences, retreats, and other informal gatherings. In such cases the celebration of the sacrament is not always accompanied by the preaching of the Word, and elders are no longer required to be present; but the officiant must be an ordained minister and elements of the liturgy must be used, as well as the words of institution of our Lord. The latter is the absolute minimum. A recent development in some Presbyterian and Reformed churches is to allow elders to serve the sacrament when (1) no ordained minister is available and (2) when they are authorized to do so by the session or consistory.

As is obvious from the above statements, when it comes to the practice of the Lord's Supper, there is considerable openness and flexibility among the various denominations—and within the denominations. The goal, in any case, is to follow the maxim of the apostle Paul that "everything should be done in a fitting and orderly way" (1 Cor. 14:40).

A BAPTIST RESPONSE

Russell D. Moore

Some may wonder whether the children of Geneva and the children of Nashville are all that far apart from one another when it comes to the question of the Lord's Supper. After all, compared to our distance from Roman Catholic, Eastern Orthodox, Lutheran, and even typical pop evangelical thought on this matter, the Reformed and Baptist models are often saying much the same thing. John Hesselink's chapter confirms such, since there is much in it to which I, and the Baptist tradition of which I am a part, can say a hearty "Amen."

First, as Hesselink notes, John Calvin was the first to maintain that the sacraments are not "automatic" means of blessing (p. 61). They are only effective when joined with the faith of the recipient. They must be empowered by the Holy Spirit, and they can only be understood in light of God's purposes in Christ. Second, as Hesselink makes clear, the Supper is more than a bare symbol, but is a "feeding" of God's people by Christ himself (p. 62). Third, Hesselink contends, with Calvin and the Calvinists, that Christ is not physically present "in" or "under" the elements of bread and wine but is seated instead physically and spatially in the heavenly places, although he is, of course, omnipresent with respect to his deity (p. 66). Finally, Hesselink offers concern about the spiritual danger of neglect of the Supper among the churches (p. 68). To all of these things, I can join my hearty approval.

My quarrel with the Reformed tradition is not so much with what is taking place but with how these blessings are conveyed to the covenant community by the messianic King, Jesus. I don't disagree with the "real presence" of Christ in the Lord's Supper (rightly defined), but I do see this presence in a different fashion

72

[handwritten: God pres't in His ppl, the Temple]

from the way Calvin and his Scholastic and Puritan successors saw it. Christ is indeed "really present" in the Lord's Supper. But it is not necessary to surmise that the Supper uniquely takes us to the heavenly places to commune with him there through the Spirit. Christ is always *really present* with his people (Matt 28:20). This is especially true in the act of gathered worship:

> But you have come to Mount Zion, to the heavenly Jerusalem, the city of the living God. You have come to thousands upon thousands of angels in joyful assembly, to the church of the firstborn, whose names are written in heaven. You have come to God, the judge of all men, to the spirits of righteous men made perfect, to Jesus the mediator of a new covenant, and to the sprinkled blood that speaks a better word than the blood of Abel.
>
> *Hebrews 12:22–24*

Moreover, the presence of Christ is specifically promised in the discipline of the congregation—a discipline centered on the fellowship of the covenant people around the messianic table. When the congregation is gathered "in My name," Jesus promises, "I am there, in their midst" (Matt. 18:20 NASB). The apostle Paul writes of the congregation "assembled in the name of our Lord Jesus" as the time when "the power of our Lord Jesus is present" (1 Cor. 5:4). The issue of the "real presence" has less to do with the elements involved, it seems to me, than with the presence of the Spirit himself, in whom Jesus comes to his people (John 14:17–18). This doesn't mean that the elements themselves are unimportant. By no means! These are the vehicles through which Jesus, through his body the church, announces to us the onset of the new covenant, thereby encouraging and strengthening our faith in him. Jesus is present with us, and we benefit from his presence when the word preached points us to his gospel. He is present with us, and we benefit from his presence when the word portrayed in the baptismal waters points us to his gospel. He is present with us, and we benefit from his presence when the communion over bread and wine points us to his gospel. In all of these things, we remain before the face of God on Mount Zion.

The "newness" of the covenant that this Supper proclaims is a further distinction between the Reformed and Baptist views. Hesselink notes the diversity of opinion within the Reformed community over paedocommunion (children at the Lord's Supper). As a Baptist Christian, I believe that the Lord's Supper "new covenant in my blood" (1 Cor. 11:25) speaks to those within the covenant, those who "all know" the Lord, "from the least of them to the greatest," those who have experienced the forgiveness of sins through the sacrifice of Christ (Jer. 31:34). Advocates of paedocommunion rightly argue that the Passover feast applies to all members of the covenant, including little children. They furthermore maintain (again, rightly, I think) that the Lord's Table defines the parameters of local church fellowship, and that all baptized members of a congregation not under discipline should be welcome to it. Opponents of paedocommunion, on the other hand, rightly maintain that the New Testament commands that those who attend the Supper must be able to "recognize" the body, and eat and drink in a worthy manner as accountable members of the assembly (1 Cor. 11:27, 29). Again, there is no argument here.

It seems to me that paedocommunion is the logical outcome of a Reformed ecclesiology. It is nonetheless ruled out by the New Testament's tying of the Lord's Table to discipline, but could it be that this is only because the New Testament restricts membership in the new covenant community to those who have been regenerated and have expressed faith in Christ? I believe this discussion to be foundational to our differences and even more important than the questions over any "real presence" versus "memorial" disagreements.

Above all, however, I look forward to the day when the children of Nashville and the children of Geneva (along with all the children of God from every tribe, tongue, and "communion") can fellowship around a supper in the new earth. Then, though perhaps not until then, we will be united around the table. On that day, I expect, the "real presence" of Jesus won't be a matter of dispute at all.

A LUTHERAN RESPONSE

David P. Scaer

Each theological tradition is entitled to define its terms, including the real presence of Christ in the Lord's Supper, as it sees fit. Since the Reformed do not identify the elements of bread and wine with Christ's actual body and blood, they understand real presence differently from the Lutherans, Orthodox, and Roman Catholics who do make this identification. According to the Reformed, believers receive Christ spiritually by faith in their souls and do not receive his body and blood with the mouth. Unbelievers do not receive Christ, though by participating in the sacrament they may cause offense or commit a sacrilege.

In working for rapprochement with the Lutherans, the Reformed have used terms familiar to Lutherans but with different meanings. "Real presence" belongs to that conciliatory vocabulary. Forthright sacramental discussion has been hampered in Germany by rulers forcing Lutherans into united territorial churches with the Reformed. After failing in the early seventeenth century, Prussian rulers succeeded in 1830 in imposing on Lutheran congregations liturgies allowing for the Reformed spiritual understanding of the Lord's Supper. In distributing the sacrament, pastors were no longer allowed to use the Lutheran formula, "This is my body," but were to say, "Christ said, 'This is my body.'" This indefinite formula allowed for the Reformed view that Jesus was present in a spiritual manner only and not in the bread.

The largest American and European Lutheran and Reformed churches have recently signed agreements allowing their members to receive Communion in each other's churches and stating that the other's views on the Lord's Supper are acceptable.

In these situations, Lutheran distinctions regarding the Lord's Supper are eventually replaced by Reformed understandings. In the minds of many, including the intellectually elite, Lutherans and Reformed are lumped together as Protestants, and past differences are seen as no more than petty historical squabbles. Martin Luther's views are seen as no different from John Calvin's. In German churches, statues and stained-glass windows of Luther, Calvin, and even Ulrich Zwingli are placed side by side as if their reformations were theologically unified. The last holdout for the classical Lutheran position are those churches that adhere to the Lutheran Confessions, of which most are in fellowship with The Lutheran Church–Missouri Synod.

With the Reformed doing their best to entice Lutherans to join them in one fold from the Reformation on, a Lutheran doesn't have to wonder what Hesselink has in mind when he writes that "Calvin had a high view of the sacraments, as high in most respects as Luther's" (p. 60). Really? When the contents of the chalice were spilled, with tears in his eyes Luther got down on his knees and licked up Christ's blood. He excommunicated a priest who placed the consecrated hosts in the same place as unconsecrated ones. It is hard to imagine Calvin doing this.

In trying to locate Calvin closer to Luther than Zwingli, Hesselink claims that Calvin did not look favorably on Zwingli's "memorialist" or "purely symbolic" interpretation of the Supper, which, he adds, was "sharply rejected by Martin Luther" (p. 59). Left unsaid is that Calvin did not disown Zwingli and that their successors accepted each other's positions in the *Consensus Tigurinus* in 1549. Zwingli's view of the sacrament as a sign or memorial may still not measure up to Calvin's view that with it the Spirit communicates spiritual gifts to believers, but both are acceptable in Reformed churches and not cause for division. Calvin may have had a higher place for the sacrament than Zwingli did; but for both, the sacramental bread remained nothing more than bread.

Like Calvin, Lutherans can speak of a spiritual reception of Christ in the Lord's Supper, but for Lutherans it is subsequent to and dependent on the oral reception of his body and blood in the bread and wine. The Reformed cannot, as Lutherans can, look at or handle the consecrated bread and say that this is Christ. Since Christ for the Reformed is confined to a spatially defined heaven, the Spirit replaces him or, at best, links Christ's flesh to the believer. Christ's divine nature, but not his human nature, may be present with the elements. In advancing his view that Christ is in a spatial heaven where faith can find him, Calvin condemned the Lutheran position (see *Inst.* IV.17.16–20). Unacceptable to the Reformed is the Lutheran insistence that Christ's divine nature works through the human nature and is fully present in it.

Some years ago, a Reformed theologian, later a president of a prestigious seminary in New England, alerted me to a foundational difference in that the Reformed go first to God to find Jesus. Lutherans take a reverse route and go through Jesus to find God. True enough, but Lutherans take one step further in going through baptism and the Lord's Supper to find Christ. In encountering Christ in the sacraments, they encounter the Spirit and the Father and come to know God as Trinity.

Like the Reformed, Lutherans speak of the sacraments as signs. For Lutherans, the signs point to the divine realities contained within them. Calvin eschews Zwingli's view that the divine realities are remote from the elements and instead holds that they signal the Spirit's working along with the sacraments and the rites. However, the elements themselves are devoid of the Spirit or divine gifts. Sacraments can be the occasion for the Spirit's works, which are made operative only by faith. Lutherans agree that faith is the only means for receiving the sacrament's benefits, but faith neither contributes to the sacrament's reality nor detracts from Christ's presence in it. By celebrating the rite, an assembly identifies itself as believers, but, contrary to Calvin's teaching, faith does not create or contribute to the character of the rite as a sacrament. For Lutherans, an unbeliever receiving the sacrament comes into an intimate relationship with Christ not as redemptive atonement but as judge, and so compounds God's judgment on him. By his unbelief, he offends not only the church but Christ, whom he has taken into both his body and soul.

Speaking of Christ's spiritual presence is just as ambivalent as speaking of his real presence. To emphasize his belief, Luther held that participants in the sacrament received not only Christ's resurrected body, which might allow for a spiritual, noncorporeal body, but the body born of the Virgin Mary.

Christ's taking on the forms of bread and wine had a prior pattern in the incarnation. Lutherans agree that by the Holy Spirit the bread becomes Christ's body by being embedded in Christ's words of institution. This is a Trinitarian work in which all the divine persons are present. In this sacrament the Spirit is present as the *Spiritus Creator*, finishing the work of creation first in the incarnation and then the Lord's Supper, not as a surrogate or replacement for the man Jesus Christ but with him. Through the Spirit's action in the Word on the bread and wine, the Father gives them to us as the body and blood of the crucified and risen Christ. The Reformed belief that the risen Christ is spatially restricted at the Father's right hand, which is seen as a place or location, virtually requires that the Spirit be the major agent in the sacramental action. He possesses the omnipresence denied to Jesus' human nature. This means that any Reformed definition of the real presence of Christ in the sacrament has to be radically different from a Lutheran understanding.

One can appreciate Hesselink's desire to bring the Reformed view as close to Luther's as possible. This he does by noting that Calvin can say "Christ's flesh enters into us to be our food" (p. 63). What might be an otherwise acceptable view to Lutherans is counterbalanced by Calvin's "resist[ing] the notion that the body and blood of Christ are contained in the elements" (p. 64). Calvin and the Reformed do not say Christ's flesh and blood enter through our mouths. Rather this happens only in our souls. For unbelievers receiving the sacrament there is no actual eating and drinking of Christ's body and blood. The Spirit "sends down the efficacy of his flesh," but not Christ himself who is contained in a place in heaven (p. 66). Lutherans do not recognize a spatial distance between heaven and earth, but heaven manifests itself on earth in the sacraments so that not only Christ's benefits but Christ himself, body and soul, God and man, are present in the Lord's Supper.

In defining the Lord's Supper, Lutherans and the Reformed make use of many of the same terms and phrases but understand them differently. This is especially true of the real presence, but beneath the surface they have different views on atonement, justification, and sanctification. Their differences with regard to the Lord's Supper are only the tip of the iceberg.

A ROMAN CATHOLIC RESPONSE

Thomas A. Baima

I enjoyed reading John Hesselink's chapter because the Reformed tradition is less known to me than the Orthodox, Anglican, or Lutheran traditions. I found the clarification he made about the varieties of positions within the Reformed tradition especially helpful. The clear connections to the Augustinian school helps Catholic Christians see that Reformed theology is not merely a reaction to the Roman Catholic position of the day but also an attempt to establish continuity with the Fathers of the church.

I found the emphasis on the role of the Holy Spirit in the sacraments to be a welcome note. On the whole, Western Christianity has neglected pneumatology. I understand better now a comment that our editor, John Armstrong, made recently that the Reformed understanding of real presence has some things in common with Eastern Orthodox theology. Fleshing out those similarities would be a discussion I would welcome.

Perhaps most instructive to the Catholic Christian who reads this chapter are the several comments that report the experience of receiving the Lord's Supper for the Reformed Christian. In college, I would frequently argue theology with my roommate, who was from the United Church of Christ, but from a congregation that had historically been part of the Evangelical and Reformed Church. One Holy Thursday, I went to church with him and observed the celebration of Holy Communion. What I observed was an experience that for him was clearly far greater than the doctrinal description he had given in our arguments.

Still, as I read the chapter, a number of questions come to mind. Central to them is the use of subjective language throughout. Hesselink quotes Calvin as saying that a sacrament "is an outward sign by which the Lord seals on our consciences the promises of his good will" (p. 60), that the sacraments were given by God to establish and increase our faith (p. 61), that "if the Spirit be lacking, the sacraments can accomplish nothing more in our minds than the splendor of the sun shining upon blind eyes" (p. 61), that the benefits of the sacraments "are … conferred, indeed, with the help of outward signs, if they allure us to Christ'" (p. 62), and that "in order to enjoy the reality of the signs our minds must be raised to heaven where Christ is" (p. 66). These are all mental effects. So, what is the presence, really?

Another question has to do with the stress on issues of space and time. We read in Hesselink's chapter of the "distant, ascended Christ" (p. 64)—that "Christ is present to us in the Supper even though physically distant from us" (p. 64), that "Christ's flesh, separated from us by such great distance, penetrates to us so that it becomes our food" (pp. 63–64). It seems that with this linear view of time Christ is in our past and in our future but not in our present. While Christ remains at the right hand of the Father, he is not trapped there the way Lazarus was at Abraham's side (Luke 16:22). He is as present as he was at the Last Supper. While I can't quite put my finger on it after studying Hesselink's chapter, there is a significant theological issue here involving both the doctrine of the incarnation and the communion of the saints.

It may, in fact, be the latter that is the problem. There seems to be a hesitation in Reformed theology to talk about the communion of saints—both those on earth and those in heaven—in the present tense. Perhaps it would be more accurate to say that there is a reluctance to speak about a relationship between the saints on earth and the saints in heaven in the present moment. The Second Vatican Council taught, "So it is that the union of the wayfarers with the brethren who sleep in the peace of Christ is in no way interrupted, but on the contrary, according to the constant faith of the Church, this union is reinforced by an exchange of spiritual gifts."[1]

So, having now opened a huge can of worms, let me simply suggest that a reconsideration of the doctrine of the communion of saints from the ancient creeds may enrich our conversation about the real presence of Christ in the Supper.

Notes: Chapter 2: Reformed View (I. John Hesselink)

1. Keith Mathison, *Given for You: Reclaiming Calvin's Doctrine of the Lord's Supper* (Phillipsburg, N.J.: P & R Publishing, 2002). Charles Hodge openly admitted that on this issue he felt closer to Bullinger, Zwingli's successor, than to Calvin. He was challenged by the able German-American Reformed theologian John Williamson Nevin in a book on the Eucharist titled *The Mystical Presence: A Vindication of the Reformed or Calvinistic Doctrine of the Holy Eucharist* (1846). An even more open Zwinglian stance was taken by the influential Southern Presbyterian theologian Robert Dabney (1820–1898). On these and other reactions to Calvin's theology in the 1800s and 1900s, see chapter 4 in Mathison's book.

2. On Beza, see Jill Raitt, *The Eucharistic Theology of Theodore Beza: Development of the Reformed Doctrine* (Atlanta, Ga.: Scholars Press, 1972). On Peter Martyr, see Joseph C. McLelland, *The Visible Words of God: A Study in the Theology of Peter Martyr, 1500–1562* (Edinburgh: Oliver & Boyd, 1957). T. F. Torrance writes in the foreword, "It is indeed his type of Reformed theology, particularly in the doctrine of the Church and Sacraments, that appealed strongly to the Church of England and the Church of Scotland, and still reveals the basic unity between the two."

3. John Calvin, *Institutes of the Christian Religion*, ed. John T. McNeill (Philadelphia: Westminster, 1960), IV.14.1. Henceforth I will simply insert quotations from the *Institutes* in the text, using the abbreviated form *Inst.*

4. Taken from *Calvin: Theological Treatises*, ed. J. K. S. Reid (Philadelphia: Westminster, 1954), 131. For other references to the crucial role of the Holy Spirit in relation to the sacraments, see *Institutes* IV.14.8, 10, 11, 22.

5. John Calvin, "Antidote to the Council of Trent," Canon IV, in *Calvin's Tracts and Treatises*, vol. 3, ed. T. F. Torrance (Grand Rapids: Eerdmans, 1958), 174.

6. I am quoting from the translation of the Latin version (1538) by Ford Lewis Battles (see my *Calvin's First Catechism: A Commentary* [Louisville: Westminster, 1987], 35). Portions of this chapter are taken from that book. The key word in this quotation is "communication" (*communicatio*), which has a far richer significance in Latin than in common English parlance. Calvin uses the same word a few lines later in the Catechism when he points out that despite Christ's absence from us, "no distance can prevent [Christ's] power from feeding his believers on himself, and bringing it about that they still enjoy ever present communication with him." This term occurs with relatively less frequency in the *Institutes*, where Calvin uses more graphic language to indicate how Christ is experienced in the Supper (however, see IV.17.20, where there is a broader reference to "that secret communication by which we grow into one with Christ"; cf. IV.17.38). The term is also used several times in Calvin's *Short Treatise on the Lord's Supper* (composed in 1540, shortly after the Catechism). Here he declares that "to deny the true communication of Jesus Christ to be offered us in the Supper is to render this holy sacrament frivolous and useless"

(*Calvin: Theological Treatises*, 146). In other contexts Calvin substitutes the word "communion" (*communio*) for "communication" in discussing the Supper, so apparently they convey the same idea.

7. Joachim Westphal, a Lutheran pastor from Hamburg, reacted violently to the Zurich Consensus, the agreement on the Lord's Supper hammered out by Calvin and Bullinger, Zwingli's successor. Westphal accused Calvin of heresy, to which Calvin responded with two treatises (see *Calvin's Tracts and Treatises*, vol. 2, ed. T. F. Torrance [Grand Rapids: Eerdmans, 1958], 244–494).

8. Later in the *Institutes* Calvin warns about people like Westphal who teach that there is a "mixture, or transfusion, of Christ's flesh with our soul." Calvin feels this danger is avoided and yet a vital truth maintained if we believe that "from the substance of his flesh Christ breathes life into our souls—indeed pours forth his very life into us—even though Christ's flesh itself does not enter into us" (IV.17.32). This is a crucial distinction.

9. Brian Gerrish concludes his study of Calvin's eucharistic doctrine with the following paragraph: "It is not at all surprising that stalwart Reformed divines have sometimes been not merely puzzled but offended by Calvin's talk about the communication of Christ's life-giving flesh. They may choose to reject it as a perilous intrusion into Reformed theology and insist that Christ's body is life-giving only because it was crucified. But in so doing they should note that Calvin's view of the Lord's Supper was bound up with a total conception of what it means to be saved and of how the historical deed of Christ reaches out to the present. It is impossible to read Calvin's ideas on baptism and the Eucharist in their own historical context and not to notice that they were developed in part as a warning against what he took to be another peril: a mentality that reduces sacred signs to mere reminders, communion with Christ to beliefs about Christ, and the living body of the church to an association of like-minded individuals. Only a careful study of later Reformed history can show which has turned out to be the greater of the two perils. But this much, I think, can fairly be said in conclusion: even if the Calvinists have the greatest difficulty in expressing what exactly that something *more* is that they experience in the holy banquet, ecumenical theology will always have need of them to throw their weight on Calvin's side of the Reformed boat" (*Grace and Gratitude* [Minneapolis: Fortress, 1993], 190).

10. See, e.g., Hermann Sasse, *This Is My Body: Luther's Contention for the Real Presence in the Sacrament of the Altar* (Minneapolis: Augsburg, 1959); Carl Braaten and Robert Jenson, eds., *Christian Dogmatics*, vol. 2 (Philadelphia: Fortress, 1984), 357ff.

11. John Calvin, "Short Treatise on the Lord's Supper," in *Calvin: Theological Treatises*, 147. As Robert Letham notes, "There is an inseparable conjunction of sign and reality" (*The Lord's Supper: Eternal Word in Broken Bread* [Phillipsburg, N.J.: P & R Publishing, 2001], 29).

12. *Calvin: Theological Treatises*, 149.

13. This quote is from a translation of the Latin edition (1545) by J. K. S. Reid (*Calvin: Theological Treatises*, 137). The earlier French version is more concise: We are able to partake of Christ's substance, though he is in heaven, "by

the incomprehensible power of his Spirit, who conjoins things separated by a distance" (*The School of Faith of the Reformed Church*, ed. T. F. Torrance [London: James Clarke, 1959], 62).

14. John Calvin, *The First Epistle of Paul to the Corinthians* (Grand Rapids: Eerdmans, 1960), 247, on 1 Cor. 11:24). Calvin also writes, "Distance does not at all prevent Christ from dwelling in us, or being one with him, since the efficacy of the Spirit surmounts all natural obstacles" ("The True Partaking of the Flesh and Blood of Christ in the Holy Supper," in *Calvin's Tracts and Treatises*, 2:519).

15. Calvin, *First Corinthians*, 246, on 1 Cor. 11:24. Thomas J. Davis points out that "flesh" in this context is not "simply a synonym for 'skin' or 'muscles,' though the bodily aspect is certainly included in the word 'flesh.' However, the word also means more than that for Calvin." In his comments on Romans 3:20, 7:5, and 7:18, Calvin explains that "the word 'flesh' served to designate what it is to be human." Thus, in the Eucharist "it is in that full humanity that Christians participate as they are joined to Christ" (*The Clearest Promises of God: The Development of Calvin's Eucharistic Teaching* [New York: AMS Press, 1995], 113).

16. Note that in these quotations the Holy Spirit is not merely the channel between Christ and his people but that he also "infuses [Christ's] life into us from heaven" ("The True Partaking of the Flesh and Blood of Christ," in *Calvin's Tracts and Treatises*, vol. 2, 518–19).

17. Christopher Kaiser has made a thorough study of what Calvin means by the notion of our lifting up our hearts to heaven and seeking Christ there in the celebration of the Eucharist and concludes that (1) Calvin was not simply using a figure of speech to describe a mental attitude; (2) that we must take Calvin's references to "the eucharistic ascent of the soul at face value"; and (3) that this eucharistic ascent "was the means of our mystical union with Christ." Calvin stressed "Christ's (and the Spirit's) role in our elevation and made the real presence of Christ in the sacrament a precondition for our ascent to Christ in heaven" ("Climbing Jacob's Ladder: John Calvin and the Early Church in Our Eucharistic Ascent to Heaven," *Scottish Journal of Theology* 56/3 [2003]: 252–53).

18. Ronald Wallace writes, "Calvin appears at times to be inconsistent in his statements about the Supper. He can in one place deny that Christ 'descends to the earth in the Supper' ... and yet in other places he speaks freely about Christ as descending through the Supper. His meaning depends on the context and the course taken by the argument which has led up to the making of the statement" (*Calvin's Doctrine of Word and Sacraments* [Edinburgh: Oliver & Boyd, 1953], 208).

19. Calvin, *First Corinthians*, 246, on 1 Cor. 11:24, emphasis added.

20. Despite such modesty, Calvin is still convinced that his view is true and is "confident" that his view "will by approved by godly hearts" (*Inst.* IV.17.7).

21. This doesn't mean we should take refuge in pious ignorance or poor theology. As Kilian McDonnell rightly points out in regard to comments like these, "Calvin knew a mystery when he saw one and he knew that the mystery was beyond man's measuring.... But the insistence on the element of mystery is no reason for foregoing an explanation: 'Knowledge of this great

mystery is most necessary and, in proportion to its importance, demands an accurate exposition' [*Inst.* IV.17.1]" (*John Calvin, the Church, and the Eucharist* [Princeton, N.J.: Princeton Univ. Press, 1967], 207).

22. *Calvin: Theological Treatises*, 49.

23. Ibid., 66. In the *Institutes*, Calvin condemns the practice of celebrating the Supper only once a year in the Catholic Church, cites Acts 2:42, and comments, "Thus it became the unvarying rule that no meeting of the church should take place without the Word, prayers, partaking of the Supper, and almsgiving. That this was the established order among the Corinthians also we can safely infer from Paul [cf. 1 Cor. 11:20]" (IV.17.44).

24. On Reformed liturgical renewal, see Howard G. Hageman, *Pulpit and Table: Some Chapters in the History of Worship in the Reformed Churches* (Richmond, Va.: John Knox, 1962); Jack Martin Maxwell, *Worship and Reformed Theology: The Liturgical Lessons of Mercersburg* (Pittsburgh, Pa.: Pickwick, 1976).

25. Mathison, *Given for You*, 292 (see esp. chapter 9 on "Practical Issues and Debates").

26. Whether wine or grape juice is used is usually a matter of preference on the part of the leaders of a given congregation. Those with high-church tendencies generally prefer wine, but the vast majority of churches use grape juice. Interestingly, Keith Mathison, a conservative Presbyterian, is adamant about the use of wine. To him this is not a matter of *adiaphora* — of indifference. He insists that wine be used and argues the case at length (sixteen pages!) in his book *Given for You*. He concludes, "Because of the irrefutable fact that wine was used by Jesus in the institution of the Lord's Supper, and because the use of wine in the Lord's Supper was an undisputed practice for the first 1800 years of the church's existence, a heavy burden of proof rests upon those who have substituted grape juice for wine" (p. 313). Robert Letham concurs and makes this interesting observation: "Wine itself conveys the intoxicating nature of the gospel" (*The Lord's Supper*, 53). That depends, of course, on whether one enjoys wine!

27. Letham, *The Lord's Supper*, 51.

28. The full exhortation, which is fairly lengthy, can be found in the RCA worship book titled *Worship the Lord* (Grand Rapids: Eerdmans, 1987), 27.

29. The history of the debate and the various papers presented by the Theological Commission, together with objections raised at General Synod, are found in *The Church Speaks*, vol. 2, ed. James I. Cook (Grand Rapids: Eerdmans, 2002), 155–64.

30. See the comments of Robert Letham, Orthodox Presbyterian minister and professor, in his book *The Lord's Supper*, 55–57.

Notes: Chapter 2: A Roman Catholic Response (Thomas A. Baima)

1. Catechism of the Catholic Church (CCC), 955.

Chapter Three

LUTHERAN VIEW

Finding the Right Word

LUTHERAN VIEW

Finding the Right Word

David P. Scaer

Sometimes the Lutheran position on the Lord's Supper is described by others as "consubstantiation," which etymologically means "one substance by the side of another." Along with bread and wine, recipients of the Supper receive Christ's body and blood. Lutherans rarely use this term and are more likely to use the phrase "the real presence" to describe their belief that the elements of bread and wine are actually Christ's body and blood and are given to and received by all who participate in the Lord's Supper. This commonly used phrase has its drawbacks, however. It can be used of the belief that Christ is only spiritually present in the Supper—not in his actual body and blood.[1] Not many Christians would dispute that Christ is present in the Lord's Supper according to his divinity, by the Spirit's power, or by being remembered. Crucial for Lutherans is that Jesus of Nazareth—born of the Virgin Mary, crucified and now raised from the dead—is given to the participants.[2]

One dictionary definition of consubstantiation fits the Lutheran view: "the substantial union of the body and blood of Christ with the eucharistic elements after the consecration"; another definition does not: "At the consecration of the Eucharist the substance of the body and blood of Christ coexists with the substance of the consecrated bread and wine." "Coexists" suggests, or at least allows, that Christ's body and blood lie side by side with the earthly elements without any essential communion between them.[3]

The Lutheran Confessions, in describing Christ's body and blood as being "in, with and under" the bread and wine, may have allowed others to use "consubstantiation" to describe this view. These prepositions were intended to affirm that the earthly elements were really Christ's body and blood and not to explain how earthly and divine elements were spatially related. In the earlier Lutheran Confessions, the three prepositions were not used together. Article Ten in the German edition of the Augsburg Confession says that "the true body and blood of Christ are truly present *under* the form [*Gestalt*] of bread and wine," a formulation which their Roman opponents found acceptable. In the Small Catechism, Luther used *under*: it "is the true body and blood of our Lord Jesus Christ *under* bread and wine." In the Large Catechism, he used two prepositions: the Sacrament of the Altar "is the true body and blood of the Lord Jesus Christ, and *in* and *under* bread and wine." Article Ten of the Apology of the Augsburg Confession uses *with*: "the body and blood of Christ are truly and substantially present and are truly distributed *with* those things that are seen, the bread and the wine." If *with* by itself allows for consubstantiation, *in*, as Christ is *in* the bread and wine, suggests impanation, the belief that Christ's body is contained in the consecrated bread like a nut in a cookie. Used together, these prepositions affirm that the elements are actually Christ's body and blood and do not have spatial significance.[4] Adequate is Luther's explanation that bread and wine "are truly the body and blood of Christ."[5]

LUTHERAN DISTINCTIVENESS
AND THE LORD'S SUPPER

Justification by faith was the first characteristic doctrine that distinguished Lutherans from Roman Catholics, but the view on the Lord's Supper that separated them from the Reformed soon claimed equal prominence. Reformed interpretations of the Supper were not all of one kind, but common to all was the teaching that the bread and wine were not Christ's body and blood. Mere symbolical, memorial, or spiritual views that did not affirm Christ's bodily presence were not tolerable to Lutherans.[6] They rejected the Roman doctrine of transubstantiation, which held that substances of bread and wine were physically changed into Christ's body and blood so that properties of bread and wine remained but not their substances;[7] however, Reformed views were seen as more threatening.

To safeguard their position, Lutherans set forth three criteria for an acceptable definition of the Lord's Supper: (1) Christ's body and blood are received by the mouth and not just by faith or the soul. (2) Unbelievers, not just believers, actually receive Christ's body and blood. (3) Views contrary to this must be condemned.[8] For Lutherans, *true* identified the sacramental elements with Christ's actual body and blood of Christ. In the distribution of the sacrament, *true* is included: "Take and eat; this is the *true* body of the Lord Jesus Christ." A mere spiritual view was unacceptable.

THE LORD'S SUPPER AMONG THE SACRAMENTS

Since Lutherans understand the Lord's Supper as a sacrament, the definition and number of sacraments come into play. Roman Catholics insist on seven and the Reformed on two. For Lutherans, this is an open issue,[9] although most follow Luther in using the word *sacrament* only of baptism and the Lord's Supper. For Luther, baptism and the Lord's Supper are constituted by the word of God—i.e., by Jesus' institution—and involve earthly elements. Baptism lays the foundation for the Lord's Supper, which in turn points the believer back to baptism. What is born in baptism is nourished by the Lord's Supper.[10]

Rather than providing a prior definition of a sacrament and then deciding which church rites meet the criteria, the Augsburg Confession lets each rite stand on its own institution and be defined by its particular functions. This allows for a gradation from rites that have Christ's explicit commands to those instituted by the church. Penance and ordination can be sacraments because in them God works to create and strengthen faith, which is seen as one action accomplished by God through the Word, that is, through Christ and the gospel. Any number of rites can be called sacraments, but each has its own necessity, function, and promise.[11]

Baptism provides for the foundation of Christian life, and the Lord's Supper is the goal. Emergency administration of baptism is required, but only regularly ordained ministers may administer the Lord's Supper. Baptism, like birth, is a once-in-a-lifetime, unrepeatable event; as nourishment for the Christian life, the Lord's Supper is received regularly. Only the baptized may receive the Supper.

The Augsburg Confession discusses baptism in Article Nine and the Lord's Supper in Article Ten, but a general discussion on the sacraments only comes later in Article Thirteen—after the articles on confession and repentance.[12] In defining sacrament, the author of these confessions, Philip Melanchthon, Luther's colleague at the University of Wittenberg, put the emphasis on God's presence in the ritual to forgive sins.[13] Since for Luther, sacraments had to do with physical, tangible things, only baptism, administered with water, and the Lord's Supper, with the elements of bread and wine, qualified. He referred to them as the "two sacraments instituted by Christ,"[14] but he spoke of penance as the practice of baptism[15] and spoke of marriage in sacramental terms. Essential in either definition was that in the sacraments God works for the salvation of believers.

In baptism, the believer is incorporated into the body of Christ; in the Lord's Supper, one receives that body. Baptism is the presupposition for the Lord's Supper, which in turn is the fulfillment of the baptism—but both offered forgiveness. One cannot be substituted for the other; nor can the order be reversed. Even the most sincere unbaptized believers dare not be admitted to the Lord's Supper. Lutherans speak of the Word making the sacrament and of the sacrament as the visible Word. The Word creates faith by hearing, and this Word changes ordinary bread and wine into Christ's body and blood and creates and confirms faith. Baptism gives a new birth by the application of the Word in water and places the recipient in Christ's death and resurrection. In the Lord's Supper, Christ comes to the believer in bread and wine. If these distinctions remain unrecognized, Christians may falsely content themselves with only hearing the Word or receiving only one of the sacraments and thus deprive themselves of the benefits God intends for them.[16]

THE SACRAMENTAL GOD

Sacraments are not New Testament innovations but rather are the ordinary ways in which God came to his Old Testament people even before the fall.[17] He was present in the tree of life to establish communion with our first parents (Gen. 2:9) and later in the rainbow (Gen. 9:13) and in the sacrifices to forgive sins (Lev. 4:1–5:13). Thus the first Jewish Christians were already sacramental in their historical reflections and liturgical practices and were prepared for recognizing Christ's presence in bread and wine. The Passover (Exod. 12:1–30),[18] the sacrifices, and the feeding with the manna in the wilderness (Exod. 16:1–36) were brought together and raised to newer and higher dimensions in the Lord's Supper. Paul explains the Lord's Supper against the background of the feeding with manna: "And all [our fathers] ate the same supernatural [NIV, spiritual] food and all drank the same supernatural drink. For they drank from the supernatural Rock which followed them, and the Rock was Christ" (1 Cor. 10:3–4 RSV).[19] The Evangelists use eucharistic language in their records of the feeding miracles.[20] The God who comes in the incarnation and the sacraments was already dwelling with Israel.

THE SACRAMENT BETWEEN ATONEMENT AND FORGIVENESS

The Lord's Supper brings its recipients face-to-face with Christ's death as the atonement so that sins can be forgiven. Christ's blood given in the Lord's Supper is first offered to God as the atonement: "This is my blood of the covenant, which is poured out for many for the forgiveness of sins" (Matt. 26:28). Christ's blood is sacrificially shed or poured out from his body as an atonement to satisfy God's charge against sinners. With the demands of the old covenant satisfied, God establishes a new covenant in which forgiveness is offered for the sins of those who participate in the Supper. It is the new covenant or testament (Luke 22:20; 1 Cor. 11:25).[21]

With his body and blood Christ is present in the church as the sacrifice to God for sin. What Christ sacrificed to God he gives as sacrament to his people. Sacrifice and sacrament are two sides of one reality. Appropriately in the liturgy the congregation greets Christ as the atonement for sin in the *Agnus Dei*: "Lamb of God, who takes away the sin of the world, have mercy on us." As the blood of lambs spared the Israelite boys from death, so Christians are spared death by Christ's blood in the Lord's Supper. In this sacrament the church proclaims the Lord's death until he returns (1 Cor. 11:24–26) and confesses that his death is the sacrifice for their sins and those of the world (John 6:51). Believers are promised eternal life and the resurrection merited by Christ's death (v. 54).[22] Unbelievers and those with unresolved sin meet him as judge. On that account, those who approach this Supper must do so with great care. In the sacrament atonement and judgment come together.

THE LORD'S SUPPER AS SIGN

Sacraments are signs to which God's Word is attached. The outward signs are affirmations that God is the Creator and point to the supernatural things contained in the sacraments—which indeed they are. They convey redemptive grace and signify that the Creator is at home in his creation. In the sacraments the Creator becomes one with his creation by taking on its forms. The sacramental union in which Jesus comes as bread and wine is one step beyond the incarnation in which God assumed flesh in Jesus of Nazareth. Corruptible created things become fit vehicles for the divine elements of Christ's body and blood. Rejected is the principle of *finitum non capax infinitum* ("the finite is incapable of holding the infinite"), an argument often raised against the Lutheran beliefs of Christ's presence in bread and wine and of God's giving of his full majesty to the human nature of Jesus (the *genus maiestaticum*). A philosophical axiom cannot be the basis of doctrine, but the terms of this axiom can be reversed to bolster the Lutheran position. It is not a matter of whether the finite is capable of the infinite but whether the infinite is capable of the finite (*infinitum capax finitum*). If this is not so, then the infinite is less than infinite.

Another axiom (namely, that only one object can occupy a particular place at one time) has no place in the Lutheran theology. Jesus can be present in one place—the local presence—but he is not bound by the ordinary rules of space and time—the illocal presence. His presence in the Lord's Supper is unique and is ordinarily called his "sacramental presence," since his body and blood are distributed by the ministers and devoured by the recipients. This is related to Jesus' omnipresence but not identical to it. God is present in all things, but for salvation he is present in some things (i.e., the sacraments) and not others. In instituting the sacrament, Jesus sat with his disciples, who received him in bread and wine, and in the same moment was present wherever God was. Finding and worshiping him in things he has not designated is idolatry. God was found and worshiped in Jerusalem but not in Bethel.

Today he is present for our salvation in *things* called sacraments to test our faith in him by our accepting his invitation to meet him in these *things*. This he does preeminently in the Lord's Supper.[23] If we do not recognize him in the elements or if we refuse his invitation, we are guilty of unbelief and do not receive the benefits he places in the sacraments. Substituting other elements for bread and wine is an act of disobedience. Such a ritual can be sacramental in the sense that the Word of God is present, but it is not a sacrament instituted by Christ. Just as God was present in the man Jesus—and in no one else—for salvation, so Jesus is present in the bread and wine to make participants beneficiaries of the salvation God accomplished in him.[24]

Luther used Augustine's definition that a sacrament was constituted by the Word's being joined to a physical element chosen by God—the Word that turned ordinary things into sacraments to forgive sins.[25] To illustrate this, Luther spoke of God's using a straw to bestow grace, though not suggesting that God had actually done or would do this.[26] He wanted to show what God's Word could do with ordinary things. The external elements of the sacraments as signs correspond to what the sacraments are and do. Like water in baptism, bread and wine are not arbitrarily chosen, but their external forms convey and correspond to the heavenly things they contain. Just as in baptism water symbolizes creation, birth, and destruction, bread is reminiscent of what humans must produce in the sweat of their brow to survive in a world of sin (Gen. 3:19). It is a reminder of our fallen condition and the necessity of eating Christ's body for salvation.

Fittingly, Jesus describes himself as "bread" (John 6:33, 35, 48, 51) and the "vine" (John 15:1), which is the source of wine. Until the Reformation, the fourth petition of the Lord's Prayer ("Give us today our daily bread" [Matt. 6:11]) was widely understood as a reference to the Eucharist. It was a prayer to God to give Jesus as the heavenly food. As we eat the bread, Jesus makes us his body and forgives us our debts. Wine anticipates heaven's joys, which already belong to believers in Jesus. He drinks of the fruit of the vine with us in the Lord's Supper and participates in the sacrament with us (Matt. 26:29).

Use of bread made without yeast is the most common practice among Lutherans. It recalls the Passover, when yeast was removed from the Israelites' houses. Another argument for the use of unleavened bread is that the Evangelists placed the institution of the Supper during the Feast of Unleavened Bread (Matt. 26:17; Mark 14:1; Luke 22:1).[27] Eastern Orthodox churches use leavened bread as a reminder that the Lord's Supper commemorates Easter, but the use of leavened or unleavened bread has not been divisive. More serious is the practice of substituting grape juice with additives for wine. Only grapes fermented as wine were available in the spring when Jesus instituted the Supper. Use of substances other than wine may be based on the idea that any alcoholic beverage, including wine, is not a fit sacramental vehicle or that the elements used are unimportant. If consumption of alcohol is a problem for some, wine with a lower alcohol content can be used.

FAITH AS THE WORTHY RECEPTION OF THE LORD'S SUPPER

Lutherans are insistent that the validity of the Lord's Supper rests on Christ's command and not on faith.[28] As important as faith is for a worthy reception of it, Christ's word in instituting the Supper—not faith—makes it a sacrament.[29] Unbelievers and those with insincere faith who receive Christ's body and blood take them to their harm.[30] The man in Corinth living in open sin with his father's wife was harming himself. Without compromising the belief that the Lord's Supper's efficacy does not depend on faith, recipients are required to believe that Jesus is offered through the earthly elements, and only by this faith do they receive the forgiveness offered through them. Christ's body and blood are received by the mouth, but their benefits are received by faith. Since faith was required to receive the Lord's Supper, Lutherans maintained the practice of confession and absolution (or penance, as it was called). Luther did not ordinarily call it a sacrament, as Melanchthon did, but he had a place for it (the fifth of six parts) in his Small Catechism between the sections on baptism and the Lord's Supper. Confession with absolution was the lifelong practice of baptism and a requirement for receiving the Lord's Supper. Only the penitent who believed in the benefits of the Lord's Supper could receive it. Baptism, absolution, and the Lord's Supper were seen as a constellation.

THE LORD'S SUPPER AS THE FOOD OF THE HOLY SPIRIT

Along with their insistence that the elements were Christ's body and blood, Lutherans spoke of this presence as supernatural, heavenly, and spiritual, though these terms were open to misunderstanding.[31] Since the manna was called a spiritual food, the sacrament of the altar could hardly be less so. The sacramental eating was a spiritual one. Mouth and teeth devour Christ's body, but it remains intact.[32] His body which was received by the mouth was "spiritually partaken through faith" in the Supper.[33] Reformed opponents held that with Christ's ascension into heaven and his session at the right hand of the Father, he could be spiritually but not actually present with his body and blood in the sacrament. Lutherans held that Christ's sitting at the Father's right hand had nothing to do with confinement to a space in heaven[34] but referred to his exercise of God's rule on earth.[35] The omnipresence of Christ's human nature provided a foundation for his sacramental presence but was not the evidence for it.

Proof for Christ's presence in the sacrament came in the words of institution that effected it. It was not dependent on a particular understanding of his omnipresence or subcategory of it. By his ascension, Christ entered into the sacramental life of the church. Wherever the Lord's Supper is celebrated, he is completely there—God and man, body and soul. Distance in time and space does not separate Christ's institution of the Supper on Maundy Thursday from its subsequent celebrations. Where a pastor and a congregation are not available, believers may participate in it in a spiritual way by meditating on it. Lutherans may not receive the Lord's Supper in other churches, but they should meditate on its mystery and benefits.

Spirit and *spiritual* can be understood in a Platonic sense of only things of the spirit being real. Physical things are not real in themselves but shadows of the world of ideas. Similarly, the Reformed see the sacramental elements as symbols of divine things and attribute the union of believers with Christ not to their actually receiving his body and blood but to the Spirit. Lutherans rejected these views; however, the Spirit's role, along with that of the Father, in the Lord's Supper must be affirmed. Bread and wine are symbols but in the sense that they contain the realities of Christ's body and blood to which they point. They symbolize a present reality and not something outside of them.

As an adjective for the Holy Spirit, *spiritual* is also a proper word. The Spirit is active in the words of consecration to create faith in the recipients and thus the Lord's Supper is a *spiritual* meal. Though a Trinitarian invocation is not included in the liturgy of the Lord's Supper, as it is in baptism, it is no less a Trinitarian act. Prayers of the traditional Lutheran liturgy are addressed to the Father: "It is truly, meet, right, and salutary, that we should at all times, and in all places, give thanks unto thee, O Lord, Holy Father, Almighty, Everlasting God."[36] Things created by the Father are transformed by the Spirit of Christ into his body and blood through which he works and confirms faith. In the Lord's Supper the *Creator Spiritus* comes as the sanctifying Spirit to turn things he created into instruments of salvation. He is present not in an action parallel to or alongside the sacrament but in Christ's words through the sacramental elements.

An argument for the Spirit's role in the Lord's Supper can be made from Paul's reference to the Israelites' partaking of the same *spiritual* food and drink, which was Christ (see 1 Cor. 10:3–4). This section introduces Paul's discourse on the Lord's Supper (1 Cor. 10:14–22). Rather than translating *pneumatikon* as "supernatural," as the RSV does, it is better translated *spiritual*, as the NIV and the ESV do, as a reference to what the Holy Spirit did. The Spirit who provided manna and water as the sacraments for Israel works sacramentally for the church in bread and wine. Liturgies of the Orthodox Church give a prominent place to the Spirit in the *epiklēsis*, by which he is invoked on the elements to make them Christ's body and blood.[37] This is not the historic Lutheran custom, but the Apology takes note of this. In the Lord's Supper, the Spirit as God's creating agent

(Gen. 1:2) raises the created things of bread and wine to a higher and more sacred level in making them Christ's body and blood. Nevertheless, at the heart of the Lutheran arguments for Christ's presence in the Supper are the words of institution: "This is my body ... this [cup] is my blood of the covenant" (Matt. 26:26, 28). Through these words Christ effects the sacrament. The word *is* is taken literally and not figuratively. Words spoken by the minister do not have their power from him, nor do they possess an autonomous power—a kind of magic—but their power resides in Christ's institution.[38] The words of Christ are the Spirit's only vehicle to work salvation.

THE PRACTICE OF THE LORD'S SUPPER

For nearly two centuries after the Reformation, the Lutheran church had a weekly Sunday celebration of the Lord's Supper. This indicated its determinative role for Christian life and its importance for doctrine. Pietism and the Enlightenment had a damaging effect on Lutheran sacramental life. Even churches seriously committed to Luther's teachings offered the Lord's Supper no more than four times a year. Ironically, the church that defined itself by its doctrine of the Lord's Supper eliminated its practice, with few exceptions, from regular worship.

Today the majority of Lutheran congregations in the United States have a weekly celebration of the Lord's Supper. Its celebration on Sunday is not seen as mandated by the commandment requiring Sabbath observance but as the celebration of the Lord's resurrection. It transcends and encompasses the time and the space between its institution and its perfect celebration in heaven. Its celebration on any day, especially festivals or saints' days, is also proper. In the Supper, Christ is temple, priest, and sacrifice, so pilgrimages to shrines and efforts to restore Israel as God's people and reconstruct Jerusalem with its temple are rendered obsolete. Participants in the sacrament have come to the heavenly Jerusalem.[39]

THE LORD'S SUPPER: WHAT'S IN A NAME?

When Lutherans speak of *the* sacrament, they are most likely speaking of the Lord's Supper. Like other designations (e.g., "the Lord's table" [1 Cor. 10:21]), it is taken over from the New Testament: "When you come together, it is not the *Lord's Supper* [*deipnon*] you eat" (1 Cor. 11:20, italics added). Use of this designation is more significant today in the light of historical doubts raised by critical scholars, who hold that Jesus may have joined his disciples for meals before his death, but its origins as a sacrament rest with his followers, who after death came to believe that he had risen. Memorial meals took on a sacred character in which bread and wine were eventually identified with Jesus himself.

Discussions among Christians about Christ's presence in the Supper must first agree that he instituted this meal as a sacrament. Without this historical conviction, the rite can hardly be called the *Lord's* Supper, and subsequent theological questions are rendered moot. Though called the Lord's *Supper* because it was instituted in an evening meal, it has since earliest times been celebrated in the morning, often at daybreak, to commemorate the resurrection. Its ritual terms were set forth on Maundy Thursday, but its origins rest in Christ's death as an atonement for sins. The Greek words translated "on the night he was betrayed" can also be rendered "on the night he was handed over" (1 Cor. 11:23)—i.e., God handed Jesus over to Satan so that by struggling with Satan and death Jesus might overcome them. By crucifixion his blood flows from his body so that both can become the heavenly elements of the sacrament. With his body and blood—i.e., as priest and sacrificial victim—Christ enters the assembly of believers to forgive their sins. Jesus is himself the Word who makes earthly elements his body and blood. Because he is all aspects of this sacrament, he is proclaimed in its every aspect (see 1 Cor. 11:26). Thus the *Lord's* people come together on the *Lord's* day to hear the *Lord's* word (i.e., the gospel), to pray the *Lord's* Prayer, and to gather around the *Lord's* table to receive the *Lord's* Supper. In all these actions and in the elements themselves Jesus is present. This meal is in every aspect the *Lord's* Supper.

Other designations for this sacrament also embrace biblical terms, though they may not have been in use in apostolic times precisely in the way we know them now. "Holy Communion" is commonly used among Lutherans. "The cup of blessing which we bless, is it not the *communion* of the blood of Christ?

The bread which we break, is it not the *communion* of the body of Christ?" (1 Cor 10:16 KJV, italics added). Those who receive the bread and the wine participate in Christ's body and blood, which provides the basis for communion with other recipients. By receiving the body of Christ, the church is constituted as a fellowship in his body. The sacrament is a *Holy* Communion because recipients share in the holy things of Christ's body and blood and through them have communion with one another and express a common faith. Without this, no real fellowship exists. Accordingly, Lutherans commune with only those who are penitent and share the same faith. Tragically, in the sacrament in which Christ unites believers to himself, and through him to others, the disunity among Christians caused by their differences becomes evident. Because Ulrich Zwingli could not say that the bread and wine of the Supper were really Christ's body and blood, Martin Luther refused to commune with him. Requiring that all recipients have a common faith is traditionally called "closed communion," after the ancient custom of dismissing those who were not eligible to receive the sacrament before the Lord's Supper was celebrated. "Open communion"—the practice of communing all who desire to participate in spite of grave differences—is more likely to be derived from understanding it as a community rite in which diverse beliefs are tolerated. A ritual practiced under these circumstances has a diminished sacramental character.

Luther in the Small Catechism called the Lord's Supper "the sacrament of the altar"—a term connected to how Lutherans place the cross or crucifix on their altars to symbolize Christ's death as a sacrifice for sins. "Altar" may have been used for the place from where the sacrament was distributed in apostolic times.[40] Even when the Supper is not celebrated, the altar as the place where Christ is in the celebration of the Lord's Supper is reverenced by bowing the head or kneeling.

"Eucharist," a term used in the *Didache*,[41] has recently come into wider use among some Lutherans. Its adjective, "eucharistic" (from the Greek *eucharistos*, "thankful"), is the most commonly used one for this sacrament. Eucharistic theology and practice deals with teaching about the Lord's Supper. "Eucharist" is derived from the words of institution: "when he had *given thanks*" (1 Cor. 11:24, italics added; cf. Matt. 26:27).[42] It is found in the accounts of the miraculous feedings of the crowds (Matt. 15:36; John 6:11)—events the Evangelists use to prepare their hearers for the Supper's institution.[43] The word also occupies a prominent place in the Proper Preface, the introductory part of the Communion liturgy: "It is truly good, right, and salutary that we should at all times and places *give thanks* to you, holy Lord, almighty Father, everlasting God." The entire service is eucharistic, the occasion in which the congregation thanks God for this inestimable gift of Christ's body and blood.

In Article 10 of the Augsburg Confession and the Apology, it is called "the Mass," a term still used in northern European Lutheran churches but rarely in America. It is derived from *missa*, the Latin word for "depart" or "go," formerly the last words in the service. Once believers have received Christ's body and blood, no greater mysteries await them on earth. Luther questioned whether private Masses qualified as a sacrament, and he denounced the Mass as a priest's offering of Christ as a sacrifice for sins, especially for those of the dead. For him this was an abomination.[44] Also objectionable was the Roman argument that since Christ's blood was in his flesh, the laity did not have to receive the cup.[45] In some places this practice has been rectified. In spite of serious differences, Luther acknowledged that Roman Catholics really received Christ's body and blood.[46]

WHAT ABOUT JOHN?

Martin Luther combined the words of institution from Matthew, Mark, Luke, and Paul in his Small Catechism definition of the sacrament of the altar: "It is the true body and blood of our Lord Jesus under bread and wine, instituted by Christ himself for us Christians to eat and drink." Strikingly absent is John, Luther's favorite evangelist. John 6 was used by the Roman Catholics to support giving only the host to the laity because blood is already in the flesh, a position compatible with their doctrine of transubstantiation. At Marburg in October 1529 in his dispute with Luther, Zwingli used John 6:63 ("the Spirit gives life; the flesh counts for nothing") to his advantage in seeing the Supper in spiritual and not physical terms.[47] Luther focused the discussion on the words of institution, especially "is" (this *is* my body; this cup *is* the new covenant in my blood).

Perhaps out of loyalty to the Reformer, Lutherans have hesitated in using John 6 in their understanding of the Lord's Supper. This hesitancy was supported by John 6:63, which seemed to require that without receiving the Lord's Supper, a person could not be saved. Lutherans made an exception to John 3:5, which made baptism an absolute necessity for salvation. In spite of their avoidance of John's gospel in their eucharistic theology, Lutherans have used such phrases as "the bread from heaven" and "the bread of life" in their eucharistic hymns and devotion. Ironically, Lutherans may have deprived themselves of the most descriptive New Testament evidences for their position that recipients of the Supper actually eat Christ's body and drink his blood and that this sacrament is vital to the Christian life. Luther's claim in the Small Catechism that forgiveness, life, and salvation are given in the sacrament strangely mirrors the teaching of John 6:50, 54 that eternal life and the resurrection come with eating Christ's body and drinking his blood.

If Lutherans can overcome their historical aversions, they will find a wealth of evidences from the entire Johannine corpus (not just John's gospel) to support their doctrine that the earthly elements of the Lord's Supper are truly Christ's body and blood. With regard to Zwingli's use of the unprofitability of the flesh as evidence against a physical understanding of the Lord's Supper, this passage more likely refers to those who without the life-giving power of the Holy Spirit cannot accept that Christ is promising to give his body for food and his blood for drink. When Jesus began to speak in such fleshly terms, many turned away from him (John 6:66). Some still do.

A BAPTIST RESPONSE

Russell D. Moore

I wouldn't want to trade places with David Scaer. The "extremes" of the spectrum represented in this book—my Baptist view and the Roman Catholic view—are relatively simple: the elements are a sign pointing to the reality thereof, or they actually are the body and blood of Jesus. By contrast, the Lutheran view of consubstantiation is exegetically, historically, philosophically, and semantically far more complex. This does not make the view untrue; it simply makes it more of a challenge to explain. Nonetheless, Scaer does so with skill and grace.

In laying out his view of the Supper as a Lutheran distinctive, Scaer helpfully notes that the Lutheran view is closer to the Roman Catholic vision of Communion than to the Reformed views. Despite the commonality among the Lutheran, Reformed, and Anabaptist streams of the Reformation on matters of authority and soteriology, Scaer is right that the heirs of Martin Luther were the least willing to "reform" the Roman Church's theology of Communion. Scaer helpfully fits the Lutheran view within the context of a sacramental theology in which the sacraments themselves do the work, apart from prerequisite faith on the part of the recipients.

This is perhaps where those of us in the Free Church tradition often find the Lutheran view the most perplexing. The sacramental theology of the Roman Catholic Church is clear and coherent—the church as the mystical body of Christ and the heir of the apostles is authorized to dispense grace. Lutherans, however, distinguish themselves from Rome by a conviction that justification comes *sola fide*, that it is received through faith alone and not through the mediation of any human ecclesial structure or authority. This tension is seen in Scaer's treatment of the Supper in the biblical context of the presence of God and atonement for sin. Scaer rightly affirms the propitiatory and sacrificial nature of the crucifixion offering of Jesus at Golgotha. Moreover, Scaer rightly ties the Supper to the Passover and the old covenant's foreshadowings of our redemption. But where he relates the Passover *event* to the Supper, I believe Scripture would tie the Passover *meal* to the Supper. The Passover *event* of sacrifice of the substitutionary lamb is fulfilled in the cross of Christ, not in the Supper. As Paul instructs the Corinthians, our Passover is Christ himself, who has already been sacrificed (1 Cor. 5:7). The church's ongoing communion over bread and wine is instead related to the Passover *festival* (1 Cor. 5:8–11).

As I noted in my chapter (pp. 33–38), the festival of the Passover was an act of proclamation, an act of remembrance and anticipation. Why should this not be the case then with the Supper when the precise same kind of wording is used for the act? The Supper points to our union with Christ in his already accomplished crucifixion, resurrection, and exaltation. Contrary to Scaer, it is not in "the sacrament" that "atonement and judgment come together"(p. 92), but rather in the cross outside the gates of Jerusalem where God's wrath and God's forgiveness meet (Rom. 3:25–26). Our appropriation of this atonement comes not through any activity (circumcision, baptism, or even Communion) but through trust in the "God who justifies the wicked" (Rom. 4:5). This faith is not severed from the Supper. The Supper prompts and encourages faith by pointing the penitent believer outside of himself to Christ, as he continues to look to the once-and-for-all atonement of Jesus.

It is perfectly understandable for Scaer to see Reformed views of the Supper as dangerous to his understanding of Communion, and even to see how he, like Luther, could not commune with those of us who hold to a view of the Supper as a sign of proclamation and promise rather than as a vehicle for the real presence of Christ. It is disappointing, however, to see his chapter equate Reformed views as similar to Platonic concepts of the relationship between spirit and matter. Plato and his philosophical heirs (both conscious and unconscious heirs) believe spirit to be inherently more "real" than matter. This is not the disagreement between us on the Supper. I believe the "real presence" of Christ—his very material human body and blood—is necessary to the life and holiness of the church. The question is whether this "real presence" is in the heavenly places, awaiting his return, or whether he comes to us physically now in the bread and wine. Scaer's Platonic allusion is no more accurate than someone saying that Lutherans are "Platonic" because they do not believe that Christ is physically present "in and under" the vocal cord vibrations of the Word preached.

Scaer's treatment of the practice of the Supper is intriguing and thought provoking. While I agree with him at many places, I am unconvinced in others. Scaer argues, for instance, that "substituting other elements for bread and wine is an act of disobedience" (p. 93). I agree, but I do not extend this to the question of whether the wine must be fermented and without additives, as does Scaer. Contrary to Scaer's argument, there are very few, if any, who would argue that an alcoholic beverage is "not a fit sacramental vehicle or that the elements used are unimportant" (p. 94). He is right that Jesus certainly used fermented wine at the Supper. The question is whether the fermentation itself is essential to the element, or whether, as it seems, the issue is the crushed fruit of the vine, which points to the blood of Jesus. I am not opposed to using "real" wine in the Supper, but I am not willing to say that alcohol content, or lack thereof, changes the act of Communion. If it does, then I must also ask if it is disobedient to use in the Supper grapes grown in regions outside of the Middle East, since it is clear that this variety of wine is what Jesus poured in the upper room.

Scaer ably defends the Lutheran insistence that the "validity of the Lord's Supper rests on Christ's command and not on faith" (p. 94). His appeal to the Corinthian correspondence, however, is not convincing. Yes, the immoral Corinthian man was harming himself and was indeed to be barred from the Lord's Table. Was this because he was in contact with the physical presence of Christ in the Supper, or because through the table he participated with the presence of Christ through his body, the covenant community? The church is not, Paul says, to "associate with" or "even eat" with such a man. Why? It is because he "calls himself a brother but is sexually immoral or greedy, an idolater or a slanderer, a drunkard or a swindler" (1 Cor. 5:11).

It seems this eating together has everything to do with faith, since a man eating at the table without faith is not a brother but an imposter. The problem with his inclusion at the meal is the church's pronouncement through Communion that he is in fact a "brother," a man of faith, when he is in reality in rebellion against the way of Christ. Again, it seems that the Supper here is an act of proclamation, while the assembly itself is the presence of Christ (1 Cor. 5:4).

Those of us who are confessional evangelical Protestants owe more than we can ever express to the biblical conviction and sheer grit of Martin Luther. This chapter should remind us that Luther and his heirs did not just protest against the Roman church but sought and still seek to provide an alternative that is in continuity with the apostles and prophets and with the church throughout the ages. When it comes to the Supper, I can only say that, while thanking God for the Word-bound conscience of Luther, I do not think he "reformed" the church enough when it comes to the relationship between the faith of the believing community and the sacraments. In short, I just wish he had nailed a bit more to the Wittenberg door.

A REFORMED RESPONSE

I. John Hesselink

It seems to be almost impossible to convince traditional-ist Lutherans—particularly those of a Missouri or Wisconsin Synod variety—that Calvin believed that Christ is really (*realiter*) and truly (*vere*) present in the celebration of the Lord's Supper. Granted, not all people in the Reformed tradition hold this view. Many are Zwinglian in their understanding of the Supper, even though they have never heard of Ulrich Zwingli. But the classical Calvinian position holds that Christ is substantially present in the Supper, though not contained in the elements. Therein lies a significant difference.

When the Reformed go on to say that the presence of Christ in the Supper is spiritual, not physical, many Lutherans often assume that spiritual presence means unreal or illusory. Or, as the Book of Concord puts it (cited in note 6 in David Scaer's chapter), "spiritually" means to the Reformed "nothing more than the spirit of Christ that is present, or the power of the absent body of Christ, or his merit." I hope my presentation has demonstrated that this understanding of the Reformed (i.e., Calvinian) view does not merit that charge. Moreover, when one dismisses the significance of the role of the Holy Spirit in uniting the believer with the risen Christ in a sacramental way, one is in effect denigrating the power and person of the Holy Spirit! In both traditions the real presence of Christ in the sacrament is acknowledged, but there is a different understanding of the modality of that presence. As Scaer points out, the phrase "real presence" is ambiguous and requires clarification (p. 87). However, in my chapter I have tried to show that "presence" means a substantial (another difficult word) partaking of the life-giving body and blood of Christ and that in the Supper there is a true communication of Christ's body and blood.

John Calvin, in any case, was closer to Luther than to Zwingli. Luther recognized this. In 1541 Calvin wrote *Short Treatise on the Lord's Supper* in an attempt to mediate between Luther and Zwingli (and Johannes Oecolampadius, the Basel Reformer who sided with Zwingli).[1] Calvin sent a copy to his friend Philip Melanchthon. It is not certain whether Melanchthon or Moritz Goltsch, a Wittenberg bookseller, gave a Latin version to Luther, who announced that "had Zwingli and Oecolampadius spoken like Calvin, there would have been no need for a long dispute."[2]

Calvin continually sought to explain his position in ways that would be understandable and acceptable to moderate Lutherans. B. A. Gerrish observes, "He repeatedly argued belief in the union of sign and reality was the actual—and sufficient—bond of agreement in sacramental theology between the Lutherans and the Swiss."[3] In 1554, Calvin wrote a letter to one of his Lutheran accusers (John Barbach), which is notable both for its irenic spirit and the succinct way he reiterates his position. Gerrish sums up the situation this way:

> If Luther, that distinguished servant of God and faithful doctor of the church, were alive today, he would not be so harsh and unyielding as not willingly to allow this confession: that what the sacraments depict is truly offered to us (*vere praestari*), and that therefore in the sacred Supper we become partakers of the body and blood of Christ. For how often did he declare that he was contending for no other cause than to establish that the Lord does not mock us with empty signs but accomplishes inwardly what he sets before our eyes, and the effect is therefore joined with the signs? This much, unless I am greatly mistaken, is agreed among you: that Christ's Supper is not a theatrical display of spiritual food but gives in reality what it depicts, since in it devout souls feed on the flesh and blood of Christ.[4]

Turning to the present, readers of this book should be alerted to the fact that in 1997 "A Formula of Agreement" was adopted by the Evangelical Lutheran Church in America, the Presbyterian Church (USA), the Reformed Church in America, and the United Church of Christ whereby they entered into full communion with each other on the basis of a document titled *A Common Calling: The Witness of Our Reformation Churches in North America Today*.[5] It was acknowledged that differences between these two communions still existed, but in the words of the Leuenberg Agreement (III.1.18), "In the Lord's Supper the risen Jesus Christ imparts himself in his body and blood, given for all, through his word of promise with bread and wine. He thus gives himself unreservedly to all who receive the bread and wine; faith receives the Lord's Supper for salvation, unfaith for judgment."[6] I realize that conservative Lutherans may regard this consensus as an unholy compromise, but it still represents a historic breakthrough on the part of two major Reformation traditions.

In conclusion, let me point out several areas where I can heartily endorse positions taken in Scaer's chapter. For example, we agree that "sacraments are not New Testament innovations but rather are the ordinary ways in which God came to his Old Testament people" (p. 90). We, too, believe that sacraments are signs to which God's Word is attached and that "the external elements of the sacraments as signs correspond to what the sacraments are and do" (p. 93). However, we would say that the role of the Holy Spirit, as far as the celebration of the Supper is concerned, is not so much to "create faith" (p. 96) as to strengthen and nourish faith; and that although the words of institution are indispensable, it is not Christ's words alone, but the Word and the Spirit that effect the sacrament (p. 97). Along with the Orthodox churches, we "give a prominent place to the Spirit in the *epiklēsis*, by which he is invoked on the elements to make them Christ's body and blood" (p. 96). Scaer concedes that this is not the historic Lutheran custom, although it is noted in the Apology. Here it appears to be a matter of emphasis.

In the light of all this and several other points of agreement, I would hope that unlike some of the sixteenth-century Lutherans—particularly the ultra-Lutherans who took over after Luther's death—even the more traditionalist Lutherans would not find our position "threatening" (p. 89) but one that should elicit a more open and sympathetic reception than in the past.

A ROMAN CATHOLIC RESPONSE

Thomas A. Baima

I like David Scaer's stress on real presence versus consubstantiation. His contextualizing of consubstantiation as "Nestorian" is an interesting insight that I want to think more about (p. 87 n. 3). Another point of particular importance was when he showed that there were some formulations of eucharistic doctrine that the Roman Catholic Church found acceptable at the beginning of the Reformation. Ecumenists have not paid enough attention to the formative period of Reformation doctrine before the polemics took over. Some kind of return to those acceptable Lutheran formulations as a basis for contemporary dialogue could be useful. Of course, the section on the sacramental God rings true to a Catholic and shows how our two traditions still share a great deal in the Western liturgical tradition.

Another aspect of Scaer's chapter—and the other two authors' as well—is the centrality of Saint Augustine in Protestant thought. Here Scaer calls us back to the Augustinian definition of a sacrament, but the larger point, often obscured by the central position that Saint Thomas Aquinas has occupied in the Catholic Church, is that all Western Christians are children of Saint Augustine. Augustine is the common father of both the Roman Catholic and Protestant communities. A new appreciation of Augustine, who was the principal source for Saint Thomas (after the Scriptures themselves), could help us find a common foundation for our theological discussions in the future.

The Lutheran stress on sacramental validity resting "on Christ's command and not on faith" (p. 94) is also clarifying for a Catholic to hear. One of our difficulties is appreciating the differences among Protestant views. We are unfair when we fail to recognize the significant differences among the different traditions of the Reformation. For example, I was surprised to learn of the Lutheran view that baptism, absolution, and the Lord's Supper form a constellation (p. 95). This notion of the relationship of penance to Holy Communion is something I reflect on in my chapter, and it is an area I would like to hear more about from Lutheran friends.

A couple of themes seem to run through all of the Protestant chapters. One overarching theme has to do with the matter of spatial and temporal relationships. It seems that the primary problem the Catholic doctrine of transubstantiation poses for Protestants of every tradition is how Jesus' body can be in multiple places. I reflect on this in my response to John Hesselink (p. 80), but here I simply identify it as a common thread running through all three chapters. Another theme was that in the first decade of the twenty-first century, all Christians are facing the problem of an overemphasized individualism and the phenomenon of "doctrine lite." We feel this acutely in the Catholic Church, and it was affirming to hear other Christian theologians identify the same problem. Perhaps it is true that misery loves company.

Reading Scaer's chapter raised some questions. It is well and good to note that there were formulas of doctrine that both the Lutherans and the Roman Catholics could accept at the start of the Reformation, but what do we do about them now? And how do we address the need, then and now, to have distinguishing formulas? We live in a time when there is great pressure to "repristineize" our churches by stressing our unique identities. Is this the way forward? Should we not return to the sources in the Great Tradition and allow those sources to critique our current practices and formulas? I believe that the distinctive elements in our separate traditions often carry the most vital insights we might offer as gifts to other Christians. The danger is that too great an emphasis on the distinctive elements runs the risk of creating a sectarian attitude. True *resourcement*, as a theological method, protects the distinctive elements by grounding them in the Great Tradition.

Another issue was the statement "a philosophical axiom cannot be the basis of doctrine" (p. 92). While this is certainly true, it is equally true that a doctrine cannot be formulated in human language without engaging philosophical questions. Any statement contains certain tacit presuppositions that affect the formula. The debate over transubstantiation versus consubstantiation is in some ways the classic example. The theological term *transubstantiation* uses Aristotelian metaphysical categories to explain theologically the doctrine of real presence. The theological term *consubstantiation* is no different. What is different is that the term *consubstantiation* involves nominalist categories drawn from William of Ockham's critique of metaphysics, involving a shift from a metaphysical position of moderate realism to the conceptualist position that universals exist only in the mind. As a result, when Luther, who was an adherent of William's teaching, engaged the question of real presence, the philosophical system he used was a form of discourse tacitly "oriented toward human understanding rather than the object itself."[1] The problem for the theologian is not one of using philosophy to frame doctrinal formulations but one of using a poor philosophy to do so. Any philosophical system used to express a revealed religion such as Christianity must have the necessary capacities to handle the subject. One way to examine the history of dogma is to evaluate the philosophical system that systematic theologians have employed to explain and explore the faith. Many of the failures of the modern period in dogmatic theology are the result of theologians employing systems that are not up to the task.[2]

Notes: Chapter 3: Lutheran View (David P. Scaer)

1. For a history of the ambiguity of the phrase, see Albert B. Collver, " 'Real Presence': A Confession of the Lord's Supper—The Origin and Development of the Term in the Sixteenth Century" (PhD Diss., Concordia Seminary, Saint Louis, Mo., 2001). Calvin did not deny the real presence but only the Roman Catholic and Lutheran understandings of the phrase (p. 335 in Collver's dissertation).

2. See the first verse of Martin Luther's eucharistic hymn, "O Lord, We Praise Thee": "May Thy body, Lord, born of Mary, That our sins and sorrows did carry, And Thy blood for us plead In all trial, fear, and need: O Lord, have mercy!" (*The Lutheran Hymnal* [Saint Louis, Mo.: Concordia, 1941], no. 313).

3. For a discussion of why Lutherans do not use consubstantiation to describe their position, see Norman E. Nagel, "Consubstantiation," in *Hermann Sasse: A Man for Our Times?*, ed. John R. Stephenson et al. (Saint Louis, Mo.: Concordia, 1998), 240–59. The term was used by the Crypto-Calvinists, those

Lutherans who after Luther's death secretly wanted to introduce a Reformed interpretation of the Lord's Supper (pp. 250–51). Consubstantiation might be described in Christological terms as "Nestorian," referring to two disconnected substances lying side by side (p. 243).

4. See the Solid Declaration of the Formula of Concord, VII.38; Epitome of the Formula of Concord, VII.3. All references to the Lutheran Confessions are found in *The Book of Concord*, ed. Robert Kolb and Timothy J. Wengert (Minneapolis: Fortress, 2000), 599.

5. Large Catechism, V.14, in *Book of Concord*, 468.

6. "For 'spiritually' means to them [the Reformed] nothing more than 'the spirit of Christ' that is present, or 'the power of the absent body of Christ, or his merit'" (Epitome of the Formula of Concord, VII.5, in *Book of Concord*, 504–5).

7. See Epitome of the Formula of Concord, VII.22, in *Book of Concord*, 505, 22.

8. Rejection of the Reformed position was included in both the Latin and German texts of the Augsburg Confession (X.2).

9. See Apology of the Augsburg Confession, XIII.2: "But we do not think that it makes much difference, if for the purpose of teaching, different people have different enumerations, as long as they properly preserve the matters handed down in Scripture. After all, even the ancients did not always number them in the same way."

10. See Large Catechism, V.4, 23, 24, in *Book of Concord*, 468, 470.

11. The Apology of the Augsburg Confession, XIII.6, 14, sees confirmation, extreme unction, and marriage as church rites and allows for them to be called sacraments in a lesser sense.

12. Article XIII of the Augsburg Confession does not list the sacraments.

13. The Apology of the Augsburg Confession, XIII.3, defines sacraments as rites commanded by God to which the promise of grace has been added. It seems as if Melanchthon understands some rites instituted by the church as having divine approval. This allowed for a broader definition in allowing which rites could be called sacraments. (The Apology was written as direct response to the Confutation in which the Roman Catholics set forth both their agreements and disagreements with the Augsburg Confession.)

14. Large Catechism, IV.1, in *Book of Concord*, 456.

15. See *Book of Concord*, 360–61. This is titled "How Simple People Should Be Taught to Confess." "A Brief Exhortation to Confession" is included at the conclusion of the Large Catechism (not included in *The Book of Concord*).

16. Karl Barth had no place in his monumental *Church Dogmatics* for the Lord's Supper simply because whatever benefit might be attached to it was already found in baptism. By concentrating on the forgiveness of sins as the constituent factor in the Lord's Supper, Lutherans may move close to that position.

17. For more discussion, see Jonathan Trigg, *Baptism in the Theology of Martin Luther* (Leiden: Brill, 1994), 21–22.

18. Paul speaks of Christ as the Passover or Paschal Lamb in the context of eucharistic practice (1 Cor. 5:7).

19. The connection between manna and the Lord's Supper is made in John 6:48–51, but a eucharistic interpretation of this passage is not beyond dispute, as discussed below.

20. See, e.g., Matthew 15:36 (italics added): "Then [Jesus] *took* the seven loaves and the fish, and when he had *given thanks*, he *broke* them and *gave* them to the disciples, and they in turn to the people" (cf. Matt. 26:26–28).

21. Lutherans are more likely to translate the Greek word *diathēkē* as "testament" rather than "covenant" to carry the idea that Christ instituted this rite before his death as his will. "Testament" and "covenant" can have overlapping meanings, though the word is ordinarily translated into English as "covenant."

22. See Small Catechism, V.5–6, in *Book of Concord*, 362. Here Luther says that with forgiveness of sins comes life and salvation.

23. Luther sees Matthew 11:28 ("Come to me, all you who are weary and burdened") as an invitation to the Lord's Supper (see Large Catechism, V.66, in *Book of Concord*, 473).

24. Notice John 6:53: "Jesus said to them, 'I tell you the truth, unless you eat the flesh of the Son of Man and drink his blood, you have no life in you.'"

25. See Large Catechism, IV.18, in *Book of Concord*, 438: "hence also it derives its essence as a sacrament, as St. Augustine also taught: *Accedat verbum ad elementum et fit sacramentum*. That is, when the Word is added to the element or natural substance, it becomes a sacrament, that is, a holy and divine matter and sign" (see also Large Catechism, V.18, in *Book of Concord*, 458, with regard to the Lord's Supper; Smalcald Articles, V.1, in *Book of Concord*, 320, with regard to baptism).

26. See Large Catechism, IV.8, 12, in *Book of Concord*, 457–58.

27. Paul points to an unrepentant sinner in the congregation as yeast in the context of the Lord's Supper. His argument would not be understood unless that congregation was using unleavened bread in the Lord's Supper. Reference to Christ as the "Passover lamb" supports this view (1 Cor. 5:7).

28. Article VII.3 of the Epitome of the Formula of Concord explicitly rejects the teaching that faith "effects and creates the presence of the body and blood of Christ in the Holy Supper" (*Book of Concord*, 580).

29. See Large Catechism, V.6: "Do you think God cares so much about our faith and conduct that he would permit them to affect his ordinance? No, all temporal things remain as God has created and ordered them, regardless of how we treat them" (*Book of Concord*, 467).

30. See Large Catechism, V.69, in *Book of Concord*, 474; the Epitome of the Formula of Concord (VII.37) also rejects as an error the teaching that unbelievers do not receive Christ's body and blood (*Book of Concord*, 508).

31. See Epitome of the Formula of Concord, VII.15.6, in *Book of Concord*, 506: Christ's body and blood is received "not in a Capernaitic fashion but rather in a supernatural, heavenly way because of the sacramental union of the elements."

32. See Epitome of the Formula of Concord, VII.26, in *Book of Concord*, 507.

33. Solid Declaration of the Formula of Concord, VII.114, in *Book of Concord*, 613.

34. Though Reformed theologians generally understood the session at God's right hand to support the view that Christ's body was confined to one place, Zwingli agreed with Luther that this was figurative speech "by which one understands that Christ Jesus is equally powerful with the Father" (Gottfried W. Locher, *Zwingli's Thought* [Leiden: Brill, 1981], 177). Reformed differences with Lutherans came from a worldview influenced by Renaissance humanistic thought.

35. See the Epitome of the Formula of Concord, VIII.17, in *Book of Concord*, 511.

36. From the *Evangelical Lutheran Hymn-Book* (Saint Louis, Mo.: Concordia, 1918).

37. In the first edition of the Apology of the Augsburg Confession (called the Quarto), Melanchthon specifically referred to this. "It is seen in their [Greek (Orthodox)] canon of the Mass, in which the priest clearly prays that the bread may be changed and become the very body of Christ," referring to the *epiklēsis* in early Eastern liturgies (see *Book of Concord*, 184 n. 269).

38. See Epitome of the Formula of Concord, VII.8, in *Book of Concord*, 505.

39. Hebrews 12:22–24 places the Lord's Supper in a heavenly dimension: "But you have come to Mount Zion, to the heavenly Jerusalem, the city of the living God. You have come to thousands upon thousands of angels in joyful assembly, to the church of the firstborn whose names are written in heaven. You have come to God, the judge of all men, to the spirits of righteous men made perfect, to Jesus the mediator of a new covenant, and to the sprinkled blood that speaks a better word than the blood of Abel." This theme is picked up in one of the offertories in *Lutheran Worship*: "I will take the cup of salvation and will call on the name of the Lord. I will pay my vows to the Lord now in the presence of all his people, in the courts of the Lord's house, in the midst of you, O Jerusalem."

40. Though the phrase "the sacrament of the altar" is not derived from the New Testament precisely in this way, the artifact from which the Lord's Supper was served was called an "altar": "We have an altar from which those who minister at the tabernacle have no right to eat" (Heb. 13:10). In the context, those who minister at the tabernacle are the priests who offer sacrifices in the Jerusalem temple, which is called a tabernacle, or tent, because it will soon pass away. The altar from which these priests are not permitted to eat is the one from which Christ's body and blood is offered to his followers.

41. A late first- or early second-century catechism.

42. The term *Eucharist* is not without its problems since it puts the emphasis on what the congregation does by remembering and thanking God and not on what God gives. It was the term favored by Zwingli.

43. In my *Discourses in Matthew: Jesus Teaches the Church* (Saint Louis, Mo.: Concordia, 2004), I have presented a number of allusions to the Lord's Supper in this gospel (pp. 157–99).

44. See Smalcald Articles, II.1, in *Book of Concord*, 301.

45. Article 21 of the Augsburg Confession expressly addresses this issue by pointing out that according to ancient church custom, the chalice was distributed to the laity. Along with transubstantiation, the practice of withholding the cup from the laity was condemned by the Lutherans (see Epitome of the Formula of Concord, VII.21–24, in *Book of Concord*, 507).

46. This was a moot issue for Roman Catholics, since for them Lutherans do not possess a valid ministry and so what they celebrated was no sacrament at all.

47. For a Lutheran perspective on this debate, see Hermann Sasse, *This Is My Body* (Minneapolis: Augsburg, 1959), esp. 232–34.

Notes: Chapter 3: A Reformed Response (I. John Hesselink)

1. The *Short Treatise* is found in *Calvin: Theological Treatises*, ed. J. K. S. Reid (Philadelphia: Westminster, 1954).

2. Concerning this incident, see B. A. Gerrish, *The Old Protestantism and the New: Essays on the Reformation Heritage* (Chicago: University of Chicago Press, 1982), 286–87 n. 53.

3. B. A. Gerrish, *Grace and Gratitude: The Eucharistic Theology of John Calvin* (Minneapolis: Fortress, 1993), 140.

4. Ibid.

5. *A Common Calling* (Minneapolis: Augsburg, 1993). Lutheran-Reformed dialogue originally took place in 1962–1966. The results were published in *Marburg Revisited* (Minneapolis: Augsburg, 1966). A statement of concord—the Leuenberg Agreement—between Lutheran and Reformed churches in Europe was published in 1973.

6. Cited in *A Formula of Agreement*, 9.

Notes: Chapter 3: A Roman Catholic Response (Thomas A. Baima)

1. Heinz Robert Schlett, "Nominalism," in *Encyclopedia of Theology*, ed. Karl Rahner (New York: Seabury, 1975), 1086.

2. For a full treatment of this subject from the viewpoint of a philosopher, see Mortimer J. Adler, *The Four Dimensions of Philosophy: Metaphysical, Moral, Objective, and Categorical* (New York: Macmillan, 1993).

Chapter Four

ROMAN CATHOLIC VIEW

Christ's True, Real, and Substantial Presence

ROMAN CATHOLIC VIEW

Christ's True, Real, and Substantial Presence

Thomas A. Baima

When I was asked to write this chapter, I had just finished using a book on comparative liturgy in the Zondervan Counterpoints Church Life series in a class at Mundelein Seminary.[1] I appreciated the value of having such a helpful dialogue among various positions, which I could share with my students. And I was thrilled to be asked to participate in this Counterpoints book.

My task in this chapter is to present the doctrine of the Lord's Supper as confessed by the Catholic Church.[2] While Orthodox teaching on Holy Communion is not presented in this volume, on a number of points it is so close to the Catholic Church's position that I will presume to include them. I do this mostly to remind readers that the kind of conversation we are having in this book must be careful to include all Christians. The Christian world is Catholic, Orthodox, Mainline Protestant, Evangelical, and Pentecostal. All of these voices cannot always be included in every conversation, but we should honestly acknowledge that the other voices are there.

The general editor of this book gave us a list of questions to consider. I have organized my chapter around these questions, which appear as section heads. I hope this will make my remarks clearer to readers who may not be familiar with the theological tradition I represent. The questions themselves indicate the very different frames of reference we each use to talk about these matters. Understanding our different frames of reference is as important as the specifics of our answers.

For a reader who wishes to explore Catholic teaching further, I would recommend the Catechism of the Catholic Church (hereafter the CCC). The CCC is not a catechism in the sense of Luther's Small Catechism; rather, the CCC is a compendium, a sourcebook of Catholic doctrine, for bishops and priests in their teaching ministry. Eight hundred pages long, it is a complete and integral presentation of Catholic doctrine, along with references to the sources of the doctrine in Scripture, Tradition, and the Magisterium. Additionally, there are a number of reliable websites that readers can consult for further study.[3]

WHAT IS THE MEANING AND SIGNIFICANCE OF COMMUNION?

This first question allows me to state at the outset some of the difficulties we have in this conversation. When asked, "What is the meaning and significance of Communion?" I must honestly say, "I don't care." I don't care about meaning and significance because it takes us off the track. The correct question should be, "What is communion [i.e., intimate fellowship]?" Let me explain why this distinction is important.

Meaning and significance are existential matters that frame the question in terms of an individual's experience of the thing being considered. If we start there, we will never come to an understanding of the Catholic view of Communion.

A BETTER QUESTION: WHAT IS COMMUNION?

A better question to use as a starting point is, "What is communion?" On this matter, Catholic Christians have a lot to say. We must use the *central truths* of the faith as the interpretive keys to *particular truths*. The central truth of Christianity is that God is Trinity. All other doctrines refer back to this central truth.

The Communion of the Triune God

If you were to attend Mass this Sunday at a local Catholic parish, the priest's first words would be, "In the Name of the

Father and of the Son and of the Holy Spirit." And if you were to attend the Divine Liturgy of Saint John Chrysostom (the ritual used by Orthodox and Eastern Catholic churches), the priest would turn to the people just prior to the Eucharistic *anaphora*, make the sign of the cross over them, and proclaim, "The grace of our Lord Jesus Christ, the love of God the Father, and the communion of the Holy Spirit be with you all." A proper Trinitarian theology is an essential condition for understanding communion. "Being is communion," according to Bishop John of Pergamon (John Zizioulas).[4] And as Christians, we know that the ground of all being—God—is a Trinity of persons: Father, Son, and Holy Spirit.

To speak of communion, it is necessary to speak of God, *who is communion itself*. This truth is often lost on Western Christians, both Catholics and Protestants, who function as practical Christomonists.[5] Our Western stress on *Christ*ology is sometimes at the expense of our *the*ology—properly, our Trinitarianism. Being *is* the communion *of the Father and the Son and the Holy Spirit*. All of the ancient creeds acknowledge this in their structure and content. All traditional Christians know that true religion stands or falls on Trinitarian doctrine. Yet this doctrine has not properly made its way into Western piety. For that reason, it is all the more important to stress that any other form of communion in the Christian life is a reflection, first of all, of the most basic communion of God being God.

This teaching may seem obvious, but so much is at stake here. At its root, Christianity proclaims that ultimate reality—*being*—is the *communion of persons*. Unity is what existence is all about. Christian existentialism is not about finding meaning but about unity—with the Father and the Son and the Holy Spirit.

The Communion of the Divine and Human in the God-Man Jesus Christ

The second key doctrine for our understanding of Holy Communion is the incarnation. The incarnation is nothing less than the communion of the divine and human in the God-Man, Jesus Christ. It is the unity in a single person of two ways of being. God and humanity are not separate, because Jesus personally unites them. Meet Jesus, and you have met God. Meet

Jesus, and you have met an authentic member of the human race. In Jesus, we become partakers in the divine nature.[6] This truth of the faith has profound consequences for our understanding of the dignity of the human person.

The Communion of the Church, Created and Sustained by the Sacraments

This notion of communion flowing from the Trinity itself and passing through the incarnate Word of God, Jesus Christ, sets the stage for the wider unity of God with all nations. If the communion of persons is how it is with God and how it is with Christ, by extension communion of persons must be how it is with the church. Now, the church is not God. It is a creature—something made by God. However, the church participates in the same communion of the Trinity and Christ because something *analogous* to the incarnation is happening in her. Christ, the head of the church, is united with the human members who make up the church, which Scripture calls "the body of Christ."[7] God and humanity are united by means of the actions of the Holy Spirit, which we call the sacraments.[8]

Sacraments are not something that the church does; rather, the sacraments make the church. When I say "make," I mean the sacraments create and sustain the church. The church is structured by the sacraments.[9] *Baptism* creates the church by building her up from new members. *Confirmation* strengthens these members to be witnesses of Christ. *Penance* and *anointing of the sick* heal the wounds of sin and suffering that afflict the members, further building them up into the living stones of the edifice. *Marriage* sanctifies human love and is described by Saint Paul as an image of the church (Eph. 5:22–33). Christ's headship is continued through *Holy Orders*—which makes the other sacraments possible. And in the *Eucharist*, Christ and members offer praise, sacrifice, and worship to the Father in the Holy Spirit.[10]

The Holy Eucharist as the Source and Summit of the Christian Life

The Eucharist has been called "the source and summit of the Christian life" by Pope Paul VI.[11] The Christian life, our Orthodox brothers and sisters remind us, is doxological. "Orthodoxy" means "right praise." What is right praise? It is a life ordered by the character of God—Father, Son, and Holy Spirit—and by the action of God in human history—creation, revelation, redemption, and consummation.

This doxological life is revealed to us in the history of the people of Israel and in the person and event of Jesus Christ. It's not a discovery of human insight but a gift, which also makes it a "given," a constitutional element of Christianity. From the doxology, which is the Eucharist, we receive life. Toward the doxology, which is the Eucharist, we journey, for unity with Christ is the goal of this life. In the doxology, which is the Eucharist, we find the foretaste and promise of the eternal life which is to come in the kingdom.

Holy Communion

Holy Communion is the moment when all of this comes together. When I receive the body and blood of Christ in the sacrament, what I receive becomes part of me. And I become part of him. The unity of the sacred elements of Communion in my body unites me to his body. And unity with the body of Christ makes me an adopted child of God.

Sacrament as the Central and Unifying Insight of the Catholic Tradition

This brings us to the central and unifying feature of Catholic Christianity (as well as Orthodox Christianity), in distinction from other forms (mainline Protestant, evangelical, or Pentecostal). Catholics call it the "sacramental economy." Economy, as used here, refers to God's work. Specifically, the sacramental economy is the work of the Holy Trinity in human history during the age of the church.

In the descriptions of the kingdom of God in the book of Revelation, we find the image of a liturgy, a worship service.[12] Worship by saints and angels is offered to the Father through the high priesthood of Jesus his Son in the communion of the Holy Spirit. Reading backward, temporally speaking, we find that the prefigure of the kingdom of God is the church, gathered for the sacred liturgy. That sacred liturgy, which the church celebrates between the time of the ascension of Christ and the second coming, recalls and makes present the saving events of his earthly ministry, especially his passion, death, and resurrection. That *anamnēsis* ("remembrance") gives glory (Gk. *doxa*) to Christ. The life of the kingdom is doxology. The Christian life in the age of the church must also be doxological.

Reading back further, through the lens of the paschal mystery, we see that pre-Christian history is also marked by this doxological dimension. The whole of the first covenant was a call to the right worship of God.[13] If we read the history of the Jewish people through this lens, we see a very clear pattern of God working in and through their history as a people, we see a sacramental economy where God blessed them. The CCC puts it this way:

> Divine blessings were made manifest in astonishing and saving events—the birth of Isaac, the escape from Egypt (Passover and exodus), the gift of the promised land, the election of David, the presence of God in the temple, the purifying exile, and the return of a small remnant. The Law, the Prophets, and the Psalms, interwoven in the liturgy of the chosen people, recall these divine blessings and at the same time respond to them with blessings of praise and thanksgiving.[14]

When this *anamnēsis* is empowered by God, it is not merely a remembering but an actualization of sacred events so that they are really present.[15] Saint John of Damascus wrote about this:

> You ask how the bread becomes the Body of Christ, and the wine ... the Blood of Christ. I shall tell you: the Holy Spirit comes upon them and accomplishes what surpasses every word and thought.... Let it be enough for you to understand that it is by the Holy Spirit, just as it was for the Holy Virgin and by the Holy Spirit that the Lord, through and in himself, took flesh.[16]

Sacrament and Sacrifice

In the short scope of this chapter, it is impossible to explore the companion doctrine of sacrifice, which is inseparable from any Catholic understanding of the Eucharist.[17] So let me just set the stage by saying that in the sacramental ethos of Catholic Christianity, when the bread and wine are separately consecrated, the death of Christ (the separation of blood from his body) is signified and through the liturgical *anamnēsis* made present. The doctrine of the real presence, however, elevates this act from mere liturgical *anamnēsis* to a real *anamnēsis*, where the same offering, the same priest, and the same sacrifice are present. As I write this, I ask my fellow authors of this volume not to latch on to this paragraph and fill their responses with quotations from the book of Hebrews. That would be a great conversation — one I would welcome — but it's not the conversation we are engaged in right now. The sacrifice and priesthood of Jesus would be a great topic for another book.

I raise the point about sacrifice solely because it is bound up in the Catholic notion of sacrament. So to adequately understand our belief, you must posit this point: the biblical pattern, or model of sacrifice, involved three things: offertory, priestly mediation, and meal.[18] The application of this Old Testament notion to the new covenant by the sacramental model entails the use of biblical images, which revealed the action of God in salvation history, to frame, interpret, and throw light on the final and definitive act of God in Jesus Christ. The great Catholic theologian Ludwig Ott wrote the following:

> Although the sacrament and the sacrifice of the Eucharist are performed by the same consecration, still they are conceptually distinct. The Eucharist is a sacrament insofar as in it Christ is partaken as nourishment for the soul; it is a sacrifice insofar as in it Christ is offered as a sacrificial gift to God.... [Saint Thomas Aquinas writes that] it has the nature of a sacrifice in that it is offered up, and it has the nature of a sacrament in that it is received, and hence, it has the effect of a sacrament in him who receives it and the effect of a sacrifice in him who offers or in those for whom it is offered [*Summa Theologica* III.79.5]. The sacrament is directed immediately to the sanctification of men [and women], the sacrifice to the glorification of God. As a sacrament, the Eucharist is a permanent reality; as a sacrifice, it is a transient action.[19]

I conclude my consideration of the sacramental economy with another quotation from the Catechism:

Jesus' words and actions during his hidden life and public ministry were already salvific, for they anticipated the power of his Paschal mystery. They announced and prepared what he was going to give the Church when all was accomplished. The mysteries of Christ's life are the foundations of what he would henceforth dispense in the sacraments, through the ministers of his Church, for [as Leo the Great wrote] "what was visible in our Savior has passed over into his mysteries."

Sacraments are "powers that come forth" from the Body of Christ, which is ever-living and life-giving. They are actions of the Holy Spirit at work in his Body, the Church. They are "the masterworks of God" in the new and everlasting covenant.[20]

The Dogma of the Real Presence

Keeping in mind the sacramental vision of Catholic Christianity, we can now approach the heart of the matter. What does the Catholic Church teach as the dogma of the real presence?

The Council of Trent summarized the teaching in its first canon on the sacrament of the Eucharist:

> If anyone denies that in the sacrament of the most holy Eucharist the body and blood together with the soul and divinity of our Lord Jesus Christ and therefore the whole Christ are truly, really and substantially contained, but says that he is in it only as in a sign or figure or by his power, let him be anathema.[21]

As you can see from the language, a dogmatic definition excludes an unacceptable teaching. To properly interpret any dogmatic text, the theologian must know what error the dogma was formulated to correct. One way to think of dogma is like an old-style prescription in medicine. One hundred years ago, doctors would write prescriptions that had to be compounded by pharmacists. In doing so, the doctor was able to customize a medicinal preparation for a particular patient's illness. The art of medicine lay in the *formulation* of the drug to treat a specific illness. When particular formulas proved successful in treating specific diseases, they were listed in formularies by the pharmacists so they could be used by other physicians.

Dogmatic formulas are the prescriptions of spiritual physicians. When an illness (heresy) afflicts the body of Christ, the pastors of the church, as spiritual physicians, formulate a doctrine. In the same way, when a doctrinal formula proves effective in treating spiritual illness, it is listed (canonized) in a decree. Such was the case with the doctrine of the real presence of Christ in the Eucharist.

There was a development of the doctrine over the centuries. Each time the real presence of Christ was denied in some way, the church replied with a formula to correct the error. Eventually, a theological term — *transubstantiation* — came to be favored in the formulation of the doctrine.

At the time of the Council of Trent, three errors had to be treated. One error was to say that the Lord Jesus was present only as a sign or figure. The Fathers would have understood this to be Ulrich Zwingli's teaching. Another error was to say that the Lord was present only by his power. This the Fathers understood to be John Calvin's teaching. There is a third error — that of Martin Luther — namely, that the presence was limited to the celebration and did not continue afterward. Not mentioned in the list but treated in the dogma was the error of Martin Bucer, namely, that the Lord is present by means of the faith of the receiver. The Fathers of the Council of Trent formulated a doctrine in such a way as to treat (with spiritual medicine) each of these errors. The components of the prescription were "true, real and substantial." But I'm getting ahead of myself.

The *Regula Fidei* — the Rule of Faith — is that Christ is really present in the sacrament of the Eucharist. In Catholic doctrine, a sacrament is a sign which brings about that which it signifies. Baptism is a sign of the washing away of sin, of death, and of rebirth. When persons are baptized, by grace and in faith their sin is washed away and they are united to Christ's death and reborn to eternal life. In the Eucharist, ordinary food is the sign of nourishment, and the separate elements are signs of Christ's sacrifice.[22] So the Faith tells us that Christ is present in the sacrament. Since this is part of the Rule of Faith, we believe it.[23]

I submit that the doctrinal problem the Council of Trent tried to address with its formulation of "true, real and substantial" was nothing short of saying that "all things are possible with God."[24] In the philosophical and theological framework of the time, the Fathers tried to explain how the impossible—the accidents remaining after the conversion of the substance—was still reasonable.[25] They were answering a charge that goes back to the Bible itself—"How can this man give us his flesh to eat?"[26]

That Jesus can do what he says is not open to question—at least if you are a traditional Christian. If, on the other hand, you don't hold the Nicene faith, if you think that Jesus died and his body was lost and the so-called resurrection is only a profound memory in the hearts of disciples, then no theology will make any sense to you. Theology begins with faith and depends on it for proper context. If you lack this faith, then your answer to the question of "How can this man give us his flesh to eat?" is simple and direct: he can't. But if Jesus is who he says he is—if he is Lord, Son of God, Savior—then we must, as traditional Christians, assume that his words in Scripture mean what they say. If Jesus, who died on the cross, is risen, then miracles still happen.

Does this shake your faith? What if you were to see the Son of Man rising from the dead?[27] This is the biblical argument for believing Jesus when he says, "This is my body." So we are left, as was the Council of Trent, in explaining how Holy Communion can be the body of Christ.

One of our problems is that we know some things about the body of Christ. We know what it looked like after the resurrection. (The Bible tells us his body looked like a gardener, or a man on the road to Emmaus, but apparently not always like Jesus of Nazareth.)[28] And we know where it is right now. He is in heaven, for he ascended and sits at the right hand of the Father. So our problem with "this is my body" centers on the word *is*.[29]

What happens in the Eucharist is not at all like a chemical reaction (e.g., hydrogen and oxygen transformed into water). The components—the reality—remain the same, but the form is changed because of the atomic fusion of the components. In the Eucharist, just the opposite occurs: the reality is changed, but the form remains the same. Also, we're not talking about a "transfiguration," though some theologians have used this term because it is a biblical word: On Mount Tabor, Jesus "was transfigured before them. His face shone like the sun, and his clothes became as white as the light"[30] No, in the sacrament of the Eucharist, there is no change in appearance. Even if you could put the elements under an electron microscope or you could observe the elements at the molecular or subatomic level, there would be no change that you could see or measure.

If that isn't what we are saying, then what are we saying? Simply that Jesus meant what he said: "This is my body." We are saying that after the consecration, the accidents of bread and wine contain the reality of the body and blood, soul and divinity of Jesus Christ.[31] So we are talking about *real* change, i.e., change at the level of reality. The Scholastic theologians called it *transubstantiation*. The CCC also uses the term *conversion*.[32] Both terms mean that the whole substance of the bread becomes the body of Christ and the whole substance of the wine becomes the blood of Christ. The Fathers of the church argue that this is possible because of the power of the Word. Saint John Chrysostom writes, "This word transforms the things offered."[33] Saint Ambrose asked, "Could not Christ's word, which can make from nothing what did not exist, change existing things into what they were not before?"[34]

Catholic theologians explain the conversion by a technical term called *adduction*.[35] Adduction means that Christ is brought into the sacrament without leaving heaven, and his presence is effected in myriad places. This explanation answers a number of objections to the doctrine of transubstantiation.

This is very important for the Catholic understanding of the sacrament. A sacrament is a sign which brings about that which it signifies. This means that the accidents are not accidental. The sign of eating and drinking—signs of nourishment—and the unity of the elements with our bodies bring about what is signified: spiritual nourishment and unity with Christ.

WHO SHOULD PARTICIPATE IN THE LORD'S SUPPER?

Anyone who is baptized and in full communion with the Catholic Church should receive Holy Communion. The real question for Catholics is when they should first be admitted to Holy Communion after baptism. The practices of Eastern and Western churches differ on this point, while both adhere to an identical doctrinal understanding. For the sake of those readers who may not be familiar with the Eastern church, let me first quickly explain the two "lungs" of traditional Christianity and then summarize the doctrinal agreement on paedocommunion. After that, I'll describe the differing praxis of the two traditions.

In the early church, adults who believed the gospel were baptized and then took part in the Eucharist. This was all fairly straightforward. Baptism was the initiation rite into the faith; Holy Communion was ongoing initiation. Gradually, as the church grew, the liturgical rites grew as well, and the initiation process became more formalized. A three-part rite became normative: baptism, chrismation (confirmation), and the Eucharist.

In the Christian East, as infants were baptized, this same order continued. In the same ceremony, the newly baptized infant is chrismated (anointed with chrism) and then given the Eucharist. (Practically, a drop or two of the precious blood is placed on their tongues. Only once they can eat solid food are they given the body of Christ, dipped in the precious blood, which is the ordinary way Eastern Orthodox and Eastern Catholics administer Holy Communion.)

The Western church followed much the same development—with an important exception. Christian initiation of infants involved a "progressive" administration of the sacraments. Baptism was given to infants, but by the thirteenth century, confirmation and communion were delayed to the age of discretion—the age of discretion at that time was debated, but twelve years of age seems to have been common.[36] Thomas A. Marsh has noted, "The mind of the Church had always been that confirmation should precede first communion. But here again the practice varied greatly until the classic sequence was officially made normative by the council of Trent (1566)."[37]

Many Protestant communities maintained this discipline when they separated from the Catholic Church in the sixteenth century. In the eighteenth century, however, a French practice developed by which confirmation was delayed until after first Holy Communion. In the nineteenth century, the practice spread to other countries. Then, at the beginning of the twentieth century, the age for the reception of first Holy Communion was set at age seven. The effect was that the order of the second and third sacrament was reversed.[38]

HOW DO CATHOLICS HANDLE
PRACTICAL PASTORAL ISSUES?

One practical pastoral issue has to do with which elements should be used in the celebration of Holy Communion. The answer for Catholics is very simple: the ones Jesus used. Real bread made from wheat and real wine made from grapes are valid matter for the sacrament. We understand ourselves to be bound by the example of Jesus. "This" in the phrase "this is my body" referred to something specific—namely, bread. "This" in the phrase "this is my blood of the covenant" referred to wine. We use the elements Jesus used.

This is so important that if other elements were to be used, Catholics would say that the sacrament was invalid. What this means is if the "this" is not bread, then it does not (cannot) become the body of Christ.

So when a pastoral situation presents itself, such as a person with a gluten allergy, and someone suggests we ought to use rice wafers instead of the regular unleavened bread for Mass, or that we ought to use grape juice for alcoholics, as good as their intentions are for wanting to include everyone in Holy Communion, intentions cannot change reality. The church lacks the authority to change the elements instituted by Jesus for the celebration of the sacraments.

HOW FREQUENTLY SHOULD COMMUNION
BE OBSERVED?

Actual practice varies among Catholics with regard to this question. Minimally, we would say that a Catholic is one who believes the truths of the gospel and has been baptized. A practicing Catholic is one who attends Mass on Sundays and holy days and who makes what is called the "Easter duty"—confessing any mortal sins and receiving Holy Communion at least once each year. A devout Catholic is one who goes to daily Mass. These simple definitions, while not official, are understood and used by Catholics the world over. For the devout Catholic, the source and summit of the Christian life is integrated into the fabric of his or her daily life. Far from being routine, Holy Communion truly becomes a special kind of "daily bread," which we pray for in the Lord's Prayer.

WHERE SHOULD COMMUNION BE SERVED?

The next question posed by the general editor was, "Where should Communion be served (for example, in the pews, at the table, etc.)?" After chuckling at some of the examples I thought of in reply, I realized that each of the examples was a time when the Eucharist had been most significant to my own faith life. So as part of a serious answer, I made a list.

I begin my list by naming the Eucharist of the bishop, because this is the ideal in the Catholic sacramental model. It is the image of the church that Ignatius of Antioch taught before his martyrdom in AD 110. This celebration reveals the ecclesiological dimension of the Eucharist. Saint Ignatius said that where you find the bishop and his Eucharist, there you find the Catholic Church. The faithful gather, with the bishop at their head, surrounded by his presbyters and assisted by the deacons. They gather before Christ, who is really present on the altar and who unites them with the Father and the Holy Spirit. Since the bishop is united with the other bishops and the pope, in the bishop's Eucharist we are able to see made manifest the mystery of the church as one, holy, catholic, and apostolic.

While the bishop's Eucharist is the ideal, the average Catholic Christian, however, usually celebrates Holy Communion in the parish church with that portion of the people of God and led by a pastor who is assigned by the bishop to minister there. But the parish is not the only place where we celebrate Holy Communion. We also do so in hospitals or nursing homes, where this sacrament brings spiritual nourishment to the sick and dying. From the intimacy of a sickroom we also move to large public gatherings, such as when the pope gathers hundreds of thousands for World Youth Day. And don't forget the profound moment of a military chaplain serving Holy Communion to his troops before combat. And we remember, too, the experience of so many Christians in the world today, who celebrate the sacred mysteries under government persecution, where the church exists in the underground.

SHOULD THE TABLE BE FENCED?

This question refers to *intercommunion*. Fencing the table, or restricting who may receive the sacraments, is a challenging issue. On the one hand, Jesus' own example of table fellowship with those who should have been excluded by Jewish law is a hallmark of his earthly ministry.[39] On the other hand, Saint Paul is very, very clear that if we eat and drink the Lord's Supper without recognizing the body, we eat and drink damnation.[40]

I talk about this in my parish in this way: if we are in communion, then we can receive Communion. If we are united with the other members of the body of Christ, the church, if we are journeying with them through this life, believing the faith, repenting of our sins, keeping his commandments, working to conform our lives to his teaching and example, submitting ourselves to the governance of the sacred pastors—in other words, if we are discerning the body—then we can and indeed should receive the body and blood of Christ in the Eucharist.

But there are times when we should not receive the Eucharist. Again, it is Saint Paul who tells us about this. If we have fallen from a right relationship with Christ through sin, we would be eating and drinking judgment, so we should not receive Communion. If we would cause scandal to our brothers or sisters, we should not receive Communion. The Bible is quite clear about these points. In the early years of the church, excommunication meant being barred from reception of Holy Communion. Reconciliation meant being restored to communion, signified by the reception of Holy Communion. Sometimes, however, excommunication (which is always meant as a discipline that will motivate a person to conversion, not simply as a punishment) resulted in permanent separation. Sometimes in the early years of the church's life, whole congregations or even local churches (dioceses) separated from full communion with the Catholic Church. Almost always, this was a result of heresy. If people were denying a truth of the Christian faith, no real communion existed between the two churches, so Holy Communion was impossible.

Today you find three different approaches to admission to Communion: open communion, closed communion, and limited intercommunion. Open communion is found in those ecclesial communities that invite anyone who is baptized or who believe in Jesus to come to the table. Closed communion is the opposite. Only members in good standing of that particular church may receive Communion. The first might be characterized by the discipline of the Episcopal Church USA. The second is the practice of the Lutheran Church–Missouri Synod or the Orthodox churches. The Catholic Church finds herself in the middle. While we usually practice closed communion, there are specific occasions where we allow a limited intercommunion with other Christians.

The decision to allow another Christian to receive Holy Communion is made on a case-by-case basis by the pastoral minister. There can be no invitation. The decision is based on the spiritual situation of the person and the relationship of their own church to the Catholic Church in terms of faith and morals.[41]

WHO SHOULD BE ALLOWED TO SERVE THE ELEMENTS?

There are two dimensions to this question. It is Catholic doctrine that only a validly ordained priest may *consecrate* the elements. This means either a presbyter or bishop is necessary to have Holy Communion. As a separate matter, the elements are normally *served* (distributed) by bishops, priests, or deacons. In cases of need, they may be assisted by acolytes and extraordinary ministers.[42]

MUST PREACHING OF THE WORD ALWAYS ACCOMPANY THE LORD'S SUPPER?

The celebration of Mass would always include the proclamation of the Word in the readings of the Scriptures. On Sundays and holy days of obligation, it is required to have a sermon. In general practice, since the Second Vatican Council, most priests preach at every Mass they celebrate, including weekdays.

Holy Communion, however, is regularly distributed outside of Mass. There is a special rite for doing so, which, while it contains readings from Scriptures, usually would not have a sermon. This rite is used by priests, deacons, and extraordinary ministers in the distribution of Holy Communion to the sick.

HOW SHOULD PEOPLE PREPARE FOR THE LORD'S TABLE?

It was Saint Paul who taught about eating and drinking in an unworthy manner.[43] Preparation for the Eucharist through penance is a constituent part of the Christian life. It is important to note here that, for Catholics, penance is a proclamation of the doctrine of grace, not works. The penitential practices of prayer, fasting, and almsgiving are aimed at creating the proper inner dispositions in the Christian that foster their configuration to Christ.

Penitential prayer is modeled after the psalms. It is a form of prayer for which we find many examples in the inspired Word. Most Catholic devotional prayers take the attitudes and themes of the psalms as their starting point. Penance is both a way of creating a disposition and a means of healing the effects of sin in a person's life. This healing comes from creating space in the soul for the development of the virtues that counteract specific sins.

Ultimately, sin is dealt with through another special sacrament called penance or reconciliation. Most people call it confession. A discussion of this sacrament would take me beyond the limits of this chapter. Suffice it to say that Jesus said, "If you forgive the sins of anyone, their sins are forgiven."[44] Catholics take him at his word.

SHOULD THE EUCHARIST BE WORSHIPED?

If Jesus is who he says he is, then he is to be believed. If the bread and wine we present at Mass become what he says they become, then they are to be worshiped. That's the simple argument for our practice of eucharistic adoration.

I have practiced eucharistic adoration since I was a child. And even as a young child, I knew very clearly that if the Lord Jesus was really present in the Host, then by worshiping it, I was worshiping him. Later, when I studied theology, I was introduced to the book of Revelation, which, as I've already mentioned, describes heaven as a worship service. In fact, in Revelation, there are two descriptions of what goes on in heaven. One is the wedding feast of the Lamb;[45] the other is worship of the Lamb on the throne.[46]

Where the celebration of the Eucharist at Mass with Holy Communion is the prefigure of the wedding feast of the Lamb, eucharistic adoration is the prefigure of the worship of the Lamb on the throne. In adoration, we do what the angels do—we fall down and worship. Through the eyes of faith, we look at the Lord. We look, hoping with the eyes of faith to see his glory, "the glory of the one and only Son, who came from the Father."[47]

In conclusion, it has been a privilege to engage this sensitive subject that has divided churches and ecclesial communities for so many years. Hopefully, by listening to each other with respect, we will be able to better understand variant positions and clear away misconceptions so that when we engage in dialogue, it is about the real issues and not a reaction to a caricature of what the other communities believe.

A BAPTIST RESPONSE

Russell D. Moore

My college roommate, James Whouley, was a devout Irish Catholic who centered his life around the celebration of the Eucharist on a weekly, if not daily, basis. As I read Thomas Baima's chapter, I could not help but remember watching with James a cable news broadcast of a televised Roman Catholic Mass attended by a number of powerful government officials. I remember seeing James's face grow red as he watched the image of William Brennan, then a United States Supreme Court Justice notorious for defying the church's stance on the sanctity of unborn human life and for authoring repeated judicial affirmations of legalized abortion, moving toward the priest officiating at the Mass. "Don't do it," James muttered repeatedly under his breath. When he saw the eucharistic host placed on Brennan's tongue, James yelled at the television: "No!" In his outraged tone of voice, I heard one who took seriously his church's teachings about the presence of Christ in the elements of bread and wine. I read something of the same voice in Baima's chapter, and I am appreciative of it.

Baima recognizes in his chapter the division between the Catholic tradition (rightly including the Orthodox and others who hold to similar views of the real presence) and other traditions. Baima rightly points out the anathemas of the Council of Trent, anathemas that make clear that my position on the Lord's Supper is not simply another "viewpoint" but a refusal to discern the body of Christ, a refusal that can damn me.

With such being the case, I cannot help but take seriously the claims of the Roman Catholic Church, even as I must dissent from them at this point. The gravity with which the

Catholic Church holds the Eucharist is seen, for example, in Baima's capable explanation of the Roman Church's position on intercommunion (pp. 133–34). I find myself often accused by other evangelical Protestants of a Baptist "bigotry" regarding our churches' historic belief that baptism is a church ordinance and prerequisite to the Lord's Table. As Baima points out, baptism is a prerequisite to the Supper in virtually every Christian communion, the dividing line being one's definition of baptism (pp. 129–30).[1]

While Baima represents well the teaching of the Roman Church on the Supper, he does not convince me that my forefathers were wrong to reject the ideas of transubstantiation and the Mass. Unfortunately, there is little opportunity for much fruitful dialogue on this point, since he and I disagree first of all on authority and only secondarily on the nature of the Supper. Since I do not receive as revelatory the teachings of the Roman magisterium, but receive Scripture alone as the final, normative authority for the church, I must ask to see where in Holy Scripture the Catholic view of the Mass is to be found. I do not think Baima makes this case.

Baima argues that skeptics who argue that God cannot transubstantiate bread and wine into the body and blood of Christ doubt the power of God. This is no doubt the case. As Baima points out, nothing is impossible for God — including the resurrection from the dead (pp. 127–28). None of us doubt, though, that God *could* transform the elements of bread and wine mystically into the presence of Christ. I don't doubt that God *could* have sent his Son to twenty-first-century Portland, Oregon, rather than to first-century Nazareth. The question is whether he has done so. Baima argues that proponents of transubstantiation "were answering a charge that goes back to the Bible itself — 'How can this man give us his flesh to eat?'" (p. 128). This is precisely the charge. Where I think Baima falters is in the answer to the question. The Jewish skeptics at Galilee failed to see that Jesus' discourse on eating his flesh and drinking his blood has everything to do with *belief*. After all, Jesus points to himself as the true Manna of God by saying clearly, "And this is the will of him who sent me, that I shall lose none of all that he has given me, but raise them up at the last day. For my Father's will is that everyone who looks to the Son and believes in him

shall have eternal life, and I will raise him up at the last day"
(John 6:39–40).

The grumbling of Jesus' overly literalistic hearers is a consistent theme in John. In John 2, when Jesus announces that he
will restore a destroyed temple in three days, the confused on-
lookers ask how this can happen when it "has taken forty-six
years to build this temple," mistakenly assuming he is referring
to the physical edifice in Jerusalem (v. 20). In John 3, Nicodemus
hears of the new birth and asks whether a man can reenter his
mother's birth canal (v. 4). In John 4, Jesus speaks of living water,
and the Samaritan woman assumes that this water will free her
from the daily routine of coming to the well (vv. 14–15). In John
8, when Jesus points to the slavery of his hearers, they assume he
means literal bond slavery to some human power (vv. 31–35).
In John 9, when Jesus says he has come to give sight to the blind
and blindness to the seeing, the Pharisees assume he is referring to congenital eye failure rather than the spiritual blindness
of those who fail to believe (vv. 38–41). In John 10, yet another
division occurs among the Jews when Jesus speaks of himself
as a shepherd who fights wolves and guards a flock, a division
that causes them to call him "raving mad" (vv. 20–21). And so it
goes. The problem with the Catholic view of the Eucharist is not
that it seeks to answer the grumbling question of the crowds by
the seashore but that it seeks to answer it on the same mistaken
terms.

Even more problematic, in my view, is the Roman Catholic
view of the sacrificial nature of the sacrament, a vision that lies
behind Baima's treatment of eucharistic adoration, the role of the
Eucharist in the redemptive process, and so forth. Baima asks us
"not to latch on to this paragraph and fill [our] responses with
quotations from the book of Hebrews," saying that "it's not the
conversation we are engaged in right now" (p. 125). Unfortunately, I feel like the state trooper who is told by the speeding mo-
torist, "Pay no attention to that radar gun reading of my speed.
I would love to have that interesting conversation but we're
talking about something completely different now, whether or
not I've violated the law." For Baptists and other Protestants,
Hebrews is entirely relevant to the discussion since the Roman
Church insists on portraying the Supper, as Baima does here
(entirely consistent with the Catechism and the historic Catholic

councils) as the reenactment of the sacrifice of Christ. I do not believe I am changing the subject when I argue that Hebrews anchors our faith to blood that has already been shed, once for all, outside the gates of Jerusalem, and offered in the heavenly places for sin (Heb. 9–10). The very nature of the sacramental system, in which the believer is repeatedly infused with the grace of Christ through the sacraments, seems to us to be precisely the problem the writer of Hebrews identifies in the shadowy, temporal animal sacrifices of the old covenant (Heb. 10:11–14). It seems that, contrary to the Catholic sacramental economy, the new covenant calls together a church that is founded on belief, a looking away from self and toward an already crucified, already resurrected Messiah. In this case, the Supper builds up the church through proclamation—a proclamation of an already accomplished salvation received through looking toward and resting in Christ (see John 3:13–15).

Baima helpfully places Communion within the larger framework of the truth that God is a communion of persons. With this I fully agree, and, as I point out in my chapter, this is a point sorely lacking in evangelical Protestantism. The communion of the church around the Lord's Supper would make no sense if the self-focused, unipersonal Allah of Islam were god of the cosmos. Could it be that Baima overreacts to Western Christianity's emphasis on Christology? Could it be that a Christ-centered Trinitarian vision is that of the New Testament, in order that the heavenly worship of Revelation pointed to by Baima comes through the bloody mediation of the One to whom the Spirit points (John 15:26), the One by whom the Father receives glory by hearing his lordship acknowledged by every tongue in the universe (Phil. 2:9–11; Col. 1:15–20)? If this is so, as Jesus promised, then the Spirit seeks to create and sustain faith by pointing us constantly to the priestly mediation and kingly triumph of our messianic King. Despite Baima's thought-provoking chapter, I still believe that this faith comes ultimately through *proclamation*—in words, in water, and in bread and wine.

A REFORMED RESPONSE

I. John Hesselink

Thomas Baima begins by pointing out that the view of the Lord's Supper or Mass he presents is the one held by all Catholic churches. He then expounds this view in a traditional and, I presume, accurate way. If we could continue this discussion, I would like to ask him what he thinks about some of the recent developments in Roman Catholic sacramentology. He does cite a few recent studies of the Mass by Catholic theologians, but his analysis does not reflect some of the attempts to rethink or re-evaluate the Scholastic notion of transubstantiation, which is the sticking point between Catholics and Protestants. We no longer think in Aristotelian categories of matter, form, and substance, and hence one idea proposed by some modern Catholic theologians, namely, to think in terms of "transignification" rather than transubstantiation, offers a fresh possibility for fruitful ecumenical dialogue.

On the Reformed side, a term used by prominent but little-known sixteenth-century Reformed theologian Peter Martyr Vermigli offers the possibility of ecumenical convergence on this thorny issue. In a treatise on the Eucharist published in 1549, he used the admittedly awkward but suggestive term "transelementation." By this he means that "the bread itself was transformed by virtue of its sacramental union with, and participation in, Christ's flesh."[1] The notion of "sacramental union" is common in Calvin and other Reformed writers.

It has also been pointed out that on certain points Calvin and Aquinas had more in common than Luther and Aquinas. They were one in believing that the ascended Christ's human body is in heaven and is not ubiquitous. Accordingly, real presence for both Aquinas and Calvin must be kept logically distinct from local presence. I think Calvin and Vermigli would agree with Aquinas when he affirms, "The body of Christ is not in this sacrament in the way a body is located in a place. The dimensions of a body in a place correspond with the dimensions of the place that contains it. Christ's body is here in a special way that is proper to this sacrament."[2] Moreover, Aquinas also believed that Christ's bodily presence is spiritual and is realized only by the power of the Holy Spirit. As I pointed out (pp. 64–67), Calvin is noted for his emphasis on the role the Holy Spirit plays in bridging the gap between the risen Christ and the believer and making it possible for us to feed on the flesh and blood of the Savior.

The differences, of course, are still significant. For one thing, the emphasis in Calvin is on spiritually feeding on Christ in heaven. In contrast to both Aquinas and Luther, Calvin rejected the belief that Christ's body is contained in the bread. An even bolder suggestion is made by the Hungarian Catholic theologian Alexandre Ganoczy. In the preface to the English translation of his book *The Young Calvin*, he maintains the following about Calvin's understanding of the sacraments:

> Calvin must be acknowledged as in accord with tradition and thus as catholic [N.B.: small *c*, I. J. H.]. By this I mean above all his doctrine of the real presence of Christ in the Lord's Supper through the activity of the Holy Spirit. On this point, according to the most recent research, even the Council of Trent could take no exception to Calvin's teaching. We could say that Calvin's pneumatology serves not only to affirm God's absolute freedom in his saving acts but also to support a dynamic understanding of the sacraments, which in many ways is quite close to the doctrine of the Eucharist in the Eastern churches.[3]

Another major issue has been the question concerning the place of sacrifice in the Supper/Mass. At the time of the Reformation this was a highly divisive issue, so much so that in the third edition of the Heidelberg Catechism (1563), still widely used in many churches in the world in the Reformed tradition, the Mass is described as "a condemnable idolatry" (*eine vermaledeite Abgotterei*). Why? Because "the Mass is basically nothing but a denial of the one sacrifice and suffering of Jesus Christ" (Q & A

80).[4] In light of a different understanding of the Catholic view of sacrifice in the Mass—and in a more ecumenical spirit—many current versions of the Catechism put this in parentheses and point out that this sentence was not in the original version of the Catechism.

As Baima points out, the concept of sacrifice "is bound up in the Catholic notion of sacrament" (p. 125). Protestants today have no problem with this, as long as it is understood that Christ is not being sacrificed in a literal sense each time the Mass is celebrated. In other words, if the sacrifice of Christ is no longer defined in terms of repetition but rather as re-presentation, there should be no stumbling block here. I would still like clarification as to what Ludwig Ott means when he says that the Mass "'is a sacrifice insofar as in it Christ is offered as a sacrificial gift to God'" (p. 125). Would Roman Catholics accept the idea of sacrifice articulated in a recent United Methodist rite that speaks of "our sacrifice of praise and thanksgiving, which we offer in union with Christ's sacrifice for us"?[5]

In any case, I appreciate the emphasis on the importance of a Trinitarian perspective in understanding the Lord's Supper as it works itself out in the Catholic notion of a "sacramental economy" (p. 123). As over against Lutherans, we are also agreed on the notion of "adduction" not understood as signifying transubstantiation but as meaning that "Christ is brought into the sacrament without leaving heaven, and his presence is effected in myriad places" (p. 129). And all four of us agree that we should celebrate the sacrament doxologically, looking forward to the wedding feast of the Lamb on the throne.[6]

A LUTHERAN RESPONSE

David P. Scaer

Thomas Baima rightly understands Christ's presence in the Lord's Supper within the wider context of the three divine persons. Trinitarian communion is expressed in the incarnation and then in all the sacraments through which Christ makes the church his body. Lutherans can affirm that "God and humanity are united by means of the actions of the Holy Spirit, which we call the sacraments" (p. 122).

In the Apology to the Augsburg Confession, baptism, the Lord's Supper, and confession and absolution are listed as sacraments; though for Luther, absolution was the practice of baptism and in this sense sacramental. Other rites recognized as sacraments by Catholics are also practiced by Lutherans as evangelical proclamations of grace to create and confirm faith. None carry the law's threats, but those who refuse them deprive themselves of grace.

Lutherans can agree that the Lord's Supper is the pinnacle to which the baptized are directed by preaching; however, for Lutherans, baptism remains effective throughout the believer's life and remains for him or her the foundational sacrament from which the church emerges. Baptism is never past tense or replaced by other sacraments or rites but determines faith's boundaries.

Baima warns his fellow contributors about referencing Hebrews in responding to his exposition of the sacrament as a sacrifice (p. 125). This opens a door to discussing his definition of the sacrament as the *anamnēsis*, "where the same offering, the same priest, and the same sacrifice are present" (p. 125). Certainly in the Supper Christ is present as offering, priest, and sacrifice.

As baptism is participation (communion) in Christ's death and resurrection, so the Lord's Supper is communion in his sacrifice by receiving his body and blood by which Christ made the sacrifice.

Sacrifice effects sacramental efficacy. What is offered to God as sacrifice is given to us as sacrament. Sacrament and sacrifice are two different sides of one reality. Christ's death is a onetime historical moment, but this sacrifice or atonement for sin is an eternal reality before God, which determines how he deals with the world. The one sacrifice for sin corresponds to only one Eucharist, which manifests itself wherever Christians celebrate it. No one but God can offer up Christ as a sacrifice, and Christ alone distributes his sacrifice as sacrament to his people. As Christ's servants, ministers are only his instruments in distributing the sacrificial benefits in the sacraments, but their persons do not contribute to the sacrament's essence and effects.

In all aspects of the sacrament—its institution, content, and administrators—it is the *Lord's* and not the church's Supper. Christ's involvement in the sacrament belongs to his promise to drink the fruit of the vine with his disciples in his Father's kingdom, which came with his resurrection. Rather than seeing the Lord's Supper as an aid to man's physical weakness, Christians ascend in the Lord's Supper to the highest glory on earth. Christ becomes part of us and we become part of him. This mysterious sacramental union between God and his church reflects the more mysterious incarnational union of God and humanity in Jesus. In the Formula of Concord (1577), the culminating confession in the Book of Concord, the article on Christ is placed right after the one on the Lord's Supper. One informs the other, and a defect in one signals a defect in the other.

Traditionally in their Communion liturgies Lutherans have no *epiklēsis*, that part of the Eastern Orthodox rites in which the Spirit is invoked on the elements to make them Christ's body and blood. This exclusion is for historical and not theological reasons. It was not part of the Catholic rites preserved by Lutherans. The Spirit is present and at work in the Lord's Supper, as he is in preaching and all sacraments and church rites, with the understanding that he is there with Christ as God and man and not as a replacement or surrogate for a Jesus confined to a spatial heaven.

Yes, the sacrament is food for the soul but also for the body. Its content is not only the crucified but also the resurrected Christ, who makes us participants in his resurrection and guarantees our own. Souls of unbelievers have no faith to be nourished by this sacrament, but their bodies devour the body and blood of him who judges unbelief. Their participation brings them before God's judgment seat. To avoid this horror and in the hope that people would in faith receive this sacrament, early Christian churches dismissed the unbaptized before the Eucharist. For this reason and to express the unity of faith, most Reformation churches shared Communion only with those of their own fellowship. This is still the common practice of most Roman Catholic churches and those Lutherans adhering to their confessions.

The Council of Trent (1545–1560) intended to refute what Catholics considered the Lutheran heresy regarding Christ's real presence. Baima quotes its first canon on the sacrament of the Eucharist (from the thirteenth session):

> "If anyone denies that in the sacrament of the most holy Eucharist the body and blood together with the soul and divinity of our Lord Jesus Christ and therefore the whole Christ is truly, really, and substantially contained, but says that he is in it only as a sign or figure or by his power, let him be anathema." (p. 126)

This document was answered in detail by Martin Chemnitz in his monumental *Examination of the Council of Trent*, in which he wanted to show where Lutherans disagreed but also where they agreed with it. The canon is acceptable, as long as "in" did not refer to impanation—the belief that the body is contained like a nut in a cookie—or transubstantiation. Lutherans had used similar language in speaking of Christ's body and blood "in" the bread and wine and adding in other documents the prepositions "with" and "under." The Augsburg Confession declares, "The true body and blood of Christ are truly present under the form of bread and wine in the Lord's Supper." Multiple prepositions affirmed Christ's presence in the Supper but not in the sense of other objects that occupy one space at a time.

For this reason, the Reformed rejected the Lutheran position. Matters could rest with simply repeating Christ's own words that the bread is his body and the cup is his blood. Luther based his defense against Zwingli on *est*, the Latin for "is." Whatever biblical arguments are brought into the debate, at least the words of Jesus should be front and center.

Baima softens Trent's "anathema" on those who do not accept this view by comparing it to a physician's diagnosing of a disease before prescribing the medicine (pp. 126–27). However, the Lutheran Confessions similarly condemn those who hold that Christ is only spiritually present or that it is no more than a sign or memorial. Some views are simply intolerable.

Not unexpectedly, as a Roman Catholic theologian, Baima wants to omit the "Roman" before Catholic (p. 119 n. 2). However, Rome compromises its catholicity in elevating its pope above all other bishops, ministers, and churches. Recent pontiffs have worked toward détente with Orthodox patriarchs and have allowed members of that fellowship to commune in their churches, but the Orthodox have not reciprocated.

Transubstantiation is a peculiarly Western philosophical definition of the Eucharist that simply cannot be equated with the Orthodox view. Baima compares transubstantiation to transfiguration (pp. 128–29). This may distort the eucharistic mystery. As the Greek word *metamorphōsis* suggests, Christ's human form was transformed so that in and through it his divine nature was manifested. It does not mean that his human nature was replaced by the divine nature—a comparison Baima uses in explaining transubstantiation. In his transfiguration, Jesus was as much man as he was in the state of humiliation, and, similarly, in the Lord's Supper his body and blood are present "in, with, and under" the bread and wine without replacing them. Just as the man Jesus is God, so the bread is his body.

Baima notes that the views of others, including the Orthodox, should also have an airing (p. 119). Their exclusion was perhaps a matter of space or the fact that their views aren't much different from those expressed therein. Like the Baptists, many Pentecostal churches reject infant baptism and share with them views on the Lord's Supper that are in line with Zwingli's. Baima does not mention the Episcopalians. Their rich eucharistic practice places them with Lutherans and Roman Catholics in the Catholic tradition, but their Thirty-nine Articles are readily recognized by the Reformed as Zwinglian and Calvinist. This is an enigma not only to those on the outside but perhaps also to them.

Claiming that Lutheran belief does not allow Christ's presence to extend beyond the liturgical celebration needs elaboration (p. 127). Taking the sacramental elements from the church to the homebound with the recitation of the words of institution was common. By hearing church bells intoned at various parts of the service, including during the words of institution, those confined to their houses participated. Only enough hosts were consecrated for those receiving the sacrament, and at the end of service, the contents of the chalice were consumed by the ministers. A mixing of consecrated and unconsecrated hosts was not allowed. For this, Luther excommunicated a minister under suspicion of Zwinglianism.

Lutherans objected to the Roman practice of carrying the sacrament in processions and its use in the evening benediction. At the imperial diet of 1530, from which emerged the Augsburg Confession, upon pain of death the Lutheran princes defied the command of Charles V to take part in the *Corpus Christi* procession. Lutherans worship Christ wherever he is, including the sacraments, and thus Luther genuflected before the baptismal font and the sacrament. Christ is not tucked away in some distant heaven, but at God's right hand he is among us in preaching and the sacraments. Like the Orthodox, Lutherans know of no devotion of Christ apart from the sacrament.

By receiving the Lord's Supper at the altar and not in the pews, Lutherans affirm their belief that with the consecration earthly elements at the altar become Christ's body and blood, and so appropriately they kneel to receive them. From the Small Catechism, Lutherans learn to call it "the sacrament of the altar." Sacramental distribution in the pews makes it appear that this is the church's supper, which is made a sacrament by the faith of believers. Perhaps the current Roman practice of having laypersons distribute the sacrament in the aisles and not at the altar will be evaluated by the current pontiff, who seems to be committed to reaffirming traditional theology and practices.

Under the influence of American Protestantism, with its Reformed bent, many Lutheran congregations have replaced the common cup with individual glasses. With concerns over communicable diseases, this practice is widespread. To express the church's unity, tradition-minded Lutherans are returning to the common cup. In the Roman Confutation, Roman Catholics accepted the Lutheran position that the earthly sacramental elements were Christ's body and blood. Further discussion may still uncover closer agreement, but the matter may be moot. Since Lutheran ministers are not ordained by bishops in fellowship with the pope, they do offer a sacrament that conveys Christ's body and blood. Ironically, Lutherans are often lumped together with the Reformed, whose views they reject and who in turn reject Lutheran views as too close to Rome's.

Perhaps the arguments offered here will suggest to some that the title describing the Roman Catholic view—"Christ's True, Real, and Substantial Presence—is also applicable to the Lutheran view. Since the Lutheran doctrine, which maintains that Christ's body is accessible through bread, best corresponds to the incarnation in which God is accessible through the man Jesus, Lutherans may have a better claim to it.

Notes: Chapter 4: Roman Catholic View (Thomas A. Baima)

1. Paul A. Basden, ed., *Exploring the Worship Spectrum* (Grand Rapids: Zondervan, 2004).

2. I leave the adjective "Roman" aside because the Catholic Church is composed of twenty-two autonomous ritual churches, only one of which follows the Roman Rite. The doctrinal position I present is held by all of them. In a number of places, I will also refer to the Orthodox churches.

3. Among the official websites I recommend are *www.vatican.va* (the Holy See), *www.fides.org* (the news service of the Congregation for the Evangelization of Peoples), *www.usccb.org* (the United States Conference of Catholic Bishops), and *www.archchicago.org* (the Archdiocese of Chicago).

4. John D. Zizioulas, *Being as Communion: Studies in Personhood and the Church* (Crestwood, N.Y.: Saint Vladimir's Seminary Press, 1985).

5. Christomonism, as the word suggests, is a monist view of God where Christ equals God. Usually a practical rather than theological heresy, Christomonists believe that Jesus is God and then ignore the truth that God is Trinity. Whenever they use the word *God*, they mean "Jesus."

6. 2 Peter 1:4.

7. 1 Corinthians 12:27.

8. CCC, 1113–30.

9. See Paul McPartlan, *The Eucharist Makes the Church* (Edinburgh, T&T Clark, 1993).

10. CCC, 1210–1666.

11. *Sacrosanctum Concilium*, 10.

12. See Revelation 7:11.

13. See Exodus 20:2–7 and Deuteronomy 5:6–21 for the texts on the Decalogue. In a particular way, the first three commandments, using either the Catholic or Protestant numbering, focus our attention on doxology.

14. CCC, 1081.

15. See CCC, 1104.

16. Cited in CCC, 1106.

17. See CCC, 1356–81.

18. See Michael McGuckian, S.J., *The Holy Sacrifice of the Mass* (Chicago: Hillenbrand, 2005).

19. Ludwig Ott, *Fundamentals of Catholic Dogma*, 4th edition, ed. James Canon Bastible (Rockford, Ill.: Tan, 1960), 402.

20. CCC, 1115–16.

21. Cited in J. Neuner, S.J., and J. Dupuis, S.J., *The Christian Faith in the Doctrinal Documents of the Catholic Church*, 7th edition, ed. Jacques Dupuis (New York: Alba House, 2000), 621. For those with Latinity: *Si quis negaverit, in sanctissimae Eucharistiae sacramento contineri vere, realiter et substantialiter, corpus et sanguinem una cum anima et divinitate Domini nostri Iesu Christi ac proinde totum Christum; sed dixerit, tantummodo esse in eo ut in signo vel figura, aut virtute: anathema sit.*

22. The separate consecration of the bread into the body of Christ and the wine into the blood of Christ signifies the crucifixion, when after Christ's death, the Roman soldier pierced the Lord's side with a spear and his blood flowed out of his body.

23. See CCC, 1381.

24. Mark 10:27.

25. See Engelbert Gutwenger, "Transubstantiation," in *Encyclopedia of Theology: The Concise Sacramentum Mundi*, ed. Karl Rahner (New York: Seabury, 1975), 1752.

26. John 6:52.

27. See John 6:61–62.

28. See John 20:15; Luke 24:13–35.

29. Aristotelian philosophy as developed by Thomistic theologians understands that every being is composed of matter and form. Matter and form together constitute the substance of a thing. Substance is what the being is, at the level of reality. In addition to the substance, each thing has "accidents." The accidents are what is apparent to the senses—what we might call "phenomena" today. Accidents can be seen, touched, and measured. To be perfectly clear, anything that is sensible or perceivable is an accident. Substance can only be apprehended by the mind through reason.

30. Matthew 17:2.

31. To be technical about the Tridentine teaching: "after the consecration, the bread and wine [the sensible accidents] contain [the reality of] the body and blood, soul and divinity of Jesus Christ."

32. See CCC, 1375.

33. Cited in CCC, 1375.

34. Ibid.

35. Adduction (from the Latin *ad* ["to"] and *ducere* ["to lead"]) is formally defined as "the action of bringing a thing to something else; spec. [the] ... bringing of our Lord's body and blood into the elements, transubstantiation" (*New Shorter Oxford English Dictionary*, vol. 1 [Oxford: Clarendon, 1993], 25).

36. See Thomas A. Marsh, "History of Confirmation," in *The New Dictionary of Sacraments and Worship*, ed. Peter Fink (Collegeville, Minn.: Liturgical, 1990), 265–67.

37. Ibid., 267.

38. Marsh goes on to note that Pope Saint Pius X (Giuseppe Sarto) in his 1910 decree made no reference to confirmation. The "traditional" pattern of reception around age twelve continued. What changed was that by fixing the age of first Holy Communion at seven, the order was reversed.

39. See Luke 5:30.

40. See 1 Corinthians 11:27–29.

41. The details of this discipline can be found in the *Code of Canon Law*, canon 844, and in the *Directory for the Application of Principles and Norms on Ecumenism*, no. 122–136.

42. "Extraordinary" means ministers who have not been ordained.

43. See 1 Corinthians 11:27–29.

44. John 20:23 TNIV.

45. See Revelation 19:1–10.

46. See Revelation 5:13.

47. John 1:14 TNIV.

Notes: Chapter 4: A Baptist Response (Russell D. Moore)

1. This is why Baptist statesman Herschel Hobbs once wrote that Baptists are not primarily "close communionists" but "close baptismists" (Herschel H. Hobbs, *What Baptists Believe* [Nashville: Broadman & Holman, 1964], 85).

Notes: Chapter 4: A Reformed Response (I. John Hesselink)

1. I am indebted for this information to an illuminating essay by George Hunsinger, professor of systematic theology at Princeton Seminary: "The Bread That We Break: Toward a Chalcedonian Resolution of the Eucharistic Controversies," in *Princeton Seminary Bulletin* 24.2 (July 2003): 254.

2. Thomas Aquinas, *Summa Theologica* 3a.75.1, vol. 58, ed. William Barden (New York: McGraw-Hill, 1965).

3. Alexandre Ganoczy, *The Young Calvin*, trans. David Foxgrover and Wade Provo (Philadelphia: Westminster, 1987), 11.

4. This is the translation found in the version published by the Christian Reformed Church in *Ecumenical Creeds and Reformed Confessions* (Grand Rapids: Board of Publications of the Christian Reformed Church, 1988).

5. Cited in James F. White, *Sacraments as God's Self Giving* (Nashville: Abingdon, 1983), 58.

6. See Revelation 5:13; 19:1–10.

CONCLUSION:
THE TWO MOST IMPORTANT QUESTIONS

John H. Armstrong

The purpose of *Understanding Four Views on the Lord's Supper* has been to provide a balanced and fair presentation of four distinct historical/theological views of Communion practiced within the Christian tradition. To be sure, there are other views, even nuances within these four views, not represented in our book. Within evangelical Protestantism alone there are modest (and sometimes acrimonious) variations of the three Protestant views presented here. As the general editor, I had to make several important choices. Obviously, I had to choose the writers for each of the four chapters. The most basic choice from the beginning was which views to include and how to frame the approach to each particular view. In the end, I chose to include the three historically representative Protestant views (essentially the Reformed, Lutheran, and Baptist), since these clearly lined up with the traditions and general practices common to our churches.

I also understood that this volume could not provide a serious basis for dialogue and fruitful debate without including the Roman Catholic view of the Lord's Supper as the Mass. This is why Thomas Baima was invited to provide an important point of contact and analysis for Protestant readers. If I had included five views, I would have added a chapter on the Eastern Orthodox perspective. There is a great deal to be learned from the East, which many of us in the Western church are only now discovering. Since readers of this book are primarily from the West,

I decided to limit the discussion to the Catholic/Protestant and Protestant/Protestant debates over Communion.

This topic is really worthy of several books. Indeed the subject has generated countless pages of text, as well as numerous debates, over the course of centuries. The bibliography at the end of the book will help readers dig deeper if they so desire. My goal has been clarity and simplicity, joined with respect and dispassionate fairness. I believe these four contributors have fulfilled this goal and have given readers an insightful overview that fits well with the design of a point-counterpoint style of presentation.

In dealing with this complex subject, the contributors have sought to understand and answer the most basic questions raised by their different views of the Lord's Supper. I am persuaded that the two most important questions remain clear: (1) What is the meaning and significance of this Supper? and (2) Why should we regularly celebrate the Lord's Supper in our church communions? All other questions flow from these two in a very important sense. Let me illustrate.

As you have discovered by now, one of the pressing questions in this debate will always be, What is the *meaning* of this bread and this cup that we partake of in the Lord's Supper? Our authors have shown how the answers vary considerably. There are clear differences among them regarding how Christ is present in the bread and the wine. This debate will clearly not be settled by these four presentations. But the presentations shed a great deal of light on the reasons different Christian churches practice the Lord's Supper as they do and teach what they do about its meaning.

Several important things can be agreed on by all Christians. By believing these things, we can be guided toward a richer understanding of the Lord's Supper and a deeper love for Christ:

- No one is warranted to neglect or denigrate the Lord's Supper just because there remains disagreement among believers regarding its meaning and practice. We can differ about our understanding of the precise way in which grace is related to the Lord's Supper *without* concluding that those within other Christian traditions that differ from our own are *outside* the grace of God. The important thing is to obey Christ in coming to this table. And the most important point is to *commune* as he taught us, not simply to *debate* the meaning of Communion.

• Not everyone who receives these elements in a church context is a true Christian. Thus, not all who have been baptized and partake of this Supper will finally be saved. This meal does *not* make one a Christian in and of itself.

• Our Savior commands all of us who are baptized Christians to partake of this meal in remembrance of him. Therefore, we must never treat the Lord's Supper as trivial. Put simply, the Lord's Supper is important, and we should be serious about it. It is bound up with Christ and his gospel. This connection makes it vitally important that all who wish to be faithful to Jesus should partake of this Supper with joy and faith.

• Both baptism and the Lord's Supper are related to one another as blessings and benefits given by Christ to his church. Baptism should be administered *once*, while the Lord's Supper should be administered *frequently*. Both of these signs nourish and strengthen our faith; thus both remain important to those of us who love Christ as Lord. To the Protestant Reformers, as this book has shown, the word *sign* meant a good deal more than the modern word means, which treats a sign as simply a mere symbol.

• Protestant Christians recognize only two sacraments, or ordinances, given by Christ to his church—baptism and the Lord's Supper. They will reject additions to these two sacraments and practice only these in a manner that will continually relate them to the gospel of grace. They also reject all human innovations and laws imposed on believers from outside the Bible.

Our Catholic brothers and sisters see seven sacraments in the Bible, but even the addition of five sacraments does not negate the fact that Catholics and Protestants agree that baptism and the Lord's Supper are vital signs that Christ clearly gave to all his people. Common ground can be found by agreeing that these offerings to God are truly sanctified, while the one sacrifice of Christ on the cross is the *only sacrifice* that saves us. Real problems exist in how we express this, especially since we have centuries of debate related to these arguments, but such a simple understanding can at least frame a proper starting point.

- Protestants and Catholics have a considerably different understanding of the Lord's Supper (and baptism), and this disagreement is important enough to warrant our continued dialogue, as well as our disagreement, in Christian love. We should not allow past debates to destroy the prospect that the future may allow for a different understanding that can develop without compromise. Though it may seem impossible now, God is able to bring about things that are "immeasurably more than all we ask or imagine" (Eph. 3:20).

- The Lord's Supper will never be fully explained or adequately defined this side of heaven. God has acted in Christ to save us—an action declared in his Word. His Spirit confirms and applies this action to our hearts. But how do we explain these great mysteries of our salvation?

In one of his hymns, Charles Wesley eloquently attempted to express the mystery of the Lord's Supper:

> *How He did these creatures raise*
> *And make this bread and wine*
> *Organs to convey His grace*
> *To this poor soul of mine;*
> *I cannot the way descry,*
> *Need not know the mystery;*
> *Only this I know—that I*
> *Was blind but now I see.*[1]

Two authors—a Baptist and an Anglican—express this agreement well. They conclude that this very mystery in the Lord's Supper can allow us to seek a position more complementary in the end:

> Somewhere along this route, surely, the whole debate on Christ's presence in the Eucharist with its hitherto contradictory positions may be found to be complementary. If it can be agreed that Christ is not physically present in the bread and wine,

then hopefully it can be agreed that he is both ob-
jectively and subjectively present. He must be ob-
jectively present, or how could anyone who eats
the bread or drinks the cup of the Lord in an unworthy manner be guilty of profaning the body
and blood of the Lord? Equally, those who eat and
drink must eat and drink in faith. The Holy Spirit
must be active, making Christ present in the Eucharist, calling forth adoration, joy, and thanksgiving from the worshiping community. The mode of
Christ's presence is best left undefined.[2]

Some will suggest that every possible avenue for common ground on the Lord's Supper has already been explored in
church history, and that there is no real basis for looking at what
divides us with any hope of fruitful change. I disagree. I don't
wish to suggest that we are *not* separated by our differences,
as this book appropriately demonstrates. But I do believe that
nonliturgical churches are increasingly looking at the biblical
teaching on sacraments with new openness, while the liturgical traditions are contextually engaging the mission of Christ in
whole new ways in the modern world. Could it be that old arguments will not suffice in this new world? Could it be that new
missional contexts will require new expressions that will open
up all of us to what God is doing in the world and the church?

Having observed the importance of the Lord's Supper and
the numerous ways in which we can and should agree about its
meaning, we must sadly acknowledge that the most evangelical
of Protestants still disagree about certain details related to the
biblical practice of Communion. The debate we have witnessed
in this book demonstrates how and where we disagree. All the
goodwill in the world will not make our views identical. No
amount of hard work or true charity can easily make our differences vanish. What then shall we do?

In my twenty years as a pastor, I found that it was always
wise to keep a congregation anchored in a common understanding of what we did at the Lord's Table. As a community, we
could encourage further discussion, and even brook some disagreement among us, but we could not afford to practice different views. Such practice would divide us and hinder the growth
of our community. The people needed to be taught the meaning

of the Lord's Supper. They needed to celebrate the Eucharist in a spirit of love and common mutuality. A congregation divided at this point is one that will not be able to come to the table as it should.

Finally, we must not miss the fact that, though we are not presently united in our views of the Lord's Supper, we *are* united in our basic Christian affirmations regarding the historical and doctrinal elements of our Christian faith as expressed in the Apostles' and Nicene Creeds. In a world increasingly divided by faith and religion, this truth seems more important than ever. While we must continue to work at understanding our differences regarding the church's practice of baptism and the Lord's Supper, we should believe that our pursuit of true unity is now more important than ever (see John 17).

In the conclusion to their wonderfully helpful book titled *Communion: The Meal That Unites?* Donald Bridge and David Phypers suggest that if any biblical understanding of the Eucharist can reconcile us, or at least bring us closer, the approaches taken by various Christian churches with regard to the Supper must finally be shaped by three great principles—which are a fitting place to end this discussion:

First, *a true celebration of the Lord's Supper must avoid any emphasis that does not express the grace of God.* The Catholic concept of "merit" and the Protestant concept of "worth" have confused people at this point. The emphasis in this Supper, if we follow Holy Scripture, should be placed on the meal as a sacrifice of praise and thanksgiving. The purpose of Communion is not to preserve any single tradition but to express God's grace to all who truly follow Jesus as Lord.

Second, *a true celebration of the Lord's Supper must express the priority of faith.* Sacramental thinking, whether Protestant or Catholic, is surely correct to remind us that God's gracious action precedes human belief. But others are equally correct to remind us that grace becomes effective in Christian disciples through the outworking of real faith. This meal must not become a work of magic but rather a proclamation of the Lord's death until he comes.

Third, *a true celebration of the Lord's Supper must give expression to the church as the body of Christ.* Those who receive God's grace are the same people who commit themselves to the body of Christ, the church. The church is not an appendage to faith. The Lord's Supper, as previously noted, is a *church meal*. This is not an individualistic business where people "make their communion" but rather a corporate activity where the whole church celebrates union with Christ and each member recognizes his or her role in the body.[3]

Notes: Conclusion: The Two Most Important Questions

1. Cited in Donald Bridge and David Phypers, *Communion: The Meal That Unites?* (Wheaton, Ill.: Shaw, 1981), 175.

2. Bridge and Phypers, *Communion*, 176.

3. These three points come directly from Bridge and Phypers, *Communion*, 182–84.

APPENDIX 1:
STATEMENTS ON THE LORD'S SUPPER
IN CREEDS, CONFESSIONS,
AND CATECHISMS

THE *DIDACHE*

Concerning the Eucharist, eucharistize thus:
First, concerning the cup:
We give you thanks, our Father,
for the holy vine of your servant David
which you revealed to us through your servant Jesus.
To you [is] the glory forever.
Second, concerning the broken [loaf]:
We give you thanks, our Father,
for the life and knowledge
which you have revealed to us through your servant Jesus.
To you [is] the glory forever.
Just as this broken [loaf] was scattered over the hills [as
     grain],
And, having been gathered together, became one;
in like fashion, may your church be gathered together
from the ends of the earth into your kingdom.
Because yours is the glory and the power
Through Jesus Christ forever.
[And] let no one eat or drink from your Eucharist
except those baptized in the name of [the] Lord,
for the Lord has likewise said concerning this:
"Do not give what is holy to the dogs."
And after being filled [by the meal], eucharistize thus:

We give you thanks, holy Father,
for your holy name
which you tabernacle in our hearts,
and for the knowledge and faith and immortality
which you revealed to us through your servant Jesus.
To you [is] the glory forever.
You, almighty Master, created all things
for the sake of your name,
both food and drink you have given to people for enjoyment
in order that they might give thanks;
to us, on the other hand, you have graciously bestowed
Spirit-sent food and drink for life forever
through your servant [Jesus].
Before all [these] things, we give you thanks
Because you are powerful [on our behalf].
To you [is] glory forever.
Remember, Lord, your church,
To save [her] from every evil
And to perfect [her] in your love
And to gather [her] together from the four winds
[as] the sanctified into your kingdom
which you have prepared for her,
because yours is the power and the glory forever.
Come, grace [of the kingdom]!
and pass away, [O] this world!
Hosanna to the God of David!
If anyone is holy, come!
If anyone is not, convert!
Come, Lord [*maranatha*]! Amen!

THE AUGSBURG CONFESSION (1530; LUTHERAN)

Article X

Of the Supper of the Lord they teach that the [true] body and blood of Christ are truly present [under the form of bread and wine], and are [there] communicated to those that eat in the Lord's Supper [and received]. And they disapprove of those that teach otherwise [wherefore also the opposite doctrine is rejected].

LUTHER'S SMALL CATECHISM [1529]: WITH EXPLANATION (ST. LOUIS, MO.: CONCORDIA, 1991)

The Sacrament of the Altar

1. The Nature of the Sacrament of the Altar

Q. What is the sacrament of the altar?

A. It is the true body and blood of our Lord Jesus Christ under the bread and wine, instituted by Christ himself for us Christians to eat and to drink.

Q. 285. What are some other names for the sacrament of the altar?

A. This sacrament is also called the Lord's Supper, the Lord's Table, Holy Communion, the Breaking of Bread, and the Eucharist.

Q. 286. Who instituted the sacrament of the altar?

A. Jesus Christ, who is true God and man, instituted this sacrament.

Q. 287. What does Christ give us in this sacrament?

A. In this sacrament Christ gives us his own true body and blood for the forgiveness of sins.

Q. 288. How does the Bible make it clear that these words of Christ are not picture language?

A. Christ's words in the sacrament must be taken at face value especially because (1) these words are the words of a testament, and even an ordinary person's last will and testament may not be changed once that person has died; (2) God's Word clearly teaches that in the sacrament the bread and wine are a communion or participation in the body and blood of Christ; (3) God's Word clearly teaches that those who misuse the sacrament sin not against bread and wine but against Christ's body and blood.

Q. 289. What are the visible elements in the sacrament?

A. The visible elements are bread and wine.

Q. 290. Do Christ's body and blood in the sacrament replace the bread and wine, so that the bread and wine are no longer there?

A. No, bread and wine remain in the sacrament.

Q. 291. How then are the bread and wine in the sacrament the body and blood of Christ?

A. The bread and the wine in the sacrament are Christ's body and blood by sacramental union. By the power of his word, Christ gives his body and blood in, with, and under the consecrated (blessed) bread and wine.

Q. 292. Do all communicants receive the body and blood in the sacrament, whether or not they believe?

A. Yes, because the sacrament depends on Christ's word, not on our faith.

Q. 293. Are the body and blood of Christ in the sacrament sacrificed again to God for the sins of the living and the dead?

A. No, the body and blood of Christ in the sacrament are the one perfect sacrifice offered to God once and for all on the cross and are now distributed to us in the sacrament together with all the blessings and benefits which this sacrifice has won for us.

Note: We speak of the "sacrament of the altar" because an altar is a place of sacrifice. Jesus sacrificed his body and blood on the cross for the sins of the world once and for all. In the sacrament of the altar, he distributes this same body and blood until the end of time.

Q. 294. What does Christ command when he says, "This do in remembrance of me"?

A. Christ commands in these words that his sacrament be celebrated in the church till the end of time as a living proclamation and distribution of his saving death in all its blessings.

Q. 295. Why are we to receive the Sacrament often?

A. We are to receive the sacrament often because (1) Christ commands, or urgently invites, us, saying, "This do in remembrance of me"; (2) his words "Given and shed for you for the forgiveness of sins" promise and offer us great blessings; (3) we need the forgiveness of our sins and the strength for a new and holy life.

Note: In the New Testament, the sacrament was a regular and major feature of congregational worship, not an occasional extra (Acts 2:42; 20:7; 1 Corinthians 11:20, 33). In Reformation times our churches celebrated the sacrament "every Sunday and on other festivals" (Apology XXIV 1).

2. The Benefit of the Sacrament of the Altar

Q. What is the benefit of this eating and drinking?

A. These words, "Given and shed for you for the forgiveness of sins," show us that in the sacrament forgiveness of sins, life, and salvation are given us through these words. For where there is forgiveness of sins, there is also life and salvation.

Q. 296. What is the benefit of the sacrament offered in this sacrament?

A. (1) The chief blessing of the sacrament is the forgiveness of sins which Christ's body and blood have won for us on the cross. (The Lord's Supper is a means of grace.) (2) Together with forgiveness, God gives all other blessings as well, that is, "life and salvation." (3) In the sacrament Christ gives victory over sin and hell and strength for the new life in him. (4) As Christians partake of this sacrament together, they make a solemn public confession of Christ and of unity in the truth of his gospel.

3. The Power of the Sacrament of the Altar

Q. How can bodily eating and drinking do such great things?

A. Certainly not just eating and drinking do these things, but the words written here: "Given and shed for you for the forgiveness of sins." These words, along with the bodily eating and drinking, are the main thing in the sacrament. Whoever believes these words has exactly what they say: "forgiveness of sins."

Q. 297. How can forgiveness, life, and salvation be obtained through bodily eating and drinking?

A. Not simply the eating and drinking, but the words of Christ together with his body and blood under the bread and wine are the way through which these blessings are given. Christ's words of promise have put these gifts into the sacrament, and the believer receives them there through faith.

Q. 298. Does everyone who eats and drinks the sacrament also receive forgiveness, life, and salvation?

A. Forgiveness, life, and salvation are truly offered to all who eat the Lord's body and blood in the sacrament, but only through faith can we receive the blessings offered there.

4. How to Receive This Sacrament Worthily

Q. Who receives this sacrament worthily?

A. Fasting and bodily preparation are certainly fine outward training. But the person is truly worthy and well prepared who has faith in these words: "Given and shed for you for the forgiveness of sins." But anyone who does not believe these words or doubts them is unworthy and unprepared, for the words "for you" require all hearts to believe.

Q. 299. Why is it important to receive the sacrament worthily?

A. It is very important because St. Paul clearly teaches: "Whoever eats the bread and drinks the cup of the Lord in an unworthy manner will be guilty of sinning against the body and blood of the Lord. A man ought to examine himself before he eats of the bread and drinks of the cup. For anyone who eats and drinks without recognizing the body of the Lord eats and drinks judgment on himself" (1 Cor. 11:27–29).

Q. 300. Is it necessary to fast before receiving the sacrament?

A. Fasting can be good training for the will, but God does not command particular times, places, and forms for this.

Q. 301. When do we receive the sacrament worthily?

A. We receive it worthily when we have faith in Christ and his words, "Given and shed for you for the forgiveness of sins."

Q. 302. When is a person unworthy and unprepared?

A. A person is unworthy and unprepared when he or she does not believe or doubts Christ's words, since the words "for you" require all hearts to believe.

Q. 303. How are we to examine ourselves before receiving the sacrament?

A. We are to examine ourselves to see whether (1) we are sorry for our sins; (2) we believe in our Savior Jesus Christ and in his words in the sacrament; (3) we plan, with the help of the Holy Spirit, to change our sinful lives.

Q. 304. May those who are weak in faith come to the Lord's Table?

A. Yes, for Christ instituted the sacrament for the very purpose of strengthening and increasing our faith.

Q. 305. Who must not be given the sacrament?

A. The sacrament must not be given to the following: (1) those who are openly ungodly and unrepentant, including those who take part in non-Christian religious worship; (2) those who are unforgiving, refusing to be reconciled. They show thereby that they do not really believe that God forgives them either; (3) those of a different confession of faith, since the Lord's Supper is a testimony of the unity of faith; (4) those who are unable to examine themselves, such as infants, people who have not received proper instruction, or the unconscious.

Note: Pastors as stewards of the mysteries of God (1 Cor. 4:1) have the greatest responsibility as to who should be admitted to the sacrament. Some of the responsibility also rests with the congregation and the communicant.

Q. 306. What is confirmation?

A. Confirmation is a public rite of the church preceded by a period of instruction designed to help baptized Christians identify with the life and mission of the Christian community.

Note: Prior to admission to the Lord's Supper, it is necessary to be instructed in the Christian faith (1 Cor. 11:28). The rite of confirmation provides an opportunity for the individual Christian, relying on God's promise given in holy baptism, to make a personal public confession of the faith and a lifelong pledge of fidelity to Christ.

THE FRENCH CONFESSION OF FAITH
(1559; PREPARED BY JOHN CALVIN)

Article XXXVI

We confess that the Lord's Supper, which is the second sacrament, is a witness of the union which we have with Christ, inasmuch as he not only died and rose again for us once, but also feeds and nourishes us truly with his flesh and blood, so that we may be one in him, and that our life may be in common. Although he be in heaven until he come to judge all the earth, still we believe that by the secret and incomprehensible power of his Spirit he feeds and strengthens us with the substance of his body and of his blood. We hold that this is done spiritually, not because we put imagination and fancy in the place of fact and truth, but because the greatness of this mystery exceeds the measure of our senses and the laws of nature. In short, because it is heavenly, it can only be apprehended by faith.

THE BELGIC CONFESSION (1561; REFORMED)

Article XXXV: The Holy Supper of Our Lord Jesus Christ

We believe and confess that our Savior Jesus Christ did ordain and institute the sacrament of the holy Supper, to nourish and support those whom he has already regenerated and incorporated into his family, which is his church. Now those who are regenerated have in them a twofold life, the one bodily and temporal, which they have from the first birth, and is common to all men; the other spiritual and heavenly, which is given them in their second birth, which is effected by the word of the gospel, in the communion of the body of Christ; and this life is not common, but is peculiar to God's elect. In like manner God has given us, for the support of the bodily and earthly life, earthly and common bread, which is subservient thereto, and is common to all men, even as life itself. But for the support of the spiritual and heavenly life which believers have, he has sent a living bread, which descended from heaven, namely, Jesus Christ, who nourishes and strengthens the spiritual life of believers when they eat him, that is to say, when they appropriate and receive him by faith in the Spirit. In order that he might represent unto us this spiritual and heavenly bread, Christ has instituted an earthly and visible bread as a sacrament of his body, and wine as a sacrament of his blood, to testify by them unto us that, as certainly as we receive and hold this sacrament in our hands and eat and drink the same with our mouths, by which our life is afterwards nourished, we also do as certainly receive by faith (which is the hand and mouth of our soul) the true body and blood of Christ our only Savior in our souls, for the support of our spiritual life.

Now, as it is certain and beyond all doubt that Jesus Christ has not enjoined to us the use of his sacraments in vain, so he works in us all that he represents to us by these holy signs, though the manner surpasses our understanding and cannot be comprehended by us, as the operations of the Holy Spirit are hidden and incomprehensible. In the meantime we err not when we say that what is eaten and drunk by us is the proper and natural body and the proper blood of Christ. But the manner of our partaking of the same is not by the mouth, but by the Spirit through faith. Thus, then, though Christ always sits at the right hand of his Father in the heavens, yet does he not, therefore, cease to make us partakers of himself by faith. This feast is a spiritual table, at which Christ communicates himself with all his benefits to us, and gives us there to enjoy both himself and the merits of his suffering, strengthening, and comforting our poor comfortless souls by the eating of his flesh, quickening and refreshing them by the drinking of his blood.

Further, though the sacraments are connected with the thing signified, nevertheless both are not received by all men; the ungodly indeed receives the sacrament to his condemnation, but he does not receive the truth of the sacrament, even as Judas and Simon the sorcerer both indeed received the sacrament, but not Christ, who was signified by it, of whom believers only are made partakers.

Lastly, we receive this holy sacrament in the assembly of the people of God, with humility and reverence, keeping up among us a holy remembrance of the death of Christ our Savior, with thanksgiving, making there confessions of our faith and of the Christian religion. Therefore no one ought to come to this table without having previously rightly examined himself, lest by eating of this bread and drinking of this cup he eat and drink judgment to himself. In a word, we are moved by the use of this holy sacrament to a fervent love towards God and our neighbor.

Therefore we reject all mixtures and damnable inventions which men have added unto and blended with the sacraments, as profanations of them; and affirm that we ought to rest satisfied with the ordinance which Christ and his apostles have taught us, and that we must speak of them in the same manner as they have spoken.

THE SECOND HELVETIC CONFESSION OF FAITH (1566; REFORMED; PREPARED BY HEINRICH BULLINGER)

Chapter XIX: Of the Sacraments of the Church of Christ

But the principal thing, which in all sacraments is offered by our Lord, and chiefly regarded by the godly of all ages (which some have called the substance and the matter of the sacraments), is Christ our Savior—that only sacrifice (Heb. 10:12); and that Lamb of God slain from the foundation of the world (Rev. 13:8); that rock, also, of which all our fathers drank (1 Cor. 10:4), by whom all the elect are circumcised with the circumcision made without hands, through the Holy Spirit (Col. 2:11,12), and are washed from all their sins (Rev. 1:5), and are nourished with the very body and blood of Christ unto eternal life (John 6:54).

THE WESTMINSTER CONFESSION OF FAITH (1646; PRESBYTERIAN)

Chapter XXVII: Of the Sacraments

Sacraments are holy signs and seals of the covenant of grace, immediately instituted by God to represent Christ and his benefits and to confirm our interest in him: as also to put a visible difference between those who belong to the church and the rest of the world; and solemnly to engage them to the service of God in Christ, according to his Word.

There is in every sacrament a spiritual relation or sacramental union, between the sign and the thing signified; whence it comes to pass that the names and the effects of the one are attributed to the other.

The grace which is exhibited in or by the sacraments, rightly used, is not conferred by any power in them; neither does the efficacy of a sacrament depend on the piety or intention of him who administers it, but on the work of the Spirit and the word of institution, which contains, together with a precept authorizing the use thereof, a promise of benefit to worthy receivers.

There are only two sacraments ordained by Christ our Lord in the gospel, that is to say, baptism and the Supper of the Lord: neither of which may be dispensed by any but a minister of the Word lawfully ordained.

The sacraments of the Old Testament, in regard of the spiritual things thereby signified and exhibited, were, for substance, the same with those of the New.

Chapter XXIX: Of the Lord's Supper

Our Lord Jesus, in the night wherein he was betrayed, instituted the sacrament of his body and blood called the Lord's Supper, to be observed in his church unto the end of the world; for the perpetual remembrance of the sacrifice of himself in his death, the sealing all benefits thereof unto true believers, their spiritual nourishment and growth in him, their further engagement in, and to all duties which they owe unto him; and to be a bond and pledge of their communion with him and with each other as members of his mystical body.

In this sacrament Christ is not offered up to his Father, nor any real sacrifice made at all for remission of sins of the quick or the dead, but only a commemoration of that one offering up of himself, by himself, on the cross, once for all, and a spiritual oblation of all possible praise unto God for the same, so that the popish sacrifice of the mass (as they call it) is most abominably injurious to Christ's one, only sacrifice, the alone propitiation for all the sins of his elect.

The Lord Jesus has in this ordinance appointed his ministers to declare his word of institution to the people, to pray, and bless the elements of bread and wine and thereby to set them apart from a common to a holy use; and to take and break the bread, to take the cup, and (they communicating also themselves) to give both to the communicants; but to none who are not then present in the congregation.

Private masses, or receiving this sacrament by a priest, or any other, alone; as likewise the denial of the cup to the people; worshiping the elements, the lifting them up, or carrying them about for adoration, and the reserving them for any pretended religious use; are all contrary to the nature of this sacrament, and to the institution of Christ.

The outward elements in this sacrament, duly set apart to the uses ordained by Christ, have such relation to him crucified, as that truly, yet sacramentally only, they are sometimes called by the name of the things they represent, to wit, the body and blood of Christ; albeit, in substance and nature, they still remain, and only, bread and wine, as they were before.

The doctrine which maintains a change in substance of bread and wine, into the substance of Christ's body and blood (commonly called transubstantiation) by consecration of a priest, or by any other way, is repugnant, not to Scripture alone, but even to common sense and reason; overthrows the nature of the sacrament; and has been, and is, the cause of manifold superstitions; yes, of gross idolatries.

Worthy receivers, outwardly partaking of the visible elements in this sacrament, do then also inwardly by faith, really and indeed, yet not carnally and corporally but spiritually, receive and feed upon Christ crucified, and all the benefits of his death; the body and blood of Christ being then, not corporally or carnally, in, with, or under the bread and wine; yet as really, but spiritually, present to the faith of believers in that ordinance, as the elements themselves are to their outward senses.

Although ignorant and wicked men receive the outward elements in this sacrament, yet they receive not the thing signified thereby; but by their unworthy coming thereunto are guilty of the body and blood of the Lord, to their own damnation. Wherefore all ignorant and ungodly persons, as they are unfit to enjoy communion with him, so are they unworthy of the Lord's table, and cannot, without great sin against Christ, while they remain such, partake of these holy mysteries, or be admitted thereunto.

THE CONFESSION OF THE WALDENSES (1655; FROM CALVINISTS IN ITALY)

Article XXX

That [Christ] has instituted the Holy Supper, or Eucharist, for the nourishment of our souls, to the end that eating effectually the flesh of Christ, and drinking effectually his blood, by a true and living faith, and by the incomprehensible virtue of the Holy Spirit, and so uniting ourselves most closely and inseparably to Christ, we come to enjoy in him and by him the spiritual and eternal life.

Now to the end that every one may clearly see what our belief is as to this point, we here insert the very expressions of that prayer which we make use of before the Communion, as they are written in our Liturgy or form of celebrating the Holy Supper, and likewise in our public Catechism, which are to be seen at the end of our Psalms; these are the words of the prayer:

> Seeing our Lord has not only once offered his body and blood for the remission of our sins, but is willing also to communicate the same unto us as the food of eternal life, we humbly beseech thee to grant us this grace that in true sincerity of heart and with an ardent zeal we may receive from him so great a benefit; that is, that we may be made partakers of his body and blood, or rather of his whole self, by a sure and certain faith.

The words of the Liturgy are these:

> Let us then believe first of all the promises which Christ (who is the infallible truth) has pronounced with his own mouth, viz., that he will make us truly partakers of his body and blood, that so we may possess him entirely, in such manner that he may live in us and we in him.

THE THIRTY-NINE ARTICLES (1563; ANGLICAN)

Article XXVIII: Of the Lord's Supper

The Supper of the Lord is not only a sign of the love that Christians ought to have among themselves one to another; but rather it is a sacrament of our redemption by Christ's death; insomuch that to such as rightly, worthily, and with faith receive the same, the bread which we break is a partaking of the body of Christ; and likewise the cup of blessing is a partaking of the blood of Christ.

Transubstantiation (or the change of bread and wine) in the Supper of the Lord cannot be proved by Holy Writ but is repugnant to the plain words of Scripture, overthrows the nature of a sacrament, and has given occasion to many superstitions.

The body of Christ is given, taken, and eaten in the Supper only after a heavenly and spiritual manner. And the means whereby the body of Christ is received and eaten in the Supper is faith.

The sacrament of the Lord's Supper was not by Christ's ordinance reserved, carried about, lifted up, or worshiped.

THE HEIDELBERG CATECHISM
(1563; REFORMED; PREPARED BY
ZACHARIAS URSINUS AND CASPAR OLEVIANUS)

Lord's Day 25: The Sacraments

Q. 65. It is by faith alone that we share in Christ and all his blessings: where then does that faith come from?

A. The Holy Spirit produces it in our hearts by the preaching of the holy gospel, and confirms it through the use of the holy sacraments.

Q. 66. What are sacraments?

A. Sacraments are holy signs and seals for us to see. They were instituted by God so that by our use of them he might make us understand more clearly the promise of the gospel, and might put his seal on that promise.

And this is God's gospel promise: to forgive our sins and give us eternal life by grace alone because of Christ's one sacrifice finished on the cross.

Q. 67. Are both the word and the sacraments then intended to focus our faith on the sacrifice of Jesus Christ on the cross as the only ground of our salvation?

A. Right!

In the gospel the Holy Spirit teaches us and through the holy sacraments he assures us that our entire salvation rests on Christ's one sacrifice for us on the cross.

Q. 68. How many sacraments did Christ institute in the New Testament?

A. Two: baptism and the Lord's Supper.

Lord's Day 28: The Lord's Supper

Q. 75. How does the Lord's Supper remind you and assure you that you share in Christ's one sacrifice on the cross and in all his gifts?

A. In this way: Christ has commanded me and all believers to eat this broken bread and to drink this cup. With this command he gave this promise: First, as surely as I see with my eyes the bread of the Lord broken for me and the cup given to me, so surely his body was offered and broken for me and his blood poured out for me on the cross.

Second, as surely as I receive from the hand of the one who serves, and taste with my mouth the bread and cup of the Lord, given me as sure signs of Christ's body and blood, so surely he nourishes and refreshes my soul for eternal life with his crucified body and poured-out blood.

Q. 76. What does it mean to eat the crucified body of Christ and to drink his poured-out blood?

A. It means to accept with a believing heart the entire suffering and death of Christ and by believing to receive forgiveness of sins and eternal life.

But it means more. Through the Holy Spirit, who lives both in Christ and in us, we are united more and more to Christ's blessed body. And so, although he is in heaven and we are on earth, we are flesh of his flesh and bone of his bone. And we forever live on and are governed by one Spirit, as members of our bodies are by one soul.

Q. 77. Where does Christ promise to nourish and refresh believers with his body and blood as surely as they eat this broken bread and drink this cup?

A. In the institution of the Lord's Supper: "The Lord Jesus, on the night he was betrayed, took bread, and when he had given thanks, he broke it and said, 'This is my body, which is for you; do this in remembrance of me.' In the same way, after supper he took the cup, saying, 'This cup is the new covenant in my blood; do this, whenever you drink it, in remembrance of me.' For whenever you eat this bread and drink this cup, you proclaim the Lord's death until he comes."

This promise is repeated by Paul in these words: "Is not the cup of thanksgiving for which we give thanks a participation in the blood of Christ? And is not the bread that we break a participation in the body of Christ? Because there is one loaf, we, who are many, are one body, for we all partake of the one loaf."

Q. 78. Are the bread and the wine changed into the real body and blood of Christ?

A. No. Just as the water in baptism is not changed into Christ's blood and does not itself wash away sins but is simply God's sign and assurance, so too the bread of the Lord's Supper is not changed into the actual body of Christ, even though it is called the body of Christ, in keeping with the nature and language of sacraments.

Q. 79. Why then does Christ call the bread his body and the cup his blood, or the new covenant in his blood? (Paul uses the words, a participation in the body and blood of Christ.)

A. Christ has good reasons for these words. He wants to teach us that as bread and wine nourish our temporal life, so too his crucified body and poured-out blood truly nourish our souls for eternal life.

But more important, he wants to assure us, by this visible sign and pledge, that we, through the Holy Spirit's work, share in his true body and blood as surely as our mouths receive these holy signs in his remembrance, and that all of his suffering and obedience are as definitely ours as if we personally had suffered and paid for our sins.

Q. 80. How does the Lord's Supper differ from the Roman Catholic Mass?

A. The Lord's Supper declares to us that our sins have been completely forgiven through the one sacrifice of Jesus Christ which he himself finished on the cross once for all. It also declares to us that the Holy Spirit grafts us into Christ, who with his very body is now in heaven at the right hand of the Father where he wants us to worship him.

[But the Mass teaches that the living and the dead do not have their sins forgiven through the suffering of Christ unless Christ is still offered for them daily by the priests. It also teaches that Christ is bodily present in the form of bread and wine where Christ is therefore to be worshiped. Thus the Mass is basically nothing but a denial of the one sacrifice and suffering of Jesus Christ and a condemnable idolatry.]

Note: This question was omitted in the first edition of the catechism. The section within brackets was added in the third edition.

In 2006, the Christian Reformed Church declared that Q. and A. 80 can no longer be held in its current form as part of its confession. While this section remains in the text, it is placed in brackets to indicate that it does not accurately reflect the official teaching and practice of today's Roman Catholic Church and is no longer confessionally binding on members of the Christian Reformed Church.

Q. 81. Who are to come to the Lord's table?

A. Those who are displeased with themselves because of their sins, but who nevertheless trust that their sins are pardoned and that their continuing weakness is covered by the suffering and death of Christ, and who also desire more and more to strengthen their faith and to lead a better life. Hypocrites and those who are unrepentant, however, eat and drink judgment on themselves.

Q. 82. Are those to be admitted to the Lord's Supper who show by what they say and do that they are unbelieving and ungodly?

A. No, that would dishonor God's covenant and bring down God's anger upon the entire congregation. Therefore, according to the instruction of Christ and his apostles, the Christian church is duty-bound to exclude such people, by the official use of the keys of the kingdom, until they reform their lives.

THE DORDRECHT CONFESSION (1632; MENNONITE)

Article X

We also believe in and observe the breaking of bread, or the Lord's Supper, as the Lord Jesus instituted the same (with bread and wine) before his sufferings, and also observed and ate it with the apostles, and also commanded it to be observed to his remembrance, as also the apostles subsequently taught and observed the same in the church, and commanded it to be observed by believers in commemoration of the death and sufferings of the Lord—the breaking of his worthy body and the shedding of his precious blood—for the whole human race. So is the observance of this sacrament also to remind us of the benefit of the said death and sufferings of Christ, namely, the redemption and eternal salvation which he purchased thereby, and the great love thus shown to sinful man; whereby we are earnestly exhorted also to love one another—to love our neighbor—to forgive and absolve him—even as Christ has done unto us—and also to endeavor to maintain and keep alive the union and communion which we have with God, and amongst one another; which is thus shown and represented to us by the aforesaid breaking of bread.

THE NEW HAMPSHIRE CONFESSION OF FAITH (1833; BAPTIST)

Article XIV: Of Baptism and the Lord's Supper

We believe that Christian baptism is the immersion in water of a believer, into the name of the Father, and Son, and Holy Spirit; to show forth, in a solemn and beautiful emblem, our faith in the crucified, buried, and risen Savior, with its effect in our death to sin and resurrection to a new life; that it is a prerequisite to the privileges of a church relation; and to the Lord's Supper, in which the members of the church, by the sacred use of bread and wine, are to commemorate together the dying love of Christ; preceded by solemn self-examination.

METHODIST ARTICLES OF RELIGION (1784)

Article XVIII: Of the Lord's Supper

The Supper of the Lord is not only a sign of the love that Christians ought to have among themselves one to another, but rather is a sacrament of our redemption by Christ's death; insomuch that, to such as rightly, worthily, and with faith receive the same, the bread which we break is a partaking of the body of Christ; and likewise the cup of blessing is a partaking of the blood of Christ.

Transubstantiation, or the change of the substance of the bread and wine in the Supper of our Lord, cannot be proved by Holy Writ but is repugnant to the plain words of Scripture, overthrows the nature of the sacrament, and has given occasion to many superstitions.

The body of Christ is given, taken, and eaten in the Supper only after a heavenly and spiritual manner. And the means whereby the body of Christ is received and eaten in the Supper is faith.

The sacrament of the Lord's Supper was not by Christ's ordinance reserved, carried about, lifted up, or worshiped.

Article XIX: Of Both Kinds

The cup of the Lord is not to be denied to the laypeople; for both parts of the Lord's Supper, by Christ's ordinance and commandment, ought to be administered to all Christians alike.

THE COUNCIL OF TRENT (ROMAN CATHOLIC)

Session 13, Chapter 4: On Transubstantiation

Because Christ our Redeemer declared that it was truly his body that he was offering under the species of bread, it has always been the belief of the church of God, which this sacred council reaffirms, that by the consecration of the bread and wine a change takes place in which the entire substance of the bread becomes the substance of the body of Christ our Lord, and the whole substance of the wine becomes the substance of his blood. This change the holy Catholic Church has fittingly and correctly called "transubstantiation."

THE CATECHISM OF THE CATHOLIC CHURCH (1994)

Part 2, Section 2, Article 3: The Sacrament of the Eucharist

1322 The holy Eucharist completes Christian initiation. Those who have been raised to the dignity of royal priesthood by baptism and configured more deeply to Christ by confirmation participate with the whole community in the Lord's own sacrifice by means of the Eucharist.

1323 "At the Last Supper, on the night he was betrayed, our Savior instituted the eucharistic sacrifice of his body and blood. This he did in order to perpetuate the sacrifice of the cross throughout the ages until he should come again, and so to entrust to his beloved spouse, the church, a memorial of his death and resurrection: a sacrament of love, a sign of unity, a bond of charity, a Paschal banquet 'in which Christ is consumed, the mind is filled with grace, and a pledge of future glory is given to us.'"

1324 The Eucharist is "the source and summit of the Christian life." "The other sacraments, and indeed all ecclesiastical ministries and works of the apostolate, are bound up with the Eucharist and are oriented toward it. For in the blessed Eucharist is contained the whole spiritual good of the church, namely Christ himself, our Pasch."

1325 "The Eucharist is the efficacious sign and sublime cause of that communion in the divine life and that unity of the people of God by which the church is kept in being. It is the culmination both of God's action sanctifying the world in Christ and of the worship men offer to Christ through him to the Father in the Holy Spirit."

1326 Finally, by the Eucharist celebration we already unite ourselves with the heavenly liturgy and anticipate eternal life, when God will be all in all.

1327 In brief, the Eucharist is the sum and summary of our faith: "Our way of thinking is attuned to the Eucharist, and the Eucharist in turn confirms our way of thinking."

1333 At the heart of the eucharistic celebration are the bread and wine that, by the words of Christ and the invocation of the Holy Spirit, become Christ's body and blood. Faithful to the Lord's command the church continues to do, in this memory and until his glorious return, what he did on the eve of his Passion: "He took bread...." "He took the cup filled with wine...." The signs of bread and wine become, in a way surpassing understanding, the body and blood of Christ; they continue also to signify the goodness of creation. Thus in the offertory we give thanks to the Creator for bread and wine, fruit of the "work of human hands," but above all as "fruit of the earth" and "of the vine"—gifts of the Creator. The church sees in the gesture of the king-priest Melchizedek, who "brought out bread and wine," a prefiguring of her own offering.

1367 The sacrifice of Christ and the sacrifice of the Eucharist are one single sacrifice: "The victim is one and the same:

the same now offers through the ministry of priests, who then offered himself on the cross; only the manner of offering is different." "In this divine sacrifice which is celebrated in the Mass, the same Christ who offered himself once in a bloody manner on the altar of the cross is contained and is offered in an unbloody manner."

1400 Ecclesial communities derived from the Reformation and separated from the Catholic Church, "have not preserved the proper reality of the eucharistic mystery in its fullness, especially because of the absence of the sacrament of Holy Orders." It is for this reason that eucharistic intercommunion with these communities is not possible for the Catholic Church. However these ecclesial communities, "when they commemorate the Lord's death and resurrection in the Holy Supper ... profess that it signifies life in communion with Christ and await his coming in glory."

1411 Only validly ordained priests can preside at the Eucharist and consecrate the bread and the wine so that they become the body and blood of the Lord.

1412 The essential signs of the eucharistic sacrament are wheat bread and grape wine, on which the blessing of the Holy Spirit is invoked and the priest pronounces the words of consecration spoken by Jesus during the Last Supper: "This is my body which will be given up for you.... This is the cup of my blood...."

1413 By the consecration the transubstantiation of the bread and wine into the body and blood of Christ is brought about. Under the consecrated species of bread and wine Christ himself, living and glorious, is present in a true, real, and substantial manner; his body and his blood, with his soul and his divinity (cf. Council of Trent: DS 1640; 1651).

1416 Communion with the body and blood of Christ increases the communicant's union with the Lord, forgives his venial sins, and preserves him from grave sins. Since receiving this sacrament strengthens the bonds of charity between the communicant and Christ, it also reinforces the unity of the church as the mystical body of Christ.

1417 The church warmly recommends that the faithful receive Holy Communion each time they participate in the celebration of the Eucharist; she obliges them to do so at least once a year.

1418 Because Christ himself is present in the sacrament of the altar, he is to be honored with the worship of adoration. "To visit the blessed sacrament is … a proof of gratitude, an expression of love, and a duty of adoration toward Christ our Lord" (Paul VI, MF66).

APPENDIX 2:
QUOTATIONS ON THE LORD'S SUPPER

QUOTATIONS FROM MARTIN LUTHER ON COMMUNION

The Babylonian Captivity of the Church (1520)

To begin with, I must deny that there are seven sacraments, and for the present maintain that there are but three: baptism, penance, and the bread. All three have been subjected to a miserable captivity by the Roman curia, and the church has been robbed of all her liberty. Yet if I were to speak according to the usage of the Scriptures, I should have only one single sacrament, but with three sacramental signs.

Note: Luther later denied the sacramental character of penance.

But for more than twelve hundred years the church believed rightly, during which time the holy fathers never, at any time or place, mentioned this "transubstantiation" (a pretentious word and idea) until the pseudo-philosophy of Aristotle began to make its inroads into the church in these last three hundred years, in which many things have been incorrectly defined, as for example, that the divine essence is neither begotten not begets; or that the soul is the substantial form of the human body. These and like assertions are made without any reason or cause, as the Cardinal of Cambrai himself admits.

QUOTATIONS FROM JOHN CALVIN ON COMMUNION

Institutes of the Christian Religion

And, indeed, we must carefully observe that the very powerful and almost entire force of the sacrament lies in these words: "which is given for you," [and] "which is shed for you." The present distribution of the body and blood of the Lord would not greatly benefit us unless they had once for all been given for our redemption and salvation. They are therefore represented under bread and wine so that we may learn not only that they are ours but that they have been destined as food for our spiritual life.

And so as we previously stated, from the physical things set forth in the sacrament we are led by a sort of analogy to spiritual things (4:17:3).

But as for the outward ceremony of the action—whether or not the believers take it in their hands, or divide it among themselves, or severally eat what has been given to each; whether they hand the cup back to the deacon or give it to the next person; whether the bread is leavened or unleavened; the wine red or white—it makes no difference. These things are indifferent, and left at the church's discretion....

Now, to get rid of this great pile of ceremonies, the Supper could have been administered most becomingly if it were set before the church very often, and at least once a week. First, then, it should begin with public prayers. After this a sermon should be given. Then, when bread and wine have been placed on the Table, the minister should repeat the words of institution of the Supper. Next, he should recite the promises which were left to us in it; at the same time, he should excommunicate all who are debarred from it by the Lord's prohibition. Afterward, he should pray that the Lord, with the kindness wherewith he has bestowed this sacred food upon us, also teach and form us to receive it with faith and thankfulness of heart, and inasmuch as we are not so of ourselves, by his mercy make us worthy of such a feast. But here either psalms should be sung, or something read, and in becoming order the believers should partake of the most holy banquet, the ministers breaking the bread and giving the cup. When the Supper is finished, there should be an exhortation to sincere faith and confession of faith, to love and behavior worthy of Christians. At the last, thanks should be given, and praises sung to God. When these things are ended, the church should be dismissed in peace (4:17:43).

Even though it seems unbelievable that Christ's flesh, separated from us by such great distance, penetrates to us, so that it becomes our food, let us remember how far the secret power of the Holy Spirit towers above all our senses, and how foolish it is to wish to measure his immeasurableness by our measure. What, then, our mind does not comprehend, let faith conceive: that the Spirit truly unites things separated in space (4:17:10).

And although my mind can think beyond what my tongue can utter, yet even my mind is conquered and overwhelmed by the greatness of the thing. Therefore, nothing remains but to break forth in wonder at this mystery, which plainly neither the mind is able to conceive nor the tongue to express (4:17:7).

I therefore say (what has always been accepted in the church and is today taught by all of sound opinion) that the sacred mystery of the Supper consists in two things: physical signs, which, thrust before our eyes, represent to us, according to our feeble capacity, things invisible; and spiritual truth, which is at the same time represented and displayed through the symbols themselves (4:17:11).

Under the apostles the Lord's Supper was administered with great simplicity. Their immediate successors added something to enhance the dignity of the mystery which was not to be condemned. But afterward they were replaced by those foolish imitators, who, by patching pieces from time to time, contrived for us these priestly vestments that we see in the Mass, these altar ornaments, these gesticulations, and the whole apparatus of useless things (4:10:19).

For baptism attests to us that we have been cleansed and washed; the eucharistic Supper, that we have been redeemed. In water, washing is represented; in blood, satisfaction (4:14:22).

Calvin's Commentaries

It is not an empty or unmeaning sign ... but those who receive this promise by faith are actually made partakers of his flesh and blood (*Commentary on the Synoptic Gospels*, 3:209).

There are three mistakes against which it is ... necessary to be on our guard; first, not to confound the spiritual blessing with the sign; secondly, not to seek Christ on earth, or under earthly elements; thirdly, not to imagine any other kind of eating than that which draws into us the life of Christ by the secret power of the Spirit, and which we obtain by faith alone (*Commentary on the Synoptic Gospels*, 3:209).

Tracts and Letters

We have no express command to constrain all Christians to use a specified day.... The practice of all well-ordered churches should be to celebrate the Supper frequently, so far as the capacity of the people will admit (*A Short Treatise on the Holy Supper of Our Lord Jesus Christ*, in *Tracts and Letters*, 2:179).

When celebrating the Supper, we shall indeed worship [Christ] as present, but with minds upraised to heaven (*The True Method of Giving Peace to Christendom and Reforming the Church*, in *Tracts and Letters*, 3:281).

QUOTATIONS FROM JOHN WESLEY ON COMMUNION (FROM SERMON 16, "THE MEANS OF GRACE," IN *JOHN WESLEY ON CHRISTIAN BELIEFS*, KENNETH CAIN KINGHORN, ED. [NASHVILLE: ABINGDON, 2002], 264–83)

The entire body of early Christians agreed that Christ had ordained certain outward means for conveying inner grace into our souls. The constant use of these means was beyond all dispute, for as long as "all who believed were together and had all things in common" and "devoted themselves to the apostles' teaching and fellowship, to the breaking of bread and the prayers."

In the course of time, however, "the love of many grew cold." Some Christians began to mistake the *means* for the *end*. They understood religion as consisting of outward marks rather than as a heart renewed after the image of God. They forgot that "the aim" of every commandment is "love that comes from a pure heart and sincere faith." They lost sight of Christ's instruction, "You shall love the Lord your God with all your heart, and with all your soul, and with all your mind." They forgot that real religion is being purified from pride, anger, and evil desire, "through faith in the power of God." Others in the church seemed to think that, although religion did not principally consist of outward means, yet there was something in their use that pleased God. They thought that the use of the outward means would make them acceptable in God's sight—even if they were not faithful in the weightier matters of the law, such as justice, mercy, and the love of God....

By the "means of grace" I mean the outward symbols, words, and actions that God ordained to be the ordinary channels through which he might convey to us his prevenient, justifying, and sanctifying grace.

I use the expression "means of grace" because I know of no better one.... We are taught in our Catechism that a sacrament is "an outward sign of inward grace, and a means whereby we receive the same."

The chief of these means of grace are *prayer* (whether in secret or with the large congregation), *searching the Scriptures* (which implies reading, hearing, and meditating on the Bible), and *receiving the Lord's Supper* (eating bread and drinking wine in remembrance of Christ). We believe that these means are ordained by God to be the ordinary channels of conveying grace to our souls.

We acknowledge that the entire value of the means of grace depends on their actual service to religion's aim. We also believe that all these means, when separated from their goal, are "less than nothing and emptiness." If the means do not actually promote the knowledge and love of God, they are not acceptable in his sight. Indeed, they are instead an abomination to God, a stench in his nostrils, and he is furious against them. Above all, if we use the means of grace as a kind of substitute for the religion they were designed to serve, it is not easy to find words to describe the enormous absurdity and wickedness of turning God's means against himself. In this way, we banish Christianity from the heart by the very means that God ordained for bringing it into the heart.

We also acknowledge that every outward means of any kind, if separated from the Spirit of God, cannot profit us at all. In themselves, the means cannot in any degree advance us toward the knowledge and love of God. Without debating the matter, we can agree that any help that we receive on the earth comes from God himself. It is God, by his almighty power, who works in us what pleases him....

All who desire an increase of the grace of God are to wait for it by partaking of the Lord's Supper.... Before God, and angels, and people, by these visible signs you openly demonstrate the same faith and express your solemn remembrance of his death, until he comes in the clouds of heaven.

Take care that you "examine yourselves," whether you understand the meaning and plan of this holy institution and whether you really yearn to be made conformable to the death of Christ. Only then, without doubting, you may "eat of the bread and drink of the cup."

Saint Paul explicitly repeats the instruction first given by our Lord: "eat" and "drink." In the Greek language, both verbs are in the imperative mood. These words do not imply a mere permission only. They are an explicit command to all those who are already filled with peace and joy in believing. They can truly say, "The remembrance of our sins is grievous unto us, the burden of them is intolerable."

From the words of Paul it is evident that Holy Communion is a standard, stated means of receiving the grace of God. In the preceding chapter, the apostle wrote, "The cup of blessing that we bless, is it not a sharing in the blood of Christ?" The bread we break, is it not a sharing in the body of Christ?" Is not the eating of this bread and the drinking of this cup the outward, visible means through which God conveys grace to our souls? Is it not all of spiritual grace, righteousness, peace, and joy in the Holy Spirit that were purchased by the body of Christ once broken, and the blood of Christ once shed for us? Therefore, let everyone who truly desires the grace of God eat of that bread and drink of that cup.

QUOTATIONS FROM CHARLES H. SPURGEON ON COMMUNION (FROM VARIOUS SERMONS)

The bread and wine, being eaten and drunk, are assimilated into the system; they minister strength to bone, sinew, muscle; they build up the man. And herein is teaching. *Christ believed in is one with us*—"Christ in us, the hope of glory." We have heard of persons talk of believers falling from grace and losing Christ. No, sir, a man has eaten bread—he ate it yesterday. Will you separate that bread from the man? Will you trace the drops that came from the cup, and fetch them out of the man's system? You shall more easily do that than you shall take Christ away from the soul that has once fed upon him. "Who shall separate us from the love of God, which is in Christ Jesus our Lord?" He is in us a well of water springing up into everlasting life. See then how large a letter Christ has written to us with these pens—how in this bread and this wine, eaten and drunk, he has taught us wondrous mysteries—in fact, the whole Christian faith is, in brief, summed up here upon this table....

Let us keep this ordinance in its pure simplicity. Let us never add anything to it by our own devising by way of fancying that we are honoring God by garnishing his table. Let us plainly show Christ's death, and as we do it plainly *we should also do it festively*. Is it not delightful to reflect that our Lord has not ordained a mournful ceremony in which to celebrate his death; it is a feast....

When are we to do it? The text says "often"—"as often as you eat this bread." The Holy Spirit might have used the words "when you eat," but he did not. He teaches us by implication that we ought to do it often. I do not think there is any positive law about it, but it looks to me as if the first Christians broke bread almost every day—"breaking bread from house to house." I am not sure that that refers to Communion, but in all probability it does. This much is certain, that in the early church the custom was to break bread in memory of Christ's passion on the first day of every week, and it was always a part of the Sabbath's service when they came together to remember the Lord in this way. How can it be thought right to leave the celebrating of this ordinance to once a year or once a quarter I cannot understand, and it seems to me that if brethren knew the great joy there is in often setting forth Christ's death they would not be content with even once a month....

The preacher is to go on preaching a dying Savior; the soul be satisfied as with marrow and fatness. There is nothing left us to occupy our thoughts, or to be the subject of our joy, as our dear dying Lord. Oh! let us feed on him. Each one, personally, as a believer—let him feed on his Savior. If he has come once, come again. Keep on coming till Christ himself shall appear. As long as the invitation stands, let us not slight it, but constantly come to Christ himself and feed on him (*The Feast of the Lord* [delivered at the Metropolitan Tabernacle, August 6, 1871]).

What does this supper mean? It means communion: communion with Christ, communion with one another....

Here on the table you have the tokens of the broadest and fullest communion. This is a kind of communion which you and I cannot choose to reject: if we are in Christ, it is and must be ours. Certain brethren restrict their communion in the outward ordinance, and they think they have good reasons for doing so; but I am unable to see the force of their reasoning, because I joyfully observe that these brethren commune with other believers in prayer, and praise, and hearing of the Word, and other ways: the fact being that the matter of real communion is very largely beyond human control, and is to the spiritual body what the circulation of the blood is to the natural body, a necessary process not dependent upon volition. In perusing a deeply spiritual book of devotion, you have been charmed and benefited, and yet upon looking at the title page it may be you have found that the author belonged to the Church of Rome. What then? Why, then it has happened that the inner life has broken all barriers, and your spirits have communed.... Blood is thicker than water, and no fellowship is more inevitable and sincere than fellowship in the precious blood and in the risen life of our Lord Jesus Christ. Here, in the common reception of the one loaf, we bear witness that we are one; and in the actual participation of all the chosen in the one redemption, that unity is in very deed displayed and matured in the most substantial manner. Washed in the one blood, fed on the same loaf, cheered by the same cup, all differences pass away, and "we, being many, are one body in Christ, and every one members one of another" (*Communion with Christ and His People: An Address at a Communion Service at Mentone*).

QUOTATIONS FROM CHURCH FATHERS ON COMMUNION

Ignatius

I desire the bread of God, the heavenly bread, the bread of life—which is the flesh of Jesus Christ, the Son of God.... And I desire the drink of God, namely his blood, which is incorruptible love and eternal life (*Epistle to the Romans*, chap. 7).

Let that be deemed a proper Eucharist, which is [administered] either by the bishop or by one to whom he has entrusted it (*Epistle to the Smyrnaeans*, chap. 8).

Justin Martyr

On finishing the prayers we greet each other with a kiss. Then bread and a cup of water and mixed wine are brought to the president of the brethren and he, taking them, sends up praise and glory to the Father of the universe through the name of the Son and of the Holy Spirit, and offers thanksgiving at some length that we have been deemed worthy to receive these things from him. When he has finished the prayers and the thanksgiving, the whole congregation present assents, saying, "Amen." "Amen" in the Hebrew language means, "So be it." When the president has given thanks and the whole congregation has assented, those whom we call deacons give to each of those present a portion of the consecrated bread and wine and water, and they take it to the absent (*First Apology*, sec. 61).

This food we call Eucharist [thanksgiving], of which no one is allowed to partake except one who believes that the things we teach are true, and has received the washing for forgiveness of sins and for rebirth, and who lives as Christ handed down to us. For we do not receive these things as common bread or as common drink; but as Jesus Christ our Savior being incarnate by God's word took flesh and blood for our salvation, so also we have been taught that the food consecrated by the word of prayer which comes from him, from which our flesh and blood are nourished by transmutation, is the flesh and blood of that incarnate Jesus (*First Apology*, sec. 66).

Those who prosper, and so wish, contribute, each one as much as he chooses to. What is collected is deposited with the president, and he takes care of orphans and widows, and those who are in want on account of sickness or any other cause, and those who are in bonds, and the strangers who are sojourners among [us], and, briefly, he is the protector of all those in need. We all hold this common gathering on Sunday, since it is the first day, on which God transforming darkness and matter made the universe, and Jesus Christ our Savior rose from the dead on the same day (*First Apology*, sec. 67).

Clement of Alexandria

The vine produces wine, as the Word produces blood. And both of them drink health to men—wine for the body, blood for the spirit (*The Instructor*, Book 1, chap. 5).

To drink the blood of Jesus is to become partaker of the Lord's immortality.... As wine is blended with water, so is the Spirit with man.... And the mixture of both—of the water and of the Word—is called Eucharist, renowned and glorious grace. Those who by faith partake of it are sanctified both in body and soul (*The Instructor*, Book 2, chap. 2).

Elsewhere the Lord, in the gospel according to John, brought this out by symbols, when he said, "Eat my flesh and drink my blood," describing distinctly by metaphor the drinkable properties of faith (*The Instructor*, Book 1, chap. 6).

Tertullian

[Jesus] declared plainly enough what he meant by the bread when he called the bread his own body. He likewise, when mentioning the cup and making the new testament to be sealed "in his blood," affirms the reality of his body (*Against Marcion*, chap. 40).

Origen

We have a symbol of gratitude to God in the bread that we call the Eucharist (*Against Celsus*, chap. 57).

OTHER CHRISTIAN QUOTATIONS ON COMMUNION (FROM *THE TABLE OF THE LORD*, CHARLES L. WALLIS, ED. [NEW YORK: HARPER & BROTHERS, 1958])

Olive Wyon (twentieth-century British author)

Every time we take part in the Eucharist, we are ourselves another link in the chain of uninterrupted celebration of the sacrament, which has never ceased, from the Last Supper down to the present moment. We are in a glorious succession. Think of Polycarp, bishop of Smyrna, who had learned much of Christ from John, the disciple of the Lord, at Ephesus, and was an intimate friend of "those who had seen the Lord." Born about the year 70 (or possibly a little earlier) Polycarp, as a young man, must have often worshiped at the Eucharist when John was officiating. How moving it must have been for him to hear the words: "This do in remembrance of me," pronounced by one who had known the Lord on earth. It was in this faith and love that Polycarp lived and prayed and served Christ, and in this faith he died. He was a very old man when persecution broke out at Smyrna. Yet when he was brought before the authorities and urged to sacrifice to Caesar, and thus to save his life, he had only one thing to say: "Eighty and six years have I served Christ, and he never did me wrong; how can I now blaspheme my King who has saved me?" When he was bound to the stake and about to be burned, he prayed: "I bless thee that thou hast thought me worthy of the present day and hour, to have a share in the number of the martyrs, and in the cup of Christ, unto the resurrection of eternal life."

Polycarp had kept the "feast of redemption" all through his long and blameless life. He had "remembered" Christ in the sacrament, but it was no more "memory" but his living Presence that strengthened him for service and endurance to the very end. Polycarp drank the "cup of Christ" when he gave his body to be burned rather than deny his Lord.

Elmer J. F. Arndt (twentieth-century seminary professor)

The sacraments declare Christ's intention to unite us to himself, to have fellowship with his own, to be at one with us.... He is present as the holy One before whom we are constrained to acknowledge our own unworthiness. He is present as the gracious One who endured the cross for our redemption. He is present as the Victor over sin and death, the living Lord of an eternal kingdom. In his presence, we are in the presence of the Eternal. Awe, reverence, wonder, adoring love possess us. Is it really surprising that the presence of the Lord and the fellowship he enters into with those who respond to him with faith cannot be contained in conceptual statement or be exhausted in verbal expression?

John G. Paton (nineteenth-century Scottish missionary to the New Hebrides)

Our first Communion on Aniwa ... was Sabbath, 24th October, 1869; and surely the angels of God and the Church of the Redeemed in Glory were among the great cloud of witnesses who eagerly "peered" down upon the scene—when we sat around the Lord's Table and partook of [Christ's] body and blood with those few souls rescued out of the heathen world.... On that Lord's Day, after the usual opening service, I gave a short and careful exposition of the Ten Commandments and of the way of salvation according to the gospel....

Beginning with the old Chief, the twelve [candidates] came forward, and I baptized them one by one.... Solemn prayer was then offered, and in the name of the Holy Trinity the Church of Christ on Aniwa was formally constituted. I addressed them on the words of the holy institution—1 Corinthians 11:23—and then, after the prayer of thanksgiving and consecration, administered the Lord's Supper—the first time since the island of Aniwa was heaved out of its coral depths!... I think, if ever in all my earthly experience, on that day I might truly add the blessed words—Jesus "in the midst."

The whole service occupied nearly three hours. The islanders looked on with a wonder whose unwanted silence was almost painful to hear.... For three years we had toiled and prayed and taught for this. At the moment when I put the bread and wine into those dark hands, once stained with the blood of cannibalism, now stretched out to receive and partake of the emblems and seals of the Redeemer's love, I had a foretaste of the joy of glory that well nigh broke my heart to pieces. I shall never taste a deeper bliss till I gaze on the glorified face of Jesus himself.

Robert P. Menzies (twentieth-century Assemblies of God theologian)

In the First World War Karl Barth was present at a Roman Catholic service somewhere in the war area. During the celebration of the mass a shell crashed into the building and burst. The priest waited till the dust cleared and the debris subsided, then quietly proceeded with the service as if nothing had happened. Apparently something much more important was being done in this service than was covered by the effects of the enemy action.... The history of Covenanting Scotland bears eloquent tribute to the power of witness that lies in public worship. When men hold conventicles in the open air, with human bloodhounds baying at their feet, and when they spread the Lord's Table literally in the presence of their enemies, they are most certainly publicizing their sense of the worth of these things.

Handley C. G. Moule (nineteenth-century Anglican bishop)

I believe that if our eyes were open to the unseen, we should indeed behold our Lord present at our Communion. There and then, assuredly, if anywhere and at any time, he remembers his promise, "Where two or three are gathered together in my name, there am I in the midst of them" (Matthew 18:20). Such special presence, the promised congregational presence, is perfectly mysterious in mode but absolutely true in fact; no creation of our imagination or emotion but an object of our faith. I believe that our Lord so present, not *on* the holy table, but *at* it, would be seen himself in our presence to bless the bread and wine for a holy use, and to distribute them to his disciples.... I believe that we should worship him, thus present in the midst of us in his living grace, with unspeakable reverence, thanksgiving, joy, and love. We should receive the bread and wine with a profound sense of their sacredness as given by him in physical assurance of our part, as believers in him and so as members of him, in all the benefits of his passion.

Alexander Balmain Bruce (nineteenth-century Scottish churchman and theologian)

In regarding Christ as the Bread of Life, we are not to restrict ourselves to the one benefit mentioned by him in instituting the feast, the remission of sins, but to have in view all his benefits tending to our spiritual nourishment and growth in grace. Christ is the Bread of Life in all his offices. As a prophet, he supplies the bread of divine truth to feed our minds; as a priest, he furnishes the bread of righteousness to satisfy our troubled consciences; as a king, he presents himself to us as an object of devotion that shall fill our hearts and whom we may worship without fear of idolatry.

The rite of the Supper ... is of use to interpret the Lord's death. It throws important light on the meaning of that solemn event. The institution of this symbolic feast was in fact the most important contribution made by Jesus during his personal ministry to the doctrine of the atonement through the sacrifice of himself. Therefore, more clearly than from any other act or word performed or spoken by him, the Twelve might learn to conceive of their Master's death as possessing a *redemptive* character. Thereby Jesus, as it were, said to his disciples: My approaching passion is not to be regarded as a mere calamity, or dark disaster, falling out contrary to the divine purpose or my expectation; not as a fatal blow inflicted by ungodly men on me and you, and the cause which is dear to us all; not even as an evil which may be overruled for good; but as an event fulfilling, not frustrating, the purpose of my mission, and fruitful of blessing to the world. What men mean for evil, God means for good, to bring to pass to save much people alive.... I pour forth my blood for a gracious end, even for the remission of sins. My death will initiate a new dispensation, and seal a new testament; it will fulfill the purpose, and therefore take the place, of the manifold sacrifices of the Mosaic ritual, and in particular of the paschal lamb, which is even now being eaten. I shall be the Paschal Lamb of the Israel of God henceforth; at once protecting

them from death, and feeding their souls with my crucified humanity, as the bread of eternal life.

William Temple (twentieth-century Anglican archbishop)

To "eat the flesh" and to "drink the blood" of the Son
of Man are not the same. The former is to receive the
power of self-giving and self-sacrifice to the uttermost.
The latter is to receive, in and through that self-giving
and self-sacrifice, the life that is triumphant over death
and united to God. Both "elements" are needed for the
full act of "communion"—which suggests that to receive
the holy Communion in one kind only is grievously det-
rimental to the full reality of the sacrament. The life that
gives itself even to death; the life that rises from death
into union with God: these are the divine gifts without
which "you have no life in you" (John 6:53). But he who
receives and makes his own those gifts has eternal life.
For those gifts are true food and drink of men; he who
receives them and makes them his own "abides in me
and I in him" (John 6:56).

It is essential to the spiritual value of this sacrament that
we do what the Lord did. It is all symbol, no doubt, but
it is expressive, not arbitrary, symbol; that is to say, the
spiritual reality signified is actually conveyed by the
symbol. The symbol is emphatically not *mere* symbol; if it
were that, we should only receive what our minds could
grasp of the meaning symbolized. It is an instrument of
the Lord's purpose to give himself to us, as well as the
symbol of what he gives. What we receive is not limited
by our capacity to understand the gift. When with the
right intention I receive the bread and the wine, I actually receive Christ, whether I have any awareness of this
at the moment or not, and always more fully than I am
aware. We, by repeating and so identifying ourselves
with his sacrificial act, become participants in his one
sacrifice, which is the perfect dedication to the Father of
the humanity which God in Christ has taken to himself.

George H. Morrison (nineteenth-century Scottish Presbyterian preacher)

The simplicity of Christ comes to its crown in the feast of the Lord's Supper. There is no gorgeous rite or showy ceremonial. There is nothing of that many-colored pageantry that had once been needful to attract the world. A cup of wine and a piece of broken bread—these are the seals and symbols of the gospel. And I never feel the simplicity of God and of God's great plan for rescuing the world ... so powerfully and so freshly as when I sit at the Communion table. There are great mysteries in our redemption. There are deep things even the angels cannot fathom. But in the center is a fact so simple that its best ritual is bread and wine.

John Frederick Jansen (twentieth-century seminary professor)

We hold to two sacraments. We do not deny that all of life is sacramental in that it points us to God's handiwork and presence. We do deny that all of life is sacramental in pointing with equal clarity to the saving love of God effected on the cross. Marriage, for example, may be called sacramental in that it points to a "Love divine, all loves excelling," but marriage is not confined to Christian faith, nor does it point to Jesus' death. For that matter, marriage is not given to all Christians. This is why Protestant Christians define as sacraments only those signs given by Jesus himself to all believers, showing and sealing the saving love of God. The two sacraments of baptism and the Lord's Supper declare that life becomes new, not because of anything we do or can do, but because of him who makes all things new. Baptism means that life has been made new—so baptism is not repeated. The Supper means that this new life must continually be sustained and nourished by him who has made it new, that he who has begun a good work in us "will bring it to completion" (Philippians 1:6).

Martin Dibelius (twentieth-century German theologian)

On his last evening, Jesus had gathered his disciples together for a supper. Only ceremonial meals were eaten at the beginning of the night; the customary hour for the main meal was earlier.... It became a farewell meal. For during the supper Jesus took a flat, round loaf of bread, broke it, as one usually did with bread, and divided the portions of the one loaf among his disciples. In the same way after supper, since goblets with wine were standing on the table, he had one of these goblets passed around among them, and each disciple drank from it. Any man of the ancient world ... would have understood the meaning of such an act even without accompanying words: the disciples were to feel themselves to be a fellowship, just as they had already been while they journeyed, ate, and drank with the Master. For eating together binds the partakers of the meal to one another.... Separation from the Master is what confronts this circle, but they are to remain united, even without him, until the day when the table fellowship is renewed in the kingdom of God. This is the foundation. Even if Jesus had not spoken of his death, he did nevertheless establish this independent fellowship. The Last Supper signifies the foundation of the church.

C. H. Dodd (twentieth-century Welsh
New Testament scholar and theologian)

In the Eucharist the church perpetually reconstructs the crises in which the kingdom of God came in history. It never gets beyond this. At each Eucharist we are there—we are in the night on which he was betrayed, at Golgotha, before the empty tomb on Easter Day, and in the upper room where he appeared; and we are at the moment of his coming with angels and archangels and all the company of heaven, in the twinkling of an eye, at the last trumpet. Sacramental communion is not a purely mystical experience to which history, as embodied in the form and matter of the sacrament, would be, in the last resort, irrelevant. It is bound up with a corporate memory of real events. History has been taken up into the supra-historical without ceasing to be history.

Evelyn Underhill (twentieth-century Anglican writer and mystic)

Here the church from the beginning has realized that Presence which is the source of her life and power; has expressed her adoration, thanksgiving, and penitence; has made her supplications for the living and the dead, offered her oblation, received the food of immortality, and remembered the prevailing sacrifice from which her life began. And here, in spite of periodical relapses ..., the Christian can still find the same essential sources of worship, refreshment, and inwardness; the same access to the inexhaustible Divine Charity, and the same invitation to oblation and communion in the offering and hallowing of bread and wine. Even were we to set aside the sacred character of its historic origin and its supernatural claim, no other rite could so well embody the ... transcendental paradox of Christianity; the universal divine action, and the intimate divine approach to every soul; the food of daily life, and the mystery of eternal life, both given at once; the historical memorial perpetually renewed, yet finding its fulfillment in a real and enduring Presence unfettered by the categories of time and space. Here the most naive worshiper finds an invitation to love and gratitude, and a focus for his devotion, which he can apprehend though never explain; and the contemplative finds a door which opens upon the ineffable mystery of God. Those deep levels of our being which live unchanged under the flow of outward life, and of which we sometimes become aware—those levels where we thirst for God and apprehend him, and know our truest selves to consist in a certain kinship with him—these levels are reached and stirred by the movement of the Eucharist.

Jonathan Edwards (eighteenth-century Congregationalist preacher, theologian, and missionary)

There is in the Lord's Supper a mutual solemn profession of the two parties transacting the covenant of grace, and visibly united in that covenant; the Lord Christ by his minister, on the one hand, and the communicants (who are professing believers) on the other.... Christ presents himself to the believing communicants as their propitiation and bread of life.... And they in receiving what is offered ... profess to embrace the promises and to lay hold of the hope set before them, to receive the atonement, to receive Christ as their spiritual food, and to feed upon him in their hearts by faith. Indeed, what is professed on both sides is the *heart*; for Christ in offering himself professes the willingness of *his heart* to be theirs who duly receive him; all the communicants, on their part, profess the willingness of *their hearts* to receive him.... Thus the Lord's Supper is plainly a *mutual* renovation, confirmation, and seal of the covenant of grace: both covenanting parties profess their consent to their respective parts in the covenant of grace.

Stephen Neill (twentieth-century Anglican theologian, historian, and evangelist)

To maintain the inner unity of fellowship, the [early] Christian group had one instrument by far more potent than any other, the regular celebration of the Eucharist. In many respects, Christian worship appears to have developed out of that of the synagogue; this, the eucharistic feast, was the one unique and irreplaceable element. Participation in it was the sign of Christian fellowship; exclusion from it was the most serious penalty that could be imposed on the erring brother. Whatever the peril, whatever the difficulty, and for slaves the difficulty must sometimes have been almost insurmountable, it was regarded as obligatory for the Christian to be present and to receive the Bread of Life. In private houses, in catacombs, often before the break of day, the Christians assembled to do what the Lord had appointed, to be fashioned anew into one bread, one body, to be set again firmly within that eternal redemption which God was accomplishing through the risen Christ. So essential was it that every member should partake of the "medicine of immortality" that portions from the one loaf were sent to those who were sick, in time of persecution to those in prison.

Emil Brunner (twentieth-century Swiss theologian)

Why did Jesus command the observation of this rite? He did not give his disciples any other similar instructions about divine worship. Why this? Is it not sufficient to preach and believe his gospel, the gospel of his atoning death? Why this ceremony in our churches? For a long time I asked myself this question ... without finding the right answer, until the answer sprang to my mind from this text [1 Cor. 10:16–17]: we must note the dual meaning of the phrase "body of Christ." On the one hand it refers to the body broken for us on the cross of Golgotha: this is symbolized or figuratively expressed in the broken bread, just as the outpoured wine represents the blood of Christ outpoured for us on the cross. That is the usual interpretation which we are familiar with from our confirmation instruction. It is correct insofar as it goes, but it is incomplete. For the body of Christ means in the New Testament something else: the church. The latter is the body of Christ because Christians are incorporated into the eternal Christ by faith and the Holy Spirit. Thus our text says: "We, who are many, are one body." There arises from us, who are a multiplicity of individuals, a unity, something whole and cohesive, kneaded together.

Thus what is effected through the common participation in the atoning death of Jesus Christ is the unity of the church.... Here is no magic, the bread is not transformed into the body, nor the wine into the blood. But a miracle does take place in that those men who formerly were their own lord and master now are ruled by the one Lord, and to form a manifold of separate individuals, each living and caring for himself, there arises a unity, one body, of which each believer is a member and Jesus Christ the Head, controlling and guiding all. In the eating of the bread and the drinking of the wine, Jesus Christ himself is present to them all and constitutes them as a unity, which he controls and directs. They become the body of Jesus Christ.

A. M. Fairbairn (nineteenth-century Scottish Congregationalist theologian)

That supper is an event which profoundly affects the imagination. Its very simplicity increases its significance. The meaning it bears to faith is marvelous on the one hand; the place it has filled, the work it has done in history, as marvelous on the other. If the vision had been granted to Christ to what it was to be and do, would it not, even when his sufferings were deepest, have turned his sorrow into joy? He would have seen his supper surviving for ages, simple in form, transcendent in meaning, a living center of unity for his scattered disciples, a source of comfort, strength, peace, purity to wearied and sinful men. In upper rooms, in catacombs, where the dust of the dead rested, and the spirits of the living met to speak to each other words of holiest cheer; in desert places and moorlands, where hunted fugitives assembled to listen to a voice which, though a man's, seemed God's; in cathedrals, where form and space spoke majestically to the eye, and lofty music to the ear; in rude huts in savage or heathen lands; in ornate churches in wealthy, busy, and intellectual cities—men of the most varied types and conditions, saintly and sinful, ignorant and educated, simple and gentle, rich and poor, peer and peasant, sovereign and subject, priest and people, forming a multitude no man can number, have for centuries met together to celebrate this supper, and be by it made wiser, happier, holier.

Arthur Evelyn Barnes-Lawrence (nineteenth-century British pastor)

How thrilling to the imagination is the feast which constitutes a bond, unquestionable and direct, with the upper room itself! Across all the conflict and stress of Asian and African church history, across all the storm-tossed ages of the world, there stretches an unbroken chain, each golden link a Eucharist, binding the last Communion feast with the first....

When we gather around the Lord's Table, we look upon, we handle, we taste the elements of bread and wine ordained by Christ. The words of consecration are those which sounded in the ears of the apostles. The purpose for which we receive it is identical with theirs. The sacrament is the same, and the gift received is the same. The fact is obviously one of the first importance.... The holy Communion answered exactly to our natural desire for historical continuity. It is of God's goodness that our love, yearning for personal contact, finds its longing met by touch and taste and hearing.... In giving to the church this sacrament, Jesus Christ anticipated the needs of love in every age.

Manna =
Angels food -
Jesus giver of life,
including angelic life?

RESOURCES FOR FURTHER STUDY

Aulen, Gustaf. *Eucharist and Sacrifice*. Trans. Eric H. Wahlstrom. Philadelphia: Muhlenberg, 1958.

Baillie, Donald M. *The Theology of the Sacraments and Other Papers*. New York: Charles Scribner's Sons, 1957.

Barclay, William. *The Lord's Supper*. Philadelphia: Westminster, 1967.

Bartels, Ernest. *Take Eat, Take Drink: The Lord's Supper Through the Centuries*. St. Louis, Mo.: Concordia, 2004.

Barth, Markus. *Rediscovering the Lord's Supper: Communion with Israel, with Christ, and Among the Guests*. Atlanta: John Knox, 1988.

Bloesch, Donald G. *The Reform of the Church*. Eugene, Ore.: Wipf & Stock, 1998.

———. *Wellsprings of Renewal: Promise in Christian Communal Life*. Grand Rapids: Eerdmans, 1974.

Bradshaw, Paul F. *The Search for the Origins of Christian Worship*. New York: Oxford Univ. Press, 1992.

Bridge, Donald, and David Phypers. *Communion: The Meal That Unites?* Wheaton, Ill.: Shaw, 1983.

Bromiley, G. W. *Sacramental Teaching and Practice in the Reformation Church*. Grand Rapids: Eerdmans, 1957.

———. *The Unity and Disunity of the Church*. Grand Rapids: Eerdmans, 1958.

Bruce, Robert. *The Mystery of the Lord's Supper: Sermons of the Sacrament Preached in the Kirk of Edinburgh by Robert Bruce in A.D. 1589*. Ed. Thomas F. Torrance. Richmond, Va.: John Knox, 1958.

Cantalamessa, Raniero. *The Eucharist: Our Sanctification*. Second edition. Trans. Frances Lonergan Villa. Collegeville, Minn.: Liturgical, 1995.

Chemnitz, Martin. *The Lord's Supper*. St. Louis, Mo.: Concordia, 1979.

Clark, Neville. *An Approach to the Theology of the Sacraments*. London: SCM, 1956.

Crockett, William R. *Eucharist: Symbol of Transformation*. Collegeville, Minn.: Liturgical, 1989.

Cullman, Oscar, and F. J. Leenhardt. *Essays on the Lord's Supper*. London: Lutterworth, 1958.

Cully, Kendig Brubaker. *Sacraments: A Language of Faith*. Philadelphia: Christian Education Press, 1961.

Davies, Horton. *Bread of Life and Cup of Joy: Newer Ecumenical Perspectives on the Eucharist*. Grand Rapids: Eerdmans, 1993.

Elert, Werner. *Eucharist and Church Fellowship in the First Four Centuries*. Trans. N. E. Nagel. St. Louis, Mo.: Concordia, 1966.

Eller, Vernard. *In Place of Sacraments: A Study of Baptism and the Lord's Supper*. Grand Rapids: Eerdmans, 1972.

Evangelical Lutheran Church in America, "The Use and Means of Grace: A Statement on the Practice of Word and Sacrament." Minneapolis: Augsburg, 1997.

Fiedler, Ernest J., and R. Benjamin Garrison. *The Sacraments: An Experiment in Ecumenical Honesty*. Nashville: Abingdon, 1969.

Forsyth, Peter Taylor. *The Church and the Sacraments*. London: Independent Press, 1964.

Freeman, Elmer S. *The Lord's Supper in Protestantism*. New York: Macmillan, 1945.

Guy, Laurie. *Introducing Early Christianity: A Topical Survey of Its Life, Beliefs and Practices*. Downers Grove, Ill.: InterVarsity, 2004.

Henry, Jim. *In Remembrance of Me: A Manual on Observing the Lord's Supper*. Nashville: Broadman & Holman, 1998.

Higgins, A. J. B. *The Lord's Supper in the New Testament*. London: SCM, 1952.

Huebsch, Bill. *Rethinking Sacraments: Holy Moments in Daily Living*. Mystic, Conn.: Twenty-Third Publications, 1989.

Jeremias, Joachim. *The Eucharistic Words of Jesus*. Trans. Norman Perrin. London: SCM, 1966.

Kereszty, Roch A., ed. *Rediscovering the Eucharist: Ecumenical Conversations*. New York: Paulist, 2003.

Kerr, High Thompson. *The Christian Sacraments: A Source Book for Ministers*. Philadelphia: Westminster, 1954.

Kodell, Jerome. *The Eucharist in the New Testament*. Collegeville, Minn.: Liturgical, 1988.

Krauth, Charles P. *The Conservative Reformation and Its Theology*. St. Louis, Mo.: Concordia, 1963.

Larere, Philippe. *The Lord's Supper: Toward an Ecumenical Understanding of the Eucharist*. Collegeville, Minn.: Liturgical, 1993.

LaVerdiere, Eugene. *The Eucharist in the New Testament and the Early Church*. Collegeville, Minn.: Liturgical, 1996.

Marty, Martin E. *The Lord's Supper*. Minneapolis: Augsburg, 1997.

Mathison, Keith. *Given for You: Reclaiming Calvin's Doctrine of the Lord's Supper*. Phillipsburg, N.J.: P & R, 2002.

McEachern, Alton M. *Here at Thy Table, Lord: Enriching the Observance of the Lord's Supper*. Nashville: Broadman, 1977.

Mitchell, Nathan. *Real Presence: The Work of the Eucharist*. Chicago: Liturgical Training Publications, 1998.

Murray, Andrew. *The Lord's Table*. New York: Revell, 1897.

Pittenger, W. Norman. *The Christian Sacrifice: A Study of the Eucharist in the Life of the Christian Church*. New York: Oxford Univ. Press, 1951.

Rahner, Karl. *The Church and the Sacraments*. New York: Hyperion, 1994.

Reu, Johann M. *Two Treatises on the Means of Grace*. Reprint. Minneapolis: Augsburg, 1952.

Rordorf, Wily et al. *The Eucharist of the Early Christians*. Trans. Matthew J. O'Connell. New York: Pueblo, 1978.

Sasse, Herman. *This Is My Body: Luther's Contention for the Real Presence in the Sacrament of the Altar*. Adelaide, South Australia: Lutheran Publishing House, 1977.

———. *We Confess the Sacraments*. Trans. Norman Nagel. St. Louis, Mo.: Concordia, 1985.

Schmemann, Alexander. *The Eucharist: Sacrament of the Kingdom*. Crestwood, N.Y.: St. Vladimir's Seminary Press, 1987.

Shurden, Walter B., ed. *Proclaiming the Baptist Vision of Baptism and the Lord's Supper*. Macon, Ga.: Smith & Helwys, 1999.

Skibbe, Eugene M. *Protestant Agreement on the Lord's Supper*. Minneapolis: Augsburg, 1968.

Stevenson, Kenneth. *Accept This Offering: The Eucharist as Sacrifice Today*. Collegeville, Minn.: Liturgical, 1989.

Stibbs, Alan M. *Sacrament, Sacrifice and Eucharist*. London: Tyndale Press, 1961.

Stookey, Laurence Hull. *Eucharist: Christ's Feast with the Church*. Nashville: Abingdon, 1993.

Stott, John R. W. *Confess Yours Sins: The Way of Reconciliation*. Philadelphia: Westminster, 1964.

Swanston, Thomas. *Come to the Feast*. Edinburgh: Handsel, 1982.

Tappert, Theodore. *The Lord's Supper: Past and Present Practices*. Philadelphia: Muhlenberg, 1961.

Teigen, Bjarne Wollan. *The Lord's Supper in the Theology of Martin Chemnitz*. Brewster, Mass.: Trinity Lutheran Press, 1986.

Thurian, Max. *The Mystery of the Eucharist: An Ecumenical Approach*. Trans. Emily Chisholm. Grand Rapids: Eerdmans, 1983.

Thurian, Max, and Geoffrey Wainwright, eds. *Baptism and Eucharist: Ecumenical Convergence in Celebration*. Geneva: World Council of Churches, 1984.

————. *Ecumenical Perspectives on Baptism, Eucharist and Ministry*. Geneva: World Council of Churches, 1983.

Vander Wilt, Jeffrey. *Communion with Non-Catholic Christians: Risks, Challenges, and Opportunities*. Collegeville, Minn.: Liturgical, 2003.

Vander Zee, Leonard J. *Christ, Baptism and the Lord's Supper: Recovering the Sacraments for Evangelical Worship*. Downers Grove, Ill.: InterVarsity, 2004.

Wallis, Charles L., ed. *The Table of the Lord: A Communion Encyclopedia*. New York: Harper & Brothers, 1958.

Welker, Michael. *What Happens in Holy Communion?* Grand Rapids: Eerdmans, 2000.

World Council of Churches, Faith and Order Paper No. 111. *Baptism, Eucharist and Ministry*. Geneva: World Council of Churches, 1982.

Wybrew, Hugh. *The Orthodox Liturgy: The Development of the Eucharistic Liturgy in the Byzantine Rite*. Crestwood, N.Y.: St. Vladimir's Seminary Press, 1990.

Yarnold, G. D. *The Bread Which We Break*. New York: Oxford Univ. Press, 1950.

A number of ancient and modern resources exist to help churches celebrate the Lord's Supper in public worship. Most historic denominations have their own guides and liturgical aids. The reader can consult any of these to get an idea of how various churches carry out the Lord's Supper in their particular liturgical setting. One book (especially designed for Protestant churches) that includes helpful resources on the Lord's Supper is *Baker's Worship Handbook: Traditional and Contemporary Service Resources*, Paul E. Engle (Grand Rapids: Baker, 1998).

ABOUT THE CONTRIBUTORS

John H. Armstrong is president of ACT 3, a ministry for the advancement of the Christian tradition in the third millennium. A pastor for more than twenty years, he now serves the church-at-large as a teacher, apologist, and evangelist. He is an adjunct professor of evangelism at Wheaton College Graduate School and teaches as a special guest at several seminaries. He is the author/editor of *The Catholic Mystery; Roman Catholicism: Evangelical Protestants Analyze What Divides and Unites Us; The Stain That Stays: The Church's Response to the Sexual Misconduct of Its Leaders; Five Great Evangelists; The Glory of Christ;* and *Reforming Pastoral Ministry*. He has been editor of *Reformation & Revival Journal*, a quarterly journal for church renewal, since 1992. His reviews and articles have appeared in numerous periodicals and multiauthored works and his online commentaries regularly appear at *www.Act3online.com*. He holds degrees from both Wheaton College and Wheaton Graduate School, and received a doctorate in 1979 from Luther Rice Seminary (Atlanta). He is married to Anita Siml Armstrong, the father of two married children and grandfather of two, and lives in Carol Stream, Illinois.

Thomas A. Baima is a priest of the archdiocese of Chicago and provost of the University of Saint Mary of the Lake/Mundelein Seminary, where he also teaches systematic theology. A native of Chicago, he received his BA from Butler University; his STB, MDiv, and STL from the University of St. Mary of the Lake; and his STD (in ecumenical studies) from the Pontifical University of Saint Thomas Aquinas in Rome. He is the author of *The Concordat of Agreement between the Episcopal Church and the Evangelical Lutheran Church in America: Lessons on the Way Toward Full Communion* and has contributed to five other books. He was the director of the Office for Ecumenical and Interreligious Affairs for the archdiocese of Chicago and served as associate pastor in several parish ministries. His teaching and research interests are in the areas of ecclesiology, ecumenism, interreligious dialogue, and missiology. He has written a number of articles and book reviews for various publications and has participated in a Catholic-Protestant forum with John H. Armstrong, the editor of this volume.

I. John Hesselink is the former Albertus C. van Raalte professor of systematic theology at Western Theological Seminary in Holland, Michigan. He also served as president of Western Theological Seminary from 1973 to 1985. He has served in a wide variety of roles—evangelist, missionary, lecturer, translator, and administrator. He received his BA from Central College (Iowa), his BD from Western Theological Seminary (Michigan), and his doctorate in theology from the University of Basel (1961). He served as a missionary to Japan from 1953 to 1973, where he also taught systematic theology. He studied under both Emil Brunner and Karl Barth, completing his doctoral degree on the law in John Calvin for Professor Barth. His research in Calvin has gained him a reputation as a respected specialist in Calvin studies. His books include *Calvin's First Catechism: A Commentary* and *On Being Reformed*. He has contributed to numerous academic and popular journals and magazines and taught historical theology at Tokyo Union Theological Seminary for twelve years. Married in 1951, John and his wife, Etta, have five children and two grandchildren and live in Holland, Michigan.

Russell D. Moore is dean of the school of theology and senior vice president for academic administration of The Southern Baptist Theological Seminary in Louisville, Kentucky. He received his BS degree from the University of Southern Mississippi, his MDiv from New Orleans Baptist Theological Seminary, and his PhD from The Southern Baptist Theological Seminary. He is the author of *The Kingdom of Christ: The New Evangelical Perspective* and co-editor of *Why I Am a Baptist*. He is a frequent contributor to various publications and is a senior editor of *Touchstone: A Journal of Mere Christianity*. He also serves as the executive director of the Carl F. H. Henry Institute for Evangelical Engagement and is a regular columnist for Baptist Press. He has served on the pastoral staffs of two churches and was an aide to a United States congressman. He and his wife, Maria, along with their three sons—Benjamin, Timothy, and Samuel—live in Louisville, Kentucky.

David P. Scaer is chairman of the department of systematic theology at Concordia Theological Seminary in Fort Wayne, Indiana. He received the MDiv and ThD degrees from Concordia Theological Seminary in St. Louis. He has written hundreds of articles in scholarly journals and popular magazines. He is the author of numerous books, including *James: The Apostle of Faith; Apostolic Scriptures and The Sermon on the Mount;* and *Discourses in Matthew: Jesus Teaches the Church Theology.* He contributed three volumes to the Confessional Lutheran Dogmatics Series: *Christology; Baptism;* and *The Law and the Gospel and the Means of Grace.* He serves as editor of *Concordia Theological Quarterly* and previously served as academic dean at Concordia Theological Seminary. He was honored by a Festschrift several years ago titled *All Theology Is Christology.* He lives with his wife, Dorothy, and five children in Fort Wayne, Indiana.

Paul E. Engle, series editor for Counterpoints Church Life, is an ordained minister who served for twenty-two years in pastoral ministry in Pennsylvania, Connecticut, Illinois, and Michigan. He is an adjunct teacher in several seminaries in this country and internationally. He is a graduate of Houghton College (BA), Wheaton College Graduate School (MDiv), and Westminster Theological Seminary (DMin). He is the author of eight books, including *Baker's Wedding Handbook, Baker's Funeral Handbook,* and *Baker's Worship Handbook.* He serves as vice president and publisher in the Church, Academic, and Reference Resources team at Zondervan. He and his wife, Margie, live in Grand Rapids, Michigan.

DISCUSSION AND REFLECTION QUESTIONS

CHAPTER 1: CHRIST'S PRESENCE AS MEMORIAL

1. Do you think the Lord's Supper as practiced in your congregation signifies the warfare between God and Satan, the victory of Christ over the demonic powers?
2. How could your congregation make the Lord's Supper a more celebrative event while maintaining the gravity of the Lord's Table?
3. Russell Moore believes the lack of attention to the Lord's Supper in many churches comes from a lack of attention to the need to preach the gospel to *believers*. Do you think the gospel of Christ crucified and resurrected—as applied to believers—is emphasized enough in our churches? How does the Lord's Supper serve to point Christians to the gospel?
4. This chapter argues that the eclipse of the Lord's Supper as the proclamation of the gospel has resulted in all sorts of substitutes—such as Hollywood films depicting the bloodshed and suffering of Jesus. Do you think things as mundane as broken bread and poured wine can demonstrate the death of Jesus as effectively as a film image?
5. Do you agree that the pellet-sized bread fragments and individual glasses of juice tend to negate the communion aspect of the Lord's Supper? How could the communal aspect of the meal be more emphasized in your church?
6. Do you agree that baptism is a biblical prerequisite to the Lord's Supper? What does this mean for churches in which members disagree about the proper mode or candidates for baptism?

CHAPTER 2: THE REAL PRESENCE OF CHRIST

1. Is Calvin's doctrine of the real presence too sophisticated or too mystical for most people to comprehend?
2. How do you respond to the exhortation in the liturgy, "Lift up your hearts!" (the *sursum corda*)? What do you experience when you celebrate the Lord's Supper?
3. What can be done to celebrate the sacrament reverently and at the same time more celebratively?
4. What are the pros and cons of admitting children to the Lord's Table?

CHAPTER 3: FINDING THE RIGHT WORD

1. At the heart of any understanding of the Lord's Supper are Christ's words "This is my body." How are these words interpreted by the various traditions and how do you understand them?
2. Calling this sacrament the Lord's Supper points to Jesus as its originator and focus. What role do the Father and the Holy Spirit have in it?
3. Most Christian traditions speak of "real presence." How do they agree or disagree in what is meant?
4. Which Old Testament rites help us to understand the New Testament institution of the Lord's Supper?
5. Should the Lord's Supper be offered to all present in a church service (open communion)? If there are restrictions on who should partake (closed communion), what should they be?
6. This rite is known as Mass, Holy Communion, Eucharist, the Lord's Supper, the Sacrament of the Altar, and the Lord's Table. In what way are these designations helpful in understanding it?

CHAPTER 4: CHRIST'S TRUE, REAL, AND SUBSTANTIAL PRESENCE

1. What does the Catholic notion of the Eucharist as the "source and summit of the Christian life," suggest for your own spirituality?

2. How do you react to Saint Ambrose's question, "Could not Christ's word, which can make from nothing that which did not exist, change existing things into that which they were not before?" Do you agree or disagree? Why? What implications does it have for how the Lord's Supper is understood?

3. Should the church demand a correspondence between an individual's faith and moral life in order for him or her to be admitted to the Eucharist? How in practice could this be carried out?

4. What new insights does the notion of *doxology* offer you as a Christian?

SCRIPTURE INDEX

Genesis
1:2 97
2:9 91
3:15 31
3:17–18. 31
3:19 93
4:3–5. 32
9:13 91
9:16 30
9:21 35
25:33–34. 35

Exodus
12:1–30. 91
12:26 15
12:27 34
12:43–50. 34
16:1–36. 91
28. 15

Leviticus
4:1–5:13 91

Numbers
11:4–5. 36

Deuteronomy
8:7–9. 36
32:32–33. 40
33:28 31

Psalms
23:5 32
81:10 36
104:15 51

Isaiah
5:1–7. 31
11:7 32
25:6 31
27:6 31

Jeremiah
2:21 31
31:34 74

Amos
9:13 31
9:14 31

Zechariah
8:12 31
9:17 139

Matthew
4:2–4. . . . . 36, 39
6:11 93
7:9 38
8:11 40
15:36 100
18:20 . . . . 73, 195
26:17 94
26:18–19. 34
26:26 . . . . 12, 97
26:27 . . . . 13, 99
26:28 . . . . 12, 91, 97
26:29 94
28:20 . . . . 39, 73

Mark
14:1 94
14:23 . . . . 16, 17
14:25 20

Luke
22:1 94
22:7 34
22:12 12
22:16 35
22:19 . . . . . 12, 14, 34, 49
22:20 . . . . 34, 91
22:28–30. 32
22:31 32

John
1:29 16
2:1–11. 31
2:20 139
3:4 139
3:13–15. 140
3:16 36

4:14–15. 139
6:1–13. 31
6:11 100
6:33 93
6:35 93
6:40 35
6:48 93
6:50 101
6:51 . . . . 92, 93
6:53 197
6:53–55. 35
6:54 . . . . 92, 101
6:56 197
6:63 . . . . 100, 101
6:66 101
8:31–35. 139
9:38–41. 139
10:20–21. 139
14:17–18. 73
15:1 93
15:1–8. 31
15:26 140
17. 158

Acts
2:42 . . . . . . 13, 14, 36, 163
2:46–47. 14
20:7 . . . . 14, 163
20:11 14

Romans
1:16 36
3:25–26. 103
4:5 103
5:8 20
12:1–2. 17
14:17 44

1 Corinthians
4:1 166
5:4 . . . . 73, 105
5:5 40
5:6–7. 40
5:7 103

5:8–11 103
5:11 . . . . 40, 104
5:12–13 40
10:3–4 . . . . 91, 96
10:4 169
10:14–22 96
10:15–17 19
10:16 . . . . 13, 40, 99
10:16–17 . . . . 24, 202
10:17 . . . . 23, 40
10:18–22 40
10:21 . . . . 12, 98
11:18 39
11:20 . . . . 98, 163
11:20–21 39
11:21 23
11:22 23
11:23 . . . . 14, 98, 194
11:24 . . . . 13, 17, 99
11:24–25 . . . . 12, 38
11:24–26 92

11:25 . . . . 74, 91
11:26 . . . 13, 20, 22, 38, 98
11:27 . . . . 39, 74
11:27–29 165
11:28 166
11:28–32 23
11:29 . . . . 39, 74
11:29–32 38
11:33 163
14:40 71
16:2 14

Galatians
5:22–23 31

Ephesians
3:10 32
3:20 156
5:22–33 122
5:23 39

Philippians
1:6 198

2:9–11 140
3:19 35

Colossians
1:15–20 140
2:11 169
2:12 169
3:3 37

Hebrews
9–10 140
10:11–14 140
10:12 169
12:16–17 35
12:22–24 73

Revelation
5:9–10 32
12 31
13:8 169
19:7 22

SUBJECT INDEX

A

adduction, 129
Ambrose, Saint, 129
anamnēsis, 49, 53, 124, 125, 144
Anglicanism, 172–73, 195, 197, 200, 201–2
anointing of the sick, 122
Apology (Justin Martyr), 15
Aquinas, Thomas, 46, 109, 141–42
Aristotelian philosophy, 150n29
Armstrong, John H., 11–12, 79
Arndt, Elmer J. F., 193–94
Assemblies of God, 195
atonement, 91–92, 104–5
Augsburg Confession, 88, 89–90, 100, 144, 148, 161
Augustine, 60, 93, 109

B

Babylonian Captivity of the Church (Luther), 182
baptism, 18, 155, 156
  Baptist theology on, 43, 50
  Lutheran theology on, 93
  Roman Catholic theology on, 122, 127, 130, 138, 156
Baptist theology
  on celebrating the Lord's Supper as a congregation, 33, 41–43
  on frequency of observing the Lord's Supper, 36–37
  the Lord's Supper as communion in, 38–43
  the Lord's Supper as proclamation in, 33–38
  the Lord's Supper as sign in, 30–33, 45–46, 54
  Lutheran response to, 48–52

New Hampshire Confession of Faith, 177
Reformed response to, 45–47
response to the Lutheran view, 102–5
response to the Reformed view, 72–74
response to the Roman Catholic view, 137–40
Roman Catholic response to, 53–55
Barbach, John, 107
Barnes-Lawrence, Arthur Evelyn, 203–4
Barth, Karl, 195
Battles, Ford Lewis, 81n6
Belgic Confession, 167–69
Benedict XVI, Pope, 53, 56n10
Beza, Theodore, 60
bread, unleavened, 94
Brennan, William, 137
Bridge, Donald, 12, 158
Bruce, Alexander Balmain, 196–97
Brunner, Emil, 202–3
Bucer, Martin, 60, 127
Bullinger, Heinrich, 169

C

Calvin, John. *See also* Reformed theology
  Baptist view and, 46, 48, 50, 52
  on communion, 183–85
  French Confession of Faith, 166–67
  on the Holy Spirit, 61, 64–67, 141–42
  Lutheran view and, 76, 77, 107
  view of the sacraments, 60–62, 72

Catechism of the Catholic Church (CCC), 178–81
Chemnitz, Martin, 146
children's participation in the Lord's Supper, 70
Christian life, the, 122–23
Chrysostom, John, 21, 121, 129
Clement of Alexandria, 192
commanded remembrance of the Lord's Supper, 13–16
commemoration in the Lord's Supper, 17
Common Calling, A, 108
common cups and loaves for the Lord's Supper, 41–42, 47, 69, 148–49
communion, the Lord's Supper as
  Baptist view on, 38–43
  Charles Spurgeon on, 189–90
  Lutheran view on, 98–100, 102
  Reformed view on, 46–47
  Roman Catholic view on, 80–81, 120–29, 123
Communion: The Meal That Unites? (Bridge and Phypers), 158
Confession of the Waldenses, 171–72
confirmation, 122, 151n38
Congregationalism, 201, 203
Consensus Tigurinus, 76
consubstantiation, 87–88, 102, 109
Council of Trent, 126, 127–28, 146, 178
Craigie, Peter, 39

D

definition of the Lord's Supper, 15
Dibelius, Martin, 199
Didache, 19, 99, 160–61
Dodd, C. H., 199–200
Dordrecht Confession, 176–77
Draft Ecclesiastical Ordinances of 1541, 68

E

Edwards, Jonathan, 201
Emerson, Ralph Waldo, 43
enabling faith, the Lord's Supper, 18
Enlightenment, the, 97
epiklēsis, 96, 145
Eucharist, the, 17, 122–23, 135–36, 178–81. See also Roman Catholic theology
  Clement of Alexandria on, 192
  Justin Martyr on, 191
Examination of the Council of Trent (Chemnitz), 146
exclusion of some from the Lord's Supper, 42–43, 51

F

Fairbairn, A. M., 203
faith
  enabled through the Lord's Supper, 18, 35–36
  required for the sacraments, 61–62, 63, 104–5, 145–46, 155
  as the worthy reception of the Lord's Supper, 94–95, 102–3, 158–59
fellowship through the Lord's Supper, 19, 23–24, 41–43, 190, 193–94
forgiveness, 91–92, 104–5
French Confession of Faith, 166–67
frequency of celebrating the Lord's Supper
  Baptist view on, 36–37
  in the early church, 14
  Lutheran view on, 97
  questions about, 22
  Reformed view on, 67–68
  Roman Catholic view on, 131

G

Ganoczy, Alexandre, 142
garden of Eden, 31–32
Gerrish, Brian, 82n9, 107
Gibson, Mel, 37
Given for You (Mathison), 59
God
  communion of the triune,
      120–21
  grace of, 158, 186–88, 201
  sacramental, 90–91
Goethe, Johann Wolfgang von, 20
Goltsch, Moritz, 107
grace of God, 158, 186–88, 201
grape juice versus wine, 41, 51,
      84n26, 94, 104, 131

H

Heidelberg Catechism, 59, 142,
      173–76
Holy Orders, 122
Holy Spirit, the
  Lutheran theology on, 77–78,
      95–97
  Reformed theology on, 61,
      64–67, 108
  Roman Catholic theology on, 79

I

Ignatius, Saint, 132, 190
Institutes of the Christian Religion
      (Calvin), 60, 61, 62, 183–85
intercommunion, 133–34, 138
intincture method, 68
Israelites, the, 15, 30–31
  Baptist view on, 33–35

J

Jansen, John Frederick, 198
Jesus Christ
  bloody death of, 37–38
  changing water into wine, 31
  church as the body of, 158–59
  communion of the divine and
      human in the God-Man,
      121–22
  conferring the kingdom of God
      on the disciples, 32
  death of, 98
  describing himself as "bread," 93
  the Lord's Supper commanded
      by, 13–16, 154–55, 192–93,
      202–3
  miracles of, 31, 35
  in Old Testament signs, 49
  presence in the Lord's Supper,
      38–39, 46, 63–64, 72–73,
      76–77, 80, 92–94, 95–97,
      98, 103–4, 106–8, 126–29,
      148, 195
  resurrection of, 128
  sacraments and, 62
  sacrifice of, 124–26, 142–43,
      144–45, 197
  temptation of, 36, 39
John, gospel of, 100–101
John of Damascus, Saint, 124
John of Smyrna, 193

K

Kaiser, Christopher, 83n17
Kass, Leon, 55n4
koinonia, 13, 24

L

laypersons, the Lord's Supper
      administered by, 51, 134
Letham, Robert, 69
Leuenberg Agreement, 108
Lord's Prayer, the, 93
Lord's Supper, the
  administered by laypersons, 51,
      134

children's participation in, 70
Christian diversity over, 12,
    153–54
commanded by Jesus Christ,
    13–16, 154–55, 202–3
commemoration in, 17, 192–93
common cups and loaves for,
    41–42, 47, 69, 148–49
as communion, 38–43, 46–47,
    98–100, 102, 120–29,
    189–90
defined, 15
discipline of the congregation
    and, 40–41, 157–59
early observance of, 14–16
exclusion of some from, 42–43,
    51
faith and, 18, 35–36, 155, 158–59
fellowship through, 19, 23–24,
    41–43, 190, 193–94
frequency of celebrating, 14, 22,
    36–37, 67–68, 97, 131
methods of distributing, 41–42,
    47, 132–34, 148–49
mystery of, 156–57, 198, 200, 203
names for, 12–13
nourishment through, 19–20,
    196–97
Old Testament and, 49, 90–91,
    124
origins of, 15–16
as a personal remembrance,
    21–22
preparation for, 20, 21–22, 135
renewal in, 17
as a spiritual remembrance, 23
as a strengthening
    remembrance, 18–20
thanksgiving in, 17–18
uniting the church, 13–16, 19,
    40–41, 154–55, 157–59,
    192–93, 199, 202–3
as a visible remembrance, 16–18
Lukacs, John, 43

Luther, Martin, 46, 62, 76, 127, 141.
    See also Lutheran theology
    on communion, 182
    rejection of the memorialist
        position by, 59
    Ulrich Zwingli and, 48, 52, 100,
        146
Lutheran theology
    atonement and forgiveness in,
        91–92, 104–5
    Augsburg Confession, 88,
        89–90, 100, 144, 148, 161
    Baptist response to, 102–5
    consubstantiation in, 87–88, 102,
        109
    faith as the worthy reception of
        the Lord's Supper in, 94–95,
        102–3, 145–46
    on frequency of celebrating the
        Lord's Supper, 97
    on the Holy Spirit, 77–78, 95–97
    Lord's Supper among the
        sacraments in, 89–90,
        144–45, 147–48
    on the Lord's Supper as sign,
        92–94
    on method of distributing the
        Lord's Supper, 148–49
    name of the Lord's Supper and,
        97–100
    Reformed response to, 106–8
    rejections of transubstantiation
        by, 88–89, 147
    response to the Baptist view,
        48–52
    response to the Reformed view,
        75–78
    response to the Roman Catholic
        view, 144–49
    Roman Catholic response to,
        109–11
    on the sacramental God, 90–91
    sacrament of the altar in, 162–66
    words of John in, 100–101

M

Marburg Colloquy of October 1529, 48, 59
marriage, 122, 198
Marsh, Thomas A., 130
Martyr, Justin, 15, 191
Martyr, Peter, 60, 141
Mass, celebration of, 134–35, 141–43
Mathison, Keith, 59, 68
McCarthy, Mary, 29
McDonnell, Kilian, 83–84n21
Melanchthon, Philip, 90, 95, 107
memorial, the Lord's Supper as a, 49–52
Mennonites, 176–77
Menzies, Robert P., 195
Methodist Articles of Religion, 177–78
Morrison, George H., 198
Moule, Handley C. G., 195
mystery in the simplicity of the Lord's Supper, 156–57, 198, 200, 203

N

names for the Lord's Supper, 12–13
Neill, Stephen, 201–2
New Hampshire Confession of Faith, 177
Noah, 30, 35
nourishment through the Lord's Supper, 19–20, 196–97

O

O'Connor, Flannery, 29, 43, 53
Old Testament and the Lord's Supper, 49, 90–91, 124
Olevianus, Caspar, 173
Origen, 192
origins of the Lord's Supper, 15–16
Ott, Ludwig, 125

P

paedocommunion, 74
participation in the Lord's Supper
  Baptist theology on, 33, 41–43
  by children, 70
  Lutheran theology on, 91–92, 104–5
  Reformed theology on, 69–70
  Roman Catholic theology on, 70, 138
Passion of the Christ, The, 37
Passover meal, the, 15–16, 30–31
  Baptist view on, 33–35, 54
  Lutheran view on, 94, 103
Paton, John G., 194
Paul, apostle, 14–15, 21, 65
  on frequency of the Lord's Supper, 22
  on the meaning of the Lord's Supper, 38–40
  on the Passover meal, 91, 96, 103
  on the practice of the Lord's Supper, 71, 187–88
  on spiritual remembrance, 23
  on unbelievers, 35
  on who should receive Communion, 133
penance, 122
personal remembrance, the Lord's Supper as a, 21–22
pesaḥ, 54
Phypers, David, 12, 158
pietism, 97
Pilate, Pontius, 49
Paul VI, Pope, 122
Polycarp, 193
prayers in preparation for the Lord's Supper, 21–22, 135
preparation for the Lord's Supper, 20, 21–22
  Roman Catholic view on, 135
presence of Jesus Christ in the Lord's Supper, the
  Baptist view on, 38–39, 46, 72–74

Moule, Handley C. G., on, 195
Lutheran view on, 76–77,
    92–94, 95–97, 98, 103–4
Reformed view on, 63–64,
    106–8
Roman Catholic view on, 80,
    126–29, 147–48
proclamation, the Lord's Supper
    as, 33–38, 49–52

R

Reformed theology
    Baptist response to, 72–74
    Belgic Confession, 167–69
    Calvinist doctrine and, 59–60
    on frequency of Lord's Supper
        celebration, 67–68
    Heidelberg Catechism, 59, 142,
        173–76
    on the Holy Spirit, 61, 64–67,
        108
    on the Lord's Supper, 62–67
    Lutheran response to, 75–78
    on manner of celebration of the
        Lord's Supper, 68–69
    pastoral issues in, 67–71
    on the real presence of Jesus
        Christ, 63–64, 106–8
    required for proper celebration
        of the Lord's Supper, 70–71
    response to the Baptist view,
        45–47
    response to the Lutheran view,
        106–8
    response to the Roman Catholic
        view, 141–43
    Roman Catholic response to,
        79–81
    on the sacraments, 60–62
    Second Helvetic Confession of
        Faith, 169
    on who may participate in the
        Lord's Supper, 69–70

renewal in the Lord's Supper, 17
resurrection of Jesus Christ, 128
Roman Catholic theology
    adduction in, 129
    Baptist response to, 137–40
    Catechism, 178–81
    celebration of Mass in, 134–35,
        141–43
    communion of the church,
        created and sustained by
        the sacraments in, 122
    communion of the divine and
        human in the God-Man
        Jesus Christ in, 121–22
    communion of the triune God
        in, 120–21
    Council of Trent and, 126,
        127–28, 146, 178
    doctrine of sacrifice in, 124–26,
        142–43
    dogma of the real presence of
        Jesus Christ in, 126–29
    on elements used in Holy
        Communion, 131
    on frequency of Holy
        Communion, 131
    the Holy Eucharist as the source
        and summit of the Christian
        life in, 122–23
    on intercommunion, 133–34
    liturgy in, 123–24
    Lutheran response to, 144–49
    meaning and significance of
        Communion in, 120
    on preaching of the word
        accompanying the Lord's
        Supper, 134–35
    on preparation for the Lord's
        Supper, 135
    Reformed response to, 141–43
    response to the Baptist view,
        53–55
    response to the Lutheran view,
        109–11

response to the Reformed view,
79–81
sacramental economy in,
123–24, 125–26
sources of information on, 120
transubstantiation in, 88–89,
109–10, 127–29, 138–39,
147, 178
on where Holy Communion
should be served, 132
on who should be allowed to
serve the elements, 134
on who should participate in the
Lord's Supper, 129–30
on worshiping the Eucharist,
135–36
Rooker, Mark, 40
Rule of Faith, 127

S

sacramental economy, 123–24,
125–26
sacraments
Lutheran theology on, 89–92,
104–5, 144–45, 145–46,
162–66
Protestant recognition of two,
155–56, 198
Reformed theology on, 60–62,
63
Roman Catholic theology on,
122, 123–26, 155–56
sacrifice, doctrine of, 124–26,
142–43, 144–45, 197
salvation, 50, 93
Second Helvetic Confession of
Faith, 169
Short Treatise on the Lord's Supper
(Calvin), 64
sign, the Lord's Supper as, 30–33,
49–52, 54, 77, 92–94
spiritual remembrance, the Lord's
Supper as a, 23

Spurgeon, Charles H., 188–90
strengthening remembrance, the
Lord's Supper as a, 18–20

T

Temple, William, 197
temptation of Jesus Christ, 36, 39
Tertullian, 192
thanksgiving in the Lord's Supper,
17–18
Thirty-nine Articles, 172–73
transubstantiation
Lutheran rejection of, 88–89, 147
in Roman Catholic theology,
109–10, 127–29, 138–39,
178
Trinitarian doctrine, 120–21, 140,
143

U

Underhill, Evelyn, 200
unification of the church through
the Lord's Supper, 13–16,
19, 40–41, 154–55, 157–59,
192–93, 199, 202–3
unleavened bread, 94
Ursinus, Zacharias, 173

V

visible remembrance, the Lord's
Supper as a, 16–18

W

Wallace, Ronald, 83n18
Wesley, Charles, 156
Wesley, John, 186–88
Westminster Confession of Faith,
59, 169–71
Westphal, Joachim, 82n7
Whouley, James, 137

Williams, Michael, 30
wine versus grape juice, 41, 51,
    84n26, 94, 104, 131
Wyon, Olive, 192–93

Y

Young Calvin, The (Ganoczy), 142

Z

Zizioulas, John, 121
Zurich Consensus, 82n7
Zwingli, Ulrich, 82n7, 101, 106, 127
    John Calvin and, 62, 76, 77
    Martin Luther and, 48, 52, 100,
        146
    memorialist position of, 50, 59